Conclusion

Conclusion

OLIVER CROMWELL—A DICTATOR'S TRAGEDY

OLIVER CROMWELL

From the painting by Samuel Cooper at Sidney Sussex
College, Cambridge.

"...those wakefull eyes:
Which through his looks that piercing sweetnesse shed."
—ANDREW MARVELL.

OLIVER CROMWELL

A Dictator's Tragedy

By

MARY TAYLOR BLAUVELT

AUTHOR OF "THE DEVELOPMENT OF CABINET
GOVERNMENT IN ENGLAND"

G. P. PUTNAM'S SONS
NEW YORK

PRINTED IN THE UNITED STATES OF AMERICA

To the Memory of My Sister

ANNA HUTTON BLAUVELT

"For she hath been a helper of many, and of myself also."

"It is not truth, but opinion, that can travaile the world without a passport. For were it otherwise, and were there not as many internal forms of the mind as there are external figures of men, then were there some possibility to persuade by the mouth of one Advocate, even Equity alone— But God's judgments upon the Greater and the Greatest have been left to posterity."

From the Preface to Sir Walter Raleigh's "History of the World" recommended by Cromwell to his son.

OLIVER CROMWELL'S IDEALS

I

"Love the sheep, love the lambs, love all, tender all, cherish and countenance all. And if the poorest Christian, the most mistaken Christian, shall desire to live peaceably and quietly under you, let him be protected."

"I had rather that Mahomedanism were permitted among us, than that one of God's children should suffer persecution."

II

"In the government of nations, that which is to be looked after is the affections of the people."

"That which you have by force, I look upon it as nothing."

In the conflict that arose between these ideals lay his Tragedy.

PREFACE

To attempt to write a life of Cromwell so soon after Mr. Buchan's great work would be in the highest degree presumptuous. But this book was in great measure written before Mr. Buchan's appeared. And it is not a life. I have paid very little attention to either military or foreign affairs, but by abstracting it from almost everything else, I have tried to emphasize the great difficulty, the impossibility of "singing a song of reconciliation between the two interests" that Oliver cared most about, the "Liberty of Men professing Godliness under a Variety of Forms and the Civil Liberty of the Nation." For while these interests are not fundamentally and permanently "inconsistent and two different things," in his day "so full of sects whether upon a religious account or upon a civil account," they were, and it was the difficulty, the impossibility, of reconciling them that led to the military despotism and drew from him the bitter cry "Misrule is better than no rule, and an ill government, a bad government, is better than none!"

So his life was a tragedy of conflicting ideals, his career a successful failure. He rose to be the head of the state, but even Mr. Belloc, prejudiced as he is against Cromwell, entitles his chapter dealing with the dictatorship "Reluctant Power." And he was not able to use that power to bring about the ends that he desired. By his sword he had saved parliamentary government for England, yet, largely because it conflicted with his other ideal, religious toleration, he was not in his own day, able to put it into successful practice. The religious toleration that he longed for came in time, but it is probable that, by associating it with a military despotism that he hated but could not escape, he retarded rather than hastened it, and his attempt to raise his countrymen to a higher moral and spiritual level was followed by the license of the Restoration period. In the main his failure was due not to his mistakes, but to the circumstances with which he had to deal, the men with whom he had to work. That was the tragedy of it. But a man should be judged not so much by what he accomplishes as by what he aims at.

I have to thank the Earl of Sandwich for showing me over Hinchingbrooke and letting me see the diary of his ancestor, the first Earl; the Rev. Elliott Simpson, Vicar of St. Mary's, Ely, for entertaining me at the Vicarage, once Cromwell's home; and especially Professor Trevelyan, who has read my manuscript. Grateful acknowledgment is also made to my lifelong friend, Miss E. Grace Briggs, who has prepared the index.

MARY TAYLOR BLAUVELT.

CONTENTS

OLIVER CROMWELL—A DICTATOR'S TRAGEDY

CHAPTER I

Family Connections

"I was by birth a gentleman, living neither in any considerable height, nor yet in obscurity."—OLIVER CROMWELL.

TOWARD the close of the fifteenth century, a certain John ap-William, a small squire from Glamorganshire, Wales, migrated to England, and settled in the thriving village of Putney on the Thames. Like many of his countrymen, he had probably been attracted to England by the fact that the new Tudor dynasty was Welsh. Indeed he seems to have been of some service to Henry VII in obtaining the throne, for which he was rewarded with copyhold lands in the neighborhood of London. His son Morgan, who inherited the Putney lands, took Williams as his surname, and as yeoman of the Welsh guard, gained a place in Court circles. He married Katherine Cromwell, the daughter of a Putney neighbor.

The Cromwells were also newcomers in Putney. They had migrated from Nottinghamshire about the time that the Williams family had migrated from Wales. They were of good yeoman stock, Walter, the father of Katherine, was a considerable landowner who combined the trades of brewer and blacksmith. But he appears not to have been a particularly creditable person, there are stories of drunken brawls, and he was finally convicted of forgery, for which he forfeited his lands. Nevertheless he had a son Thomas, who was to become known to History as Henry VIII's principal agent in the destruction of the monasteries, the holder of innumerable offices, and finally as Earl of Essex.

To Morgan Williams and Katherine Cromwell was born a son Richard who, probably attracted by his uncle's fame, preferred to be known as Richard Cromwell, rather than as Richard Williams. To avoid confusion he was in the habit of signing himself Richard Cromwell, alias Williams, and for generations members of the family sometimes used this signature. This Richard Cromwell, alias Williams, assisted his uncle in dealing with Papistically inclined clergymen, and destroying monasteries, and secured his share of the spoils, in 1538 the

17

Benedictine priory of Hinchingbrooke, near Huntingdon, in 1540 the site of the abbey of Ramsey and some of its most valuable manors.

May Day 1540 was a great day in Richard Cromwell's life, for in the tournament held in the King's presence at Westminster, he was one of the six champions chosen to defend the honor of England against all comers. We read how these champions of England "came into the lists that day richly apparelled, their horses trapped all in white velvet, with certain knights and gentlemen riding afore them, apparelled all with white velvet and white sarsanet, and all their servants in white doublets and hosen, cut all in the burgundian fashion." The festivities lasted six days, during which time the challengers "feasted not only the King and Queen and the whole court, but also all the knights and burgesses of the Commons' House in the Parliament, and on the morrow after they had the Mayor of London, the aldermen and all their wives to dinner."

In this gorgeous pageant none distinguished himself more than Richard Cromwell. In recognition of his prowess, the King not only made him a knight, but also took a ring from his own finger with a great diamond in it, and dropping it, said to Sir Richard "Formerly thou wast my Dick, but hereafter thou shalt be my Diamond." And when Richard Cromwell picked it up, he was commanded by the King to wear such a one in the fore-jamb of the lion in his crest, instead of in the javelin.

If those were happy days for young Richard, no doubt they were also happy for his uncle Thomas, now Earl of Essex. For the festivities were in honor of the marriage that he had arranged between Henry VIII and Anne of Cleves, and the nephew who had chosen to bear his name had acquitted himself well, and been duly honored. But they were his last happy days. For him these marriage festivities were the beginning of the end. Only five weeks later he was arrested in the Council Chamber, and committed to the Tower, on a charge of high treason. He had gone further than his master could go with him.

For in breaking from Rome, Henry VIII had contemplated no doctrinal change. He had cast off the authority of the Pope, not only because he had denied him the wife that he desired, but also because he had felt that to be master of the English nation, he must be master of the English Church. But, as it has been well said, he was still "a good Catholic who wanted to be his own Pope." He had been the Defender of the Faith against Luther, and his attitude toward German Protestantism had not changed.

In the matter of the monasteries his minister had served him well.

They had outlived their usefulness, and he wanted their money; it would save him from wrangling with Parliament over supplies, and leave him something to give to his friends. But Cromwell had gone further, he had left "the mean, indifferent, virtuous and true way of reforming religion," was trying to bring about doctrinal changes, and an alliance with the Protestant princes of Germany. To further this policy he had married him to a wife, whom he found "nothing fair." German wife, German doctrine and German alliance must go. Therefore the minister who was responsible for them must go.

A Bill of Attainder was the easiest way to get rid of him; it did not require that charges should be proved, and gave the defendant no chance to speak in his own defense. He had few friends and many enemies, so it was not difficult to get such a Bill through Parliament.

Only one man dared to wear mourning at Court for Thomas Cromwell, and perhaps only one man cared to. That man was his nephew, Sir Richard. Notwithstanding this, perhaps even partly because of it, King Henry who "knew a man when he saw him," continued to lavish favors upon him, made him a gentleman of the Privy Council, Constable of Berkeley Castle, and gave him more land. He married the daughter of a Lord Mayor of London, and died in 1546.

His son and heir, Sir Henry, known as the Golden Knight, was a typical Elizabethan. Like his father, he married the daughter of a Lord Mayor of London. At Hinchingbrooke, on the spot where a Benedictine monastery had stood since the Conquest, he built for himself the beautiful stately mansion, which stands to this day, much as he left it. There in 1564 he entertained Queen Elizabeth in royal state. Four times he was Sheriff of Huntingdonshire. At the time of the Spanish Armada he was marshal of the county, and to the four soldiers that he was bound to furnish, he added twenty-six horsemen at his own cost, and exhorted the trained bands "to practice the right and proper use of their weapons, and fight for the success of the religion of Christ against the devilish superstition of the Pope." When he died in 1603 his eldest son Oliver succeeded to Hinchingbrooke, and proceeded to dissipate his substance in riotous living.

The Golden Knight himself had thrown away his fortune with too lavish a hand, so the portions of younger children were not large. To his second son Robert was given a modest estate in Huntingdon, about a mile from Hinchingbrooke, worth only about £300 a year, perhaps the equivalent of £1200 now. Royalist lampoons call Robert Cromwell a brewer, but while he may have done some brewing for his neighbors as well as himself, in the main his life was that of a gentleman farmer. He managed his small estate, sat for Huntingdon in the Parliament of 1593, was bailiff for the borough, and one of the Justices of the Peace for the county.

About 1591 he married Elizabeth, the young widow of William Lynn, and daughter of William Steward of Ely. It was not the first time that the Cromwells, alias Williamses, had come in contact with the Stewards of Ely. For in 1538, on a certain "Tuesday in the morning," Robert's grandfather Richard, who was making a tour of the monasteries to ascertain what Abbots and Priors would conform to the King's will, wrote to his uncle Thomas, "Your Lordship, I think, shall shortly apperceive the Prior of Ely to be of a froward sort, by evident tokens; as at our coming home, shall be at large related unto you." Because this Prior, his name was Steward, had been "of a froward sort," the last Catholic Prior became the first Protestant Dean of Ely. Moreover he was given leases of the Church lands, and made farmer of the tithes of Ely. Mrs. Robert Cromwell's father, descended from a brother of the Prior Dean, had inherited this position. She brought her husband a fortune of sixty pounds a year.

The house in which the Robert Cromwells lived had once been a home of the Austin Friars. Its site, just off the High Street, fronting the old Roman road, still called Ermine Street, is known. There is a fine stone house there now, with extensive back premises and a beautiful garden. On the wall fronting the street there is an inscription to the effect that here Oliver Cromwell, called the Protector, was born. However it is not the house in which he was born, nor is the garden the garden that he looked upon. But on the twenty-fifth of April 1599, he was born, probably in a house that stood on this site. We say probably, because there is a tradition that he was born at Hinchingbrooke, his mother having gone there for her confinement, because of the greater comfort and better air. But as Oliver was her fifth child this is not likely. On the twenty-ninth of April he was christened at St. John's church, Huntingdon. St. John's is no longer standing, but the record of the christening is preserved at All Saints', whose exterior is almost as it was in 1599.

CHAPTER II

Childhood and Youth

O F Oliver's childhood we have little definite information, yet from what we know of the times and of the family connection it is possible to reconstruct it after a fashion. It was a large family into which he was born. His parents had ten children, three boys and seven girls, but of these two boys and one girl died young. So Oliver was left an only son with six sisters, but there is no evidence that as the only boy among so many girls he was spoiled. Certainly his worst enemies have never accused him of being unmanly.

He grew up in that flat, comparatively treeless Fen country which, with its great expanse of sky and water, tends to give one a very vivid sense of the presence of the Infinite. Not as something over-awing and crushing, but as something near, tender, helpful and kind, something within one as well as around one, conducive therefore neither to egotism, nor yet to helplessness. One feels one's self just a part of that great Whole in Whom we live and move and have our Being. Perhaps that had something to do with those brooding mystical eyes of his.

And he grew up among those prosperous, intelligent, pious middle class people who at that time dominated the eastern counties. It was his good fortune to be born in a position which brought him more or less into contact with all classes of society. As the son of a small gentleman farmer he would mingle freely with townsmen and trades-people, but Hinchingbrooke would always be in the background of his life, the splendor of his grandfather, the prodigal expenditure of his uncle Oliver, and the memories of the part that his family had played during the whole Tudor period.

In his own family the religious differences that were to set England on fire were probably already apparent. As yet the whole family was in the Established Church, but there were Cavalier and Puritan elements. We must bear in mind that the term Puritan was applied in those days, generally in derision, not only to those who held to peculiar doctrines and forms of worship (of these there were at that time very few), but to all those who were more religious, or had higher or more rigid moral standards than their neighbors.

There was nothing of the Puritan in Oliver's grandfather, or in his uncle Oliver, and perhaps not much in the other Cromwell uncles. But while we know little of his father, there is reason to believe that he was a sober, perhaps rather stern religious man, of the type that in those days would be called a Puritan; the portrait preserved of him at Hinchingbrooke, if genuine, would certainly indicate that. We know assuredly that his mother was a woman of great piety. And strangely enough, all his aunts, the Golden Knight's daughters, had married into Puritan families. Aunt Joan was the wife of Sir Thomas Barrington of Barrington Hall, Essex. Seven of her family were to sit in the Long Parliament. Aunt Elizabeth had been the wife of William Hampden of Great Hampden, Bucks; when Oliver was born, she was a young widow, with two little boys, one of whom, John, five years older than Oliver, was to become known to History. Aunt Frances had married Richard Whalley of Kerton, Nottinghamshire. In later days her son Henry was to become Judge Advocate, her son Edward was one of those who signed Charles I's death warrant. After the Restoration he fled to New England, where he had a sorry time of it.

A portrait of Oliver as a child of three represents him as a winsome self-composed little chap, eyes already sad, mouth already firm. Yet Royalist biographers tell us that even then he was "of a cross and peevish disposition," while a more friendly writer credits him with "a quick and lively apprehension and sagacious wit, and a solid judgment." Probably neither of them knew anything about it, yet both statements may have been in a measure true. In later life we know that he had a hot temper and considerable nervous irritability which an unfriendly critic might interpret as "cross and peevish"; we know also that he had a solid judgment. Perhaps he showed both in childhood.

As Hinchingbrooke was less than a mile from his home, there must have been frequent visits, first to Grandfather, later to Uncle Oliver. There is a story, not likely to have been invented, that on one of his earliest visits the whole household was thrown into consternation, because he could not be found. Every one joined in the search, and he was finally discovered on the roof, whither an ape had carried him. Thus, Royalist historians were to write, was England all but delivered from him.

But a change was to come to Hinchingbrooke. For in January 1603, when Oliver was not quite four years old, Grandfather Cromwell died. It was probably the first experience that he had had of death, and it would make an impression upon him. For Sir Henry's funeral was the most impressive and most costly that that countryside had ever seen. Sons and daughters gathered, and doubtless talked of the part that their father had played in the history of his country, especially at the time of the Armada. That was less than fifteen years ago, they all remembered it well. Cousin John Hampden was almost nine, he could understand, even Oliver could understand a little. And it must never be forgotten that that story was always in the background of his life.

Three months later he would hear of another death, that of good Queen Bess. "Queen Elizabeth of famous memory": he was to say of her fifty years later, "we need not be ashamed to call her so." Yet at the time it probably did not make much impression upon him, he was too young. But it made an impression upon England. Those of us who remember the passing of Victoria can form a faint idea of how England was affected by the passing of Elizabeth. That the great romantic age was over, that the undisciplined adventurous spirit of Englishmen must find other and more prosaic outlets, was of course not appreciated. But England did understand that it was the end of an epoch and that the situation was complicated by the fact that the heir to the throne was a foreigner.

If the child did not exactly take in the Queen's death, he must have taken in her successor. For on April 27th, 1603, Oliver being then four years and two days old, King James, on his way to assume the English crown, stopped two nights at Hinchingbrooke, and Uncle Oliver entertained him in such state as never subject had entertained monarch before. A new window was built in the great banqueting hall for the occasion,* the whole neighborhood was invited, there were all manner of elaborate ceremonies, Cambridge doctors were there with loyal addresses, Knights were created. Uncle Oliver was already a Knight, but at the coronation he was to be made a Knight of the Bath. The royal guests were loaded down with gifts, horses, hounds, a golden cup of fabulous value, and there was money to be distributed among their retinue. "Marry, man, thou hast treated me better than any one since I left Edinboro'," were King James' parting words.

Certainly little Oliver had never seen anything so wonderful before, it was a thing for a child to dream about. And perhaps he did dream about it. At any rate there is a story, though it was probably invented long afterward, that one night a tall woman appeared at his bedside,

---

* The banqueting hall was destroyed by fire about a century ago, but the window has been preserved, and is in another part of the house.

and told him that he was destined to become the most powerful man in England. If he ever dreamed such a dream, it might easily have been the night after his return from that visit to Hinchingbrooke. It was natural after such an experience to dream of future greatness, of a time when he might be greater than Uncle Oliver, greater than Grandfather Henry, or Great grandfather Richard, perhaps even greater than the King himself. But the legend has it that when he told his dream, his father went even beyond old Jacob, when his son Joseph reported a similar experience, for he not only reproved him, but thrashed him soundly. Such dreams, whether night dreams or daydreams, were not encouraged in the family of Robert Cromwell.

There were other royal visits to Hinchingbrooke, and there is a tradition that in the following year, 1604, Prince Charles, then Duke of York, a year younger than Oliver, was taken there on his way to London, that the children played together and Oliver got the better of him in fisticuffs. In the light of subsequent events, it would have been easy and natural to invent such a story. But as little Charles was a sickly child, probably suffering from rickets, and at that time scarcely able to walk, it is not probable. Yet it is not unlikely that Oliver and Charles met first as children, in Sir Oliver's hall at Hinchingbrooke.

There is no reason to suppose that the Robert Cromwells were a bookish family, but no Cromwell could fail to be interested in public affairs. So Oliver would hear much talk on weighty matters during those early years of James I. More probably than he could take in. Whatever popularity the King may have had in his immediate family, must have disappeared when they heard of the Hampton Court Conference, where Puritan divines, who wished to stay in the Church, merely asking that they might be allowed to omit certain forms, which they thought savored of Rome, were met with the response, "I will make them conform, or harry them out of the land." No doubt Oliver heard his father and Uncle Oliver discuss this, and perhaps Uncle Oliver sided with the King, his father against him.

But there could be no division in the family when word came that the King, who had refused to tolerate the Puritans, was tolerating the Catholics. Brothers who remembered the Armada, and the part that their father had taken against it, could hardly differ on that subject. And then in November 1605 came the Gunpowder Plot. Even a boy under seven would be roused by that, and the more so as Uncle Oliver was a member of the Parliament that was to be blown up.

Then, when he was eleven years old, word would come of the

assassination of Henry IV of France. This produced great consternation in England. For while the separation from Rome had roused a strong nationalist spirit, such as Englishmen had not known before, it had also made them international in a sense in which they had not been before. The question in which they were most interested was not English but European. The whole history of Europe was the struggle between Protestantism and Catholicism, and even although he had decided that Paris was worth a mass, Henry IV was still the hope of Protestantism.

The school to which young Oliver went was founded in 1187 by David, Earl of Huntingdon. Still used as a grammar school, it stands today much as it was in the twelfth century, more so than it was in Oliver's day. For at that time it had been made to conform to the Elizabethan style, but the alterations have since been done away with, so that it is now, as it originally was, a small Norman building, ecclesiastical in style, standing close to the side walk, just opposite All Saints' Church.

The master in Oliver's day, Dr. Thomas Beard, was a great man in Huntingdon, and not unknown throughout England. He not only managed the school, but "painfully preached the Word of God in the town on the Sabbath Day dewly, to the great comfort of the Inhabitants." He must have emphasized the anti-Papal teachings that the boy had received at home, for he was sure that the Pope was Anti-Christ, and had written a book to prove it. He also taught his pupils that God invariably punishes evil doers in this life, as well as in the life to come. On this subject he was also to write a book "The Theatre of God's Judgments, Dedicated to the Mayor and Burgesses of Huntingdon, Because, Mr. Mayor, you have been my Scholar, and brought up in my house." By a judicious selection of examples from history he proved his case.

Although Oliver was to advance somewhat beyond the crudity of this teaching, even in later life he showed that it had made a great impression upon him. Success was to him always a proof that God approved of his undertaking, failure a call to examine himself, and see if his course and his motives had been right, and he generally found them wrong. In childhood he may or may not have seen visions and dreamed dreams, but in later life God was to speak to him not in dreams or visions, but in the course of events. "God makes Himself known," he told the first Parliament of the Protectorate, "by the judgments that He executes— And what are all our Histories, and other traditions of actions in former times, but God manifesting Himself, that He hath shaken, and tumbled down, and trampled upon, everything that He hath not planted?"

Tradition would have it, that even in his school days he thought on future greatness, that he acted the part of a king in a school play, placing the crown himself upon his head, and adding "majestical and mighty words" of his own to the text. Any boy to whom such a part had been assigned might have amused himself and his friends in that way. But all that we really know of his school life is that Dr. Beard's discipline was strict, that he corrected the errors of the young Cromwell "with a diligent hand, and a careful eye," and taught him enough, so that on the twenty-third of April 1616, two days before his seventeenth birthday, he was able to matriculate at Sidney Sussex College, Cambridge. It was the day that Shakespeare died. It is possible that Cromwell knew as little of Shakespeare as Shakespeare knew of Cromwell. Had Cromwell known Shakespeare, he could hardly have failed to have been interested in the historical plays. But had Shakespeare known Cromwell, he might have made an historical play of him, perhaps more powerful than any that he ever wrote.

In Cambridge Oliver was still under Puritan influences. The university as a whole was much more Puritan than Oxford, and Sidney Sussex was one of those colleges that Laud was afterwards to describe as nurseries of Puritanism. The Master, Dr. Samuel Ward, had taken part in the recent King James translation of the Bible, and was soon to be a member of the Synod of Dort in which Calvinism was to triumph over Arminianism. He was "learned and conscientious, a severe disciplinarian who exacted elaborate accounts of sermons, and whipped offenders in Hall."

Cromwell's tutor, Magister Richard Howlett, appears to have been made of not quite such stern stuff. Twenty-two years later, when he became Dean of Cashel, Ireland, a former pupil, Dr. Bramhall, by that time Bishop of Derry, wrote of him, "I never knew him quarrel with any man in my time. A moderate man in his tenets, far from Dr. Ward's rigidity and his ways." Archbishop Usher found him "an able man and very fit for government."

Magister Howlett observed that young Cromwell was "not so much given to speculations as to actions." That is in keeping with what we know of him later. Perhaps while he did not formulate his impressions, as Milton was to do a few years later, he too rather vaguely thought that the speculation valued at Cambridge was vain. Royalist biographers tell us that "he was easily satiated with study, taking more delight in horse and field exercises, being one of the chief matchmakers, and players of football, cudgels or any other boisterous sports." As an athlete he was probably not unpopular with his fellow students, and learned better how to manage men and horses than if he had applied himself more strictly to his studies. And managing men and horses was to be the passion of his life.

Those were the days when Hobson drove the mail coach between Cambridge and London, and kept horses for hire in Cambridge, Hobson whom Milton was to immortalize in two poems, Hobson who was to immortalize himself by the water supply that he was to give to Cambridge, and still more by the fact that while he allowed each customer to choose his horse, he must always choose the one that stood next to the barn door, so that the phrase "Hobson's choice" has become a part of the language. No doubt Oliver knew him, perhaps he sometimes hired his horses.

And while there is no evidence that he ever was of the stuff of which students are made, the efforts of Dr. Beard and Magister Howlett were not altogether in vain. Although he knew little of modern languages, as Protector he was able to carry on a conversation with the Dutch Ambassador in Latin, bad Latin perhaps, but understandable. A contemporary tells us that he did good work in mathematics, and his kinsman, the poet Waller, says that he was "very well read in Greek and Roman story," and though he was himself no scholar or even reader, he always respected scholars, and in the days of his power did what he could to help them.

He really was hardly long enough at Cambridge to settle down and learn much. On the twenty-fourth of June 1617, only a little more than a year after he matriculated, his father was buried from All Saints', Huntingdon. Four days before, his sister Margaret, next younger than himself, had married Valentine Walton, perhaps the marriage had been hastened that it might take place before the father's death. Whether Oliver got home in time to see his sister married and his father die, we do not know, but he certainly went home very soon afterwards, and "returned no more to Cambridge." That same year his Grandfather Steward died at Ely. He was only eighteen, but he must take his father's place in the family and in the community as soon as possible.

But not quite yet. As a country gentleman likely to become a Justice of the Peace and a Parliament man, it was desirable that he should have a little knowledge of law, so he went to London, and "betook himself to the study of law at Lincoln's Inn, in order that nothing might be wanting to make him a complete gentleman, and a good commonwealth man." His name does not appear on the books of Lincoln's Inn, probably because he did not study with the intention of becoming a lawyer, but only that he might obtain that general knowledge of law, which his position seemed to demand.

How long he was in London we do not know, but it is probable that he was there on that cold frosty morning in October 1618 when Sir Walter Raleigh was beheaded, Sir Walter Raleigh who wrote one of the very few books that we know for certain that Oliver read and admired, that "History of the World" that he was afterward to commend to his son, as a "body of History that would add much more to his understanding than fragments of story." If he was in the crowd that gathered around the scaffold he may have heard the old man say to one who told him that he should die facing the east, "What matter how the head lie, so that the heart be right?" And Cromwell must have felt, as most Englishmen of his time did, that whatever the great adventurer's errors had been, his heart had been right, that heart that was always set on England's greatness. To him as to the majority of his countrymen, his death must have seemed a national dishonor. For he had been done to death because Spain willed it. The King of England had made friends with the land of the Inquisition and the Armada, the land of Mary Tudor's husband. And England's blood was boiling.

The indications are that it was not only the study of the law that kept Oliver in London, for on August 22nd, 1620, being then in his twenty-second year, he was married in St. Giles's Church, Cripplegate, the church in which Milton was afterward to be buried, to Elizabeth, daughter of Sir James Bourchier, a merchant whose city house was in London, but who also owned property at Felsted in Essex.

The bridegroom was about five feet ten, his body "well compact and strong," his head, a friend says, "so shaped, that you might see in it a store house and a ship, both of a vast treasury of natural parts." His light brown hair was worn in long curls over his shoulders. His blue eyes were keen and penetrating, perhaps always sad, in later life to become very sad. His nose was so large that Royalist pamphleteers were to speak of it as the beak of a vulture, while friends jested about it. The mouth also was large and tender. "His temper exceeding fiery as I have known," writes John Maidston, his steward, "but the flame of it, kept down for the most part, was soon allayed with those moral endowments he had. He was naturally compassionate towards objects in distress, even to an effeminate measure, though God had made him a heart, wherein was left little room for fear, but what was due to Himself, of which there was a large proportion, yet did he exceed in tenderness toward sufferers. A larger soul, I think, has seldom dwelt in house of clay than his was."

Of the bride we know less than we could wish. Her portrait suggests a comely dignified personality. She took no part in public affairs, but tradition says that she was a notable housekeeper. Perhaps she and Oliver became acquainted through the Hampdens, who were related to both of them. It looks as though it were a love match, for the bridegroom's fortune was not sufficient to attract a wealthy merchant's daughter, if she had not cared for him. It was certainly a love marriage, she found her life "but half a life in his absence," while he "loved to write to his dear, who was very much in his heart." On the day after Dunbar there were many necessary letters to write, but he found time to write to her "Truly, if I love you not too well, I think I err not on the other hand much. Thou art dearer to me than any other creature, let that suffice."

CHAPTER III

Family Life

OLIVER took his wife home to live with his mother and unmarried sisters in Huntingdon. His means were limited, for two-thirds of the income from Robert Cromwell's estate had been left to his widow for twenty-one years, to provide for her daughters. However his wife must have brought him something, for the day after his marriage he contracted, under penalty of £4000, to settle upon her, as her jointure, the parsonage house of Hertford, in Huntingdonshire, with its glebe lands and tithes. It is interesting to notice that this document is signed "Oliver Cromwell, alias Williams."

All the sisters except Elizabeth, the oldest, married in time. Perhaps the most interesting marriage was that of Jane, six years younger than Oliver, to John Desborough, who was to be so closely connected with him in later life. Just when these marriages took place we do not know, but a time came when the family in the Huntingdon house consisted of only Oliver, his wife and children, his mother and sister Elizabeth. Three Elizabeths in one house, for mother, wife and sister were all called by the name of the great Queen in whose reign they were born.

It was a Puritan household, but not on that account somber and drab. In manners, dress and even most amusements, the Puritan country gentleman was not unlike other country gentlemen of his time. While in early life Oliver did not, perhaps could not, employ a good tailor, and was a little careless about his dress, the general style of it did not differ from that of his Uncle Oliver. He always wore his hair long, as did all men of his class, Puritans as well as others.

He was an athletic country gentleman of sporting tastes. We have seen how at Cambridge he "delighted in horses, and in pastimes abroad in the field." He continued to do so all his life, so that in his elegy on his death Andrew Marvell could write

> "All, all is gone of ours or his delight
> In horses fierce, wild deer or armor bright."

He was always a lover of horses. It was as a leader of cavalry that he was first to become known to fame, and all through his campaigns his letters show him to have been as solicitous for his horses as for his men. In the days of his greatness, he had better horses than any English king had had before him; it was understood throughout Europe that no present gave him greater pleasure than a fine horse, so we may be sure that in his Huntingdon days he had as good horses as he could afford. We do not know what his views on horse racing were, and at present there is no evidence that he ever entered his horses for the races. But Sir Charles Firth thinks it not impossible that a record may sometime turn up of a prize won by a horse owned by Mr. Oliver Cromwell.

He was also greatly addicted to hunting, hawking and bowling, these too were pleasures that he was to keep up throughout his life. One of his earliest extant letters is to a Mr. John Newdigate, concerning a hawk which had come into Mr. Newdigate's, and which he supposed to be Cromwell's. It was not his, but Cromwell thanks Mr. Newdigate for his courtesy in keeping it for him, and promises that if it ever falls his way, he will do him service in the like, or any other way. Years afterward Mr. Newdigate's nephew found this letter and preserved it, endorsing it "Oliver Cromwell, that wicked successful rebel, his letter to my uncle. No business but about hawks, but I keep it to show his hand and stile."

Later he was to develop a fondness for painting, but how much opportunity there was for this in early life, we do not know. It was easier to indulge his passion for music. For in the seventeenth century it was not necessary for an Englishman to travel, to have power or money in order to be able to hear good music. England was a nation of musicians and music lovers. Girls, Burnet tells us, were taught to sing and play on the lute, or some such instrument, before they could say their Pater Noster, or Ten Commandments, the best way their parents thought to get them husbands. That Bunyan's pilgrim should compose and sing his own songs as he went, seemed natural to contemporary Englishmen. For all over England people in all walks of life were composing songs and airs, writing masques, singing to stringed instruments, with remarkable perfection. A foreign visitor comments on "the beautiful music of violas and pandoras, for in all England it is the custom that even in small villages the musicians wait on you for a small fee. In the morning, about wakening time, they stand outside the chamber, playing religious hymns."

Later Oliver was able to indulge his fondness for music on a larger scale. As Protector it was his delight to gather the greatest musicians of Europe about him. "Rare music both of instruments and voices" was always part of the entertainment at his court. When Puritan visitors deprived a student of Christ Church of his place, friends who knew that he had a bass voice "very strong and exceeding trilling," planned that he should sing in the Protector's presence. After that no examination in politics, theology or ecclesiastical preferences was necessary. Oliver restored him.

Of reading there is no evidence that Cromwell was especially fond (though plenty that he respected those who were), or that he really ever knew any book except the Bible. To the end of his life he wrote and spoke its language, but that was not in his days peculiar to him, or even to the Puritan. Every intelligent person knew the Bible, everyone used its language, Strafford and Falkland almost as much as Cromwell. In its infinite variety they could always find phrases that would speak the language of their hearts better than any words of their own could have done. The Authorized Version, published in 1611, soon superseded all other translations. And almost as important as the new translation itself, was the fact that it soon began to be published in a portable and fairly cheap edition. It became the standard for the language. For as English literature was not taught in the schools and universities, it was not accessible to many people. So Cromwell lived at a time when the Bible was not only the religion, but the poetry and the story book, almost the sole literature of the masses of his countrymen.

Therefore it is not remarkable that his speeches in Parliament were "always intertwined with sentences from Scripture." A contemporary tells us that was "to give them greater weight and the better to insinuate them into the affections of the people." But probably not designedly so. Cromwell quoted Scripture because it was natural for him to do so, because he could not help doing so. But there is no doubt but that in this way he did "insinuate into the affections of the people." The words of Scripture were in their minds and hearts as they were in his. To them as to him there was no cant about such quotations.

And to Cromwell, as to almost all his contemporaries, the Bible was from cover to cover the literal Word of God, its authors merely amanuenses of the Holy Ghost. Miracles were not doubted, for science had not yet proclaimed a reign of law. And while to the Protestant the miracle that seemed contrary to nature belonged only to Bible times, he still clung to the belief that God timed natural events so as to reward the godly, and punish the ungodly, sent rain and fair weather in answer to the prayers of the faithful, put a cloud over the moon to cover Cromwell's retreat to Dunbar, allowed Tiverton to burn because its inhabitants had profaned the Lord's day.

And if God was very real and very near to the men of the seventeenth century, the Devil was equally real and equally near. The belief in witchcraft was almost universal. James I had written a dialogue on the subject, Shakespeare had repeatedly referred to it, Sir Thomas Browne denounced those who denied its existence as not only infidels, but atheists. Lord Bacon declared that the three declinations from religion were heresies, idolatries and witchcraft. As late as 1665 Sir Matthew Hale, the sanest and best balanced judge on the Bench, declared in court that he had no doubt at all that there were such creatures as witches, "for first, the Scriptures affirmed so much, secondly the wisdom of all nations had provided laws against such persons, which is an argument of their confidence of such a crime."

This belief was particularly rife around Huntingdon. Indeed the Golden Knight's second wife, not Oliver's grandmother, was supposed to have been done to death by witchcraft, and three witches had been burned for it. Their property, forfeited to Sir Henry, had been used by him to provide annual sermons in Huntingdon by alumni of Queens' College, Cambridge, against the sin of witchcraft, sermons which continued to be preached until 1785. But that was before Oliver was born. Whether he shared the general belief or not, we do not know, but it would have been a miracle if he escaped it.

There would be a great deal of talk in the Cromwell family, and the talk would run largely on public affairs. Uncle Oliver was in every Parliament of the reign, so he could give them first hand information. How the Spaniards had invaded the territory of the King's son-in-law the Elector Palatine, and how the King, so far from fighting the King of Spain because of this, was drawing nearer and nearer to him. How immorality of all sorts was tolerated at Court, how masques were performed, in which drunken ladies took, or tried to take, the leading parts. How all offices were for sale, how the King listened to no one except his favorite, George Villiers, successively Earl, Marquis and Duke of Buckingham. How he called him Steenie, because to him his face, like St. Stephen's, shone like that of an angel. A few years before this man had gone about in an old black suit, broken out in places. Now all who wished to obtain promotion, or even secure themselves from dismissal, must pay court to him. For the King, his "dear Dad and Gossip," promoted only on his recommendation.

Then, worst trouble of all, would come word of how Buckingham had taken Prince Charles to Spain, and how he might come back a

Catholic with a Spanish bride, or, such was the treachery of the Spaniard, might not come back at all. And then the reaction when none of these things happened, when he did come back, still a Protestant, and without the Infanta. Uncle Oliver would tell them how Buckingham, in dazzling apparel, had received the Lords and Commons, not in the Painted Chamber, but in the great hall of the palace like a king, as he was in all but the name. How he had stood as a monarch stands, surrounded by the peers in their robes, the King and the Prince behind him. How he had given a most entertaining narrative of the visit to Spain, couched in such language as to increase England's hatred for that country. How this had even made him popular, so that a Committee of the Whole House had asked the King that the Duke might be encouraged to proceed in his faithful service to the State.

And then the Parliament, not content with not having a Spanish Queen, must have a Spanish war for the relief of the Protestants of the Palatinate. And the King, urged by favorite, son and Parliament had consented. Shortly afterward the poor old man, whose motto had been "Blessed are the peace-makers," died, probably not much regretted. England was inclined to look upon the dignified moral son with more favorable eyes.

But then again would come bad news, the marriage with Henrietta Maria. After all was a French Queen very much better than a Spanish Queen? Then the story of how twelve thousand Englishmen had been taken from their employment by the press gang, put under the command of the German Mansfield, landed on the coast of Holland with only five days' provisions, and ordered to march on to the Palatinate. They never got there, simply died of disease and starvation. No doubt the suffering was due largely to the fact that Parliament had not voted supplies, but Parliament had not voted supplies because it had not been called together lest it should object to the French marriage.

Soon there would be even worse things to talk about. English ships had been loaned to France to reduce the Protestants of Rochelle. So after the first Parliament of Charles I, Uncle Oliver would bring back word that the short-lived popularity of Buckingham was over, that he was hated worse than ever, and had been named as unfit for his post. Further that the Commons had refused supplies for the war that fifteen months ago was so popular, partly because they could not trust the duke, but partly also because they had misunderstood the whole matter, had supposed that the Palatinate could be recovered simply by a successful attack upon Spain, had not realized that Austria and other countries were to be reckoned with. And for a general European war they had no mind.

But there was something that was troubling Cromwell more even than the state of public affairs. Dr. Sincott, the local Huntingdon physician, reported that for many years he had been his patient, and that he was "a most splenetick man, had phansies about the cross in the town; that he had been called up to him at midnight, and such unreasonable hours very many times, upon such a strong phansy, as made him believe that he was then dying." Oliver was worrying about his soul, was undergoing conversion.

Royalist historians tell us that his youth was given over to dissipation, that he was a notorious toss pot and drabber, even that he was sent to London to study law, because his mother feared that he might corrupt the home. "The first years of his manhood," says Sir Philip Warwick, who lived for a time in Huntingdon, "were spent in a dissolute course of life, in good fellowship and gaming, which afterwards he seemed very sensible of and sorrowful for, and, as if it had been a good spirit that had guided him therein, he used a good method upon his conversion, for he declared that he was ready to make restitution unto any man who would accuse him, or whom he could accuse himself to have wronged." In the records of St. John's Church, Huntingdon, now preserved at All Saints', there are statements that in 1621 and again in 1628, Oliver Cromwell submitted to some form of Church discipline. These entries were evidently made at a later date, they are inserted in another hand after the scrivener has copied the record for the year, no day or month is given, and there is evidence of erasure. Yet as Dr. Gardiner has suggested, there may have been in the mind of the writer, a vague memory of something that had actually happened.

As for the Royalist historians, they probably knew little of his youth, and they naturally sought to blacken his memory, and the censure of a seventeenth century Church, even if undergone, does not necessarily imply any very grave iniquity. The circumstances of his life do not allow much time for dissipation, yet it is possible that there was a period in which he did not altogether succeed in keeping himself under control. Sir Philip Warwick speaks of gaming, he may have gambled somewhat, his general sociability may have led him into some temptations, his quick temper into occasional violence and injustice. To the end of his life he was given to horseplay, and he may sometimes have carried it too far.

In 1638 he himself wrote to his cousin Mrs. St. John, "You know what my manner of life hath been. Oh, I lived in, and loved darkness rather than light, I was a sinner, the chief of sinners. This is true, I hated goodness, but God had mercy on me."

But that is the way that the Puritan was wont to feel and write after he had experienced conversion. And it is noticeable that Cromwell does not accuse himself of outward actions, but only of an inward state of mind. The modern psychologist would say that he suffered from a disintegrated personality. He who "needed not that any one should testify to Him of man, for He Himself knew what was in man" would say that he had not yet "come to himself." For he had not yet entered into that life of communion with God which, as a mystic, he believed to be necessary; he had not attained unto a constant practice of the presence of God, therefore he could not honestly say that he loved what He loved, hated what He hated. Conversion was the center of the Puritan creed. And conversion, according to Milton, meant not only or mainly to be saved from evil deeds, but to be saved from drifting, from levity of mind. It was generally preceded by a certain melancholy, an often exaggerated sense of sin. Even as an elderly man Oliver believed something of this to be necessary. "Whoever yet," he wrote to his daughter Bridget, "tasted that the Lord is gracious, without some sense of self-vanity and badness?" It was necessary to realize that one had sinned much and been much forgiven in order to love much.

Cromwell's melancholy has often been compared to Lincoln's, but both in cause and in duration, it seems to have been very different. With Lincoln it was a naturally melancholy temperament, not concern for his own soul. "The universe made him sad," he never got over it, to the end he "dripped melancholy." With Cromwell it was concern for his soul, but his was a sanguine temperament, so just as soon as he believed that his heart was right in the sight of God, the melancholy left him. Anxieties he was to have in plenty, but no more melancholy. But this happy ending was still some years ahead of him.

Children came rapidly. By 1626, Oliver being then twenty-seven years old, there were four of them, Robert, Oliver, Bridget and Richard. The family was still in the Church of England, the children were all properly christened at St. John's, as their father had been. When the time came to christen Richard, Oliver wrote, October 14th, 1626, to his "approved good friend, Mr. Henry Downhall, at his chambers in St. John's College, Cambridge, "Make me so much your servant, as to be godfather to my child. I would myself have come over to you to have made a more formal invitation, but my occasions would not permit; therefore hold me in that excused. The day of your trouble is Thursday next, let me entreat your company on Wednesday."

There was probably a christening feast that Wednesday night. Uncle Richard Cromwell, for whom the child was named, and who was probably another godfather, would be there. He was a near neighbor, he had bought land in Huntingdon in 1607. Uncle Oliver would come from Hinchingbrooke, and perhaps some of the Steward and Bourchier kin from Ely and London.

Sir Oliver had just come from the Parliament of 1626, had heard Sir John Eliot denounce the mismanagement of the expedition to Cadiz, then had heard Dr. Turner accuse Buckingham by name, and Sir William Walters declare that the cause of all their grievances was that "all the King's Council ride upon one horse." He would probably tell them of this, and of how the King had summoned the Lords and Commons to him at Whitehall, and told them that they were striking not at Buckingham, but at his father's government and his, and had added, "Remember that Parliaments are altogether in my power for their calling, sitting or dissolutions, therefore as I find the fruits of them good or evil, they are to continue, or not to be." In spite of this, there had been an attempt to impeach Buckingham. That had been dropped, but the Commons had prepared a Remonstrance, which they insisted must precede supply. "We protest to your Majesty, and to the whole world, that until this great person be removed from intermeddling with the great affairs of State, we are out of hope of any good success, and do fear that any money that we shall and can give, through his employment be turned rather to the hurt and prejudice of this your kingdom than otherwise." Rather than let this Remonstrance pass, the King had dissolved Parliament, though it had not yet granted supplies.

All these things Uncle Oliver would tell them. But as Cambridge men, what would probably excite Mr. Oliver Cromwell and Mr. Henry Downhall most was that, even while the impeachment was pending, Buckingham had been elected Chancellor of their university. Court influence of course. There had been opposition, he had been elected by a very small majority, and there were those who maintained that a severe scrutiny would show that he had not been elected at all.

More bad news was to follow. England, already at war with Spain and Austria, had drifted into a war with France. To pay for all these wars a Free Gift had been asked and refused. Therefore a Forced Loan was imposed, which was simply taxation without consent of Parliament. For refusal to subscribe to this loan, some eighty gentle-

men were imprisoned, four of whom were connected with the Cromwell
family, Aunt Joan's husband Sir Francis Barrington, Sir William
Masham, husband of one of Aunt Joan's daughters, John Hampden's
uncle Sir Edward Hampden, who was to die in prison. And John
Hampden himself, who said "that he could be content to lend as well
as others, but he feared to draw upon himself that curse in Magna
Charta, which should be read twice a year against those that infringe
it."

And because there was no money the soldiers had to be billeted
upon the people. They were often very troublesome. Crimes of which
ordinary justice should have taken cognisance were punished by
martial law.

Meanwhile Buckingham's attempt to seize the Isle of Rhé off
Rochelle had ended in a most dismal failure. Evidently war could not
be carried on without ample supplies, and these could be obtained only
through Parliament. As Charles would not give up the war, a new
Parliament was summoned. In this Parliament of 1628, Oliver Cromwell, twenty-nine years old, always a year older than the century,
Carlyle says, represented the borough of Huntingdon.

In June 1627 his uncle Oliver had been forced to pay the penalty
of his extravagance, and sell Hinchingbrooke to the Montagus, who,
as Earls of Sandwich, still hold it. Oliver's election therefore could
hardly be due mainly to family influence. Somehow or other he must
have acquired the respect and confidence of his fellow townsmen.
That hardly agrees with Royalist stories of dissipation during these
years.

CHAPTER IV

Puritanism and Parliamentarism

WHEN Oliver Cromwell entered public life, two questions were agitating not only England, but all of Western Europe. Was Catholicism or Protestantism to prevail, and if Protestantism what form of Protestantism? Was the government to be an absolute monarchy, or were the people, or at least a part of the people, to have a share in it? Everywhere the second grew in a measure at least out of the first, for everywhere the answer to the first depended largely upon who was to answer it.

To many of us of the twentieth century, whether we have settled down to a comfortable or hopeless agnosticism, or are still crying "Where is He, that I may find Him?" the religious battles of the seventeenth century seem to have arisen from trivial causes, and therefore to have been hardly worth fighting. No longer are we interested in the various doctrines that divided our ancestors. To us the questions are so much deeper, "Does God exist at all? Is there life beyond the grave?" So not only the fierce battles between Calvinism and Arminianism, but even the fear and hatred of Rome, are to us almost incomprehensible.

To understand, it is necessary to invoke the historical imagination, to realize that the fathers of Oliver's generation could remember and tell their sons of the fires of Smithfield, the Spanish Inquisition, Alva's Court of blood in the Netherlands, St. Bartholomew's Day and the Spanish Armada, that they themselves could remember the Gunpowder Plot, and that the Thirty Years' War, which seemed to them nothing but a life and death struggle between Protestantism and Catholicism, was going on. For the Counter Reformation had done its work, everywhere Catholicism seemed to be gaining ground. Rome and Spain had not relaxed their efforts to bring England back into the fold, and the danger was not only religious but political, it involved the political independence, the very existence of England as a nation.

Pius V's method had been to excommunicate Elizabeth in the hope of raising a revolt among her Catholic subjects. Campion and Parsons had labored to increase the number of such subjects. Success would

39

mean the death or dethronement of Elizabeth. Parsons had even gone so far as to speculate, in case of that event, what form of the Inquisition should then be brought in "whether that of Spain, (whose rigour is misliked by some), or that which is used in divers parts of Italy, (whose coldness is apprehended by more), is not so easy to determine; but the time itself will speak, when the day shall come. Perhaps some mixture of it will not be amiss for England." It was even proposed that the restored Catholic Bishops should have power to negative or confirm elections to the House of Commons. Thus Rome would never again lose her hold upon England.

While they may have over-estimated the danger, it was natural, under such circumstances, that Englishmen should have feared the Catholic population in their midst, and it is only fair to say that the penal laws against them were, under Elizabeth, dictated more by patriotic than by religious feeling. It is true that men were punished who had committed no crime, except as the state had made the practice of their religion a crime, men the great majority of whom probably never would have committed any other crime. But the underlying motive was patriotic and political rather than religious. They belonged to a church which had from the beginning been hostile to the government of Elizabeth, and later had seemed to sanction the overthrow of that government. What wonder if every member of that church had become an object of fear and suspicion? Who could tell which one of them might some day undertake the crime sanctioned by his church? It must be remembered also that to Elizabeth and the statesmen who surrounded her throne, the Reformation itself was patriotic and political, rather than religious and spiritual.

So there were laws excluding recusants from all positions in either the national or local governments, laws which even forbade them to travel more than five miles from home without a license from the local magistrates. There were fines for not attending the services of the Church of England, but they were collected very irregularly. The Mass was regarded as treason, every priest who celebrated it was doomed to death. However this statute seems to have been directed only against the propaganda that might come with publicity of worship. While no Catholic service was held openly except at the chapels of foreign ambassadors, Mass continued to be celebrated in private houses, nor was there any systematic attempt to banish priests from England.

Much to his credit, James I had no desire to be a persecutor. He wished to put an end to both religious persecution and religious wars.

Therefore when he came to the throne, to a considerable extent he refused to enforce the penal laws against the Catholics. As a result there was a great increase in the number of recusants, an increase perhaps more apparent than real, since it was probably largely owing to the fact that secret Catholics became avowed Catholics. Nevertheless England was alarmed, so the laws were again enforced. Then came the Gunpowder Plot, the work of a few desperate gentlemen, but it was not unnatural that Protestant England should believe that the whole Catholic population was more or less in sympathy with it.

For it was known that the Pope had not relaxed his efforts to bring England back into the fold. Indeed he was redoubling them, it was reported that he "stayed two full hours in prayer every day for the conversion of England," for he was convinced that if he could gain England, he would gain all. In 1614 the Spanish Ambassador to the Court of St. James had declared that if English Protestantism fell, Continental Protestantism would fall with it, the Dutch States would submit to Spain, French Huguenots and German Protestants would disappear, and with them the civil wars that were devastating their respective countries. The King of Denmark, the only Protestant state left, would follow the example of his brother-in-law of England. Thus Christendom would again be united, one fold and one shepherd.

Clement VII however had adopted a different method. Instead of stirring up the subjects to insurrection, he would convert the sovereign; the subjects who had changed before at the royal command would do so again. So before the death of Elizabeth, he approached James, offering to support his claim to the English throne, on condition that his eldest son, Prince Henry, be educated as the Church should direct. Later there had been proposals to marry first Prince Henry, and after his death Prince Charles, to a Spanish Infanta, these proposals in the early part of the reign being conditioned upon the education of the Prince under Catholic influences.

And James' conduct was not such as to reassure his subjects. His desire to secure the peace of Europe by putting an end to religious wars, had led him to draw near to Spain, so that Raleigh had fallen a victim to that country, the Spanish ambassador Gondomar seemed to excited Englishmen to have more influence with the King than any Englishman except Buckingham, there had been the negotiations for the Spanish marriage of the Prince of Wales, the journey of the Prince and Buckingham to Spain, and Charles I's actual French marriage had not been much more acceptable.

Moreover there were Catholic influences at work in high places, which were not unnaturally exaggerated. Buckingham's mother and other prominent people had gone into the Roman Church, there had been a time when Buckingham himself had seemed inclined to do the same. There was a feeling that the King could deny his Catholic Queen nothing, there were ninety Catholics in places about the Court, over one hundred and ninety Catholic landowners were influential in the country. Papal envoys were received at Whitehall, and were believed to be working for the conversion of England.

That England needed to be converted to something was beyond a doubt. For in many parts of the country there was danger that the separation from Rome might mean a relapse into heathendom. By Henry VIII and Elizabeth that separation had been regarded as political rather than religious, to them the Church of England was little more than an instrument by which independence from Rome and Spain might be secured. As for the mass of the people in the country districts, especially in the north and west, they had largely given up the old faith, and had not as yet acquired anything in its place. They went to Church and took the sacraments to prove their loyalty or to escape fines, repeated the Creed or the Lord's Prayer as a talisman. Or they might mutter certain syllables, neither Latin nor English, a vague reminiscence of the religion of their forefathers, for "many still superstitiously refused to pray in their own language."

Against this rising tide of heathenism two forces were at work, Puritanism and the High Church. Roughly speaking the one attempted to work from within out, the other from without in, and it was this difference of method which led to controversy and civil war.

In 1628 most of the Puritans were, like the Cromwell family, still in the Established Church. There was an Independent congregation in London, founded in 1616 by Hans Jacob, and now presided over by John Lathrop, formerly a Church of England clergyman. There were a few Baptists, chiefly in London and Norwich, and there were a few adherents of a peculiar sect known as Familists or Ranters. But with the exception of the Catholics, the church was almost synonymous with the nation. Within the Church however there were two parties, the High Church and the Puritan.

The name Puritan was at first applied by dissolute courtiers and hangers on at ale-houses to all those who protested against the vice and corruption of the age, and endeavored to lead or to induce others to lead a righteous and godly life. Baxter tells us that his father, "because he read Scripture on the Lord's Day, and reproved Drunkards and Swearers was reviled commonly by the name of Puritan

Precisian and Hypocrite," and this though he "never spake against the Bishops, nor even so much as prayed but by a Book or Form, being not even acquainted with any that did otherwise." "If any out of morality and civil honesty discountenanced the abominations of those days," says Mrs. Hutchinson, "he was a Puritan." "In my conscience," said Cromwell, speaking in Parliament in 1658, "it was a shame to be a Christian within these fifteen, sixteen, seventeen years in this nation, either in Cæsar's house or elsewhere. It was a shame, it was a reproach to a man, and the badge of Puritan was put upon it."

The Puritans laid great stress upon conversion, but to them conversion meant much more than amendment of life. The change must come from within out, amendment of life must be based upon amendment of soul. There must be a conviction of the immediate action of the Holy Spirit upon the heart, and of His constant presence in the life, the whole being must be brought into tune with the Infinite, the whole will must be conformed to the Divine will. Not only to George Fox and the Quakers, but to the best of the Puritans, by whatever name they were called, Christ must be the living Christ, not only a man who lived sixteen hundred years ago, but the Christ who lived now in them, the Hope of Glory.

Some of the more cultured Puritans were even broad enough to realize that the inward state at which they aimed could be attained without a knowledge of the historic Jesus. "By Christianity," said Mrs. Hutchinson, "I mean the universal habit of grace which is wrought in a soul by the regenerating spirit of God whereby the whole creature is resigned up to the Divine Will, and its actions directed to the obedience and glory of its maker—this is that sacred fountain which baptizeth all the gentle virtues that so immortalize the names of Cicero, Plutarch, Seneca, and all the old philosophers."

Puritanism has often been accused of hypocrisy. Of course it could and sometimes did degenerate into hypocrisy, but Puritanism was, in its origin, chiefly a protest against hypocrisy. It was not enough that the outward action should be right, the heart must be right in the sight of God. "It is an exaggerated, but an illuminating way of putting it," says Mr. Wingfield-Stratford, "that the Puritans made the discovery of the soul," and he attributes the excellence of English seventeenth century portrait painting largely to the Puritan insight into the depths of the soul.

But every creed degenerates, takes upon itself the imperfections of human nature, as the number of its adherents increases. So it was natural that as Puritanism, like every other creed, spread sometimes

among those who had small souls to develop, it should gather to
itself some who were too much given to censoriousness and self-
satisfied complacency. For while the Puritan held that it was possible
for the outward action to be right when the heart was not right,
he also held that when the heart was right, the outward action would
conform to it. And of course there were Puritans who were a little
too sure that they knew what the right outward action was for the
brother as well as for themselves.

However, Mr. Percy Scholes in his exhaustive study of "The Puritans
and Music" has proved conclusively that it was no part of the
seventeenth century Puritan creed to regard recreation or any art
or form of beauty as in itself sinful. Cromwell seems to have
expressed the general Puritan position of his day when he wrote that
he wished his son Richard to "approve himself to the Lord in his
course, and to search His statutes for a rule to conduct," but added,
"This will not abridge of lawful pleasures, but teach such an use
of them as will have the peace of a good conscience going along
with it."

If the Puritans objected to Christmas and other festivals of the
Church, it was because they regarded them as survivals or transforma-
tions of pagan holidays, not commanded in the Bible. And they made
the first day of the week a Sabbath day, because they thought that
was commanded in the Bible. But they realized that recreation was
necessary, so having taken away some of the accustomed opportunities
for it, the Parliament of 1647 decreed that every second Tuesday was
to be a holiday, and that no master should withhold his apprentice
or other servant from recreation on that day. Thus the stern Puritan
government gave the English working man facilities for recreation
which he was to lose under the Merry Monarch.

Again if the Puritans, in the day of their power, objected to
instrumental music, especially organ music, as a part of the church
service, it was because they regarded it as a sensuous pleasure, which
tended to distract the attention from the words sung, in which they
felt that the real worship consisted, and in this many Catholics and
Anglicans agreed with them. But the Puritans cultivated secular
music to a surprising extent. Bunyan's pilgrims played the viol
and the lute, Ready-to-Halt and Much-Afraid danced together (mixed
dancing!), and "footed it well, and also the girl was to be commended,
for she answered the music handsomely." Colonel Hutchinson as
a boy had the best dancing masters, and he provided them for his
children. Cromwell's wife and daughters danced. And although

Whitelocke, his ambassador to Sweden, refused an invitation of Queen Christina to a dance, because it happened to be on the "Lord's day," when she invited him on a week day he went and danced with her, whereby she perceived that "the Hollanders were lying fellows, for they had told her that there were no gentlemen in the Parliament party, but she saw by his dancing that he was a gentleman, as were many others of his party." There have been lying fellows since then. But when the Queen asked Whitelocke whether dancing was prohibited in England, he admitted that there were some who did not approve of it, but there was no law against it.

If the seventeenth century Puritans objected to the theater, except in extreme cases like that of Prynne, it seems to have been because the theater at that time was objectionable. The objection did not extend to masques and private theatrical performances. And when Cromwell wished to brand a certain Scotch regulation as extremely foolish, he likened it to that of a "man who would keep all the wine out of the country, because loose men would be drunk."

As for clothes Colonel Hutchinson wore embroidered suits, General Harrison scarlet and silver lace, and Dr. John Owen, at one time Cromwell's principal adviser in ecclesiastical affairs and Vice-Chancellor of Oxford under Cromwell as Chancellor, walked down the Oxford High "his hair powdered, cambric band with large costly band strings, velvet jacket, breeches set round at knee with ribbons pointed, and Spanish leather boots with cambric tops."

That the stress laid by the Puritans on conversion sometimes led to too much self-examination, excessive depression and morbidness, cannot be denied. Violent conversion, following upon intense conviction of sin, certainly implies a disintegrated personality. A time would come when it would be recognized that there were those who were children of God from the beginning, who had no need to bathe, but only to cleanse the feet from the dirt that would cling to them in the journey through this world of temptation and sin. That even when the previous life had been evil, conversion meant nothing but turning with heart, mind and soul from it to another, and for this no great emotional experience was absolutely necessary, the mind and will might precede the heart. Even in 1635 Baxter could hold the doctrine of conversion, without thinking it necessary to date the new birth.

But Puritanism was not the only force that was combating English paganism and immorality. The High Church was also busy. Many of its leaders were actuated by the same desire for high spirituality that directed the Puritan movement. But their method was the reverse of that of Puritanism, they worked from without in, rather than from within out. In some ways they had a broader knowledge of human nature than had the Puritans who would tear up evil by the roots. For with Plato they believed that "the true order of going was to use the beauties of earth as steps, upon which we mount upward, from fair forms to fair actions, from fair actions to fair notions, until we arrive at the notion of Absolute Beauty, and so become friends of God." The senses and imagination must be used to reach the heart. God must be worshiped in the Beauty of Holiness, the Righteousness of Holiness would follow.

So as many of the church buildings had fallen into decay, and "lay very nastily," they must be put in order and beautified. Reverence for the building itself and every detail of it must be inculcated and since, while the Prayer Book in some measure at least had been generally used, there had been considerable variety in the services, so that in some cases they seemed grotesque and uncouth, they must now be made uniform, reverent and beautiful. While the superstitions of Rome must be rejected, the beautiful forms with which she had come into the presence of the Unknown God must be restored, except when they were in direct contradiction to the teaching of the Reformed Church. Because the Church of Rome was painted was no reason why the Church of England should go undressed.

The Puritans were alarmed. Was it the intention to bring them back step by step to Rome? But it was not only fear of Rome that led to their opposition to these innovations (it must be remembered that they were innovations). They were also afraid that such forms instead of being aids to, might become substitutes for the worship of the God who is a Spirit, and Who must be worshiped in spirit and in truth, that instead of quickening the spiritual life, they might be made the opiates of the soul, that as Prynne put it, they were "likely to take the imprisoned soul, and lap it in Elysium," divorce religion from the realities of life and its problems. Perhaps they felt as St. Paul did, when he saw the Galatians substituting Jewish forms and ceremonies for "Jesus Christ, who had been openly set forth to them, crucified among them."

If the High Churchman could claim that he had History on his side, that all religions in all ages and in all countries had found forms, customs, institutions, necessary for their survival, the Puritan could answer "Because of this all religions, after the first enthusiasm has passed, have a tendency to become mere forms, with little influence upon heart and life." So while George Herbert could rejoice that "Beauty had taken up her place" in the Church of England, could find even in the stones of the pavement of his little church at Bemerton, symbols by which he came to the knowledge of God, and showed it forth in his life, Mrs. Hutchinson, as cultivated as he, saw in the service "nothing but a mere solemn kind of stage play." If only George Herbert had been allowed to worship in his way and Mrs. Hutchinson in hers, there would have been no difficulty. But Laud insisted upon uniformity, nor were the Puritans less strenuous in their opposition to forms than he was in his insistence upon them.

The center of the High Church was worship, their clergy therefore priests. To them the Puritan said "Ye worship ye know not what"; it was the function of the clergy to teach them what to worship. Therefore preaching, teaching, became the center of the Puritan service, to them the clergyman was prophet rather than priest. In many of the churches there was almost no preaching; the clergyman was lazy or incompetent, and contented himself with reading the service. So many Puritans would go to the next parish church to hear a sermon, when they had none of their own. The Cromwells probably did not do that, they were satisfied with Dr. Beard.

While there were some great preachers in the High Church, in general preaching was not much encouraged. This was largely because it tended to become doctrinal, and the doctrines set forth were those which the High Church was inclined to combat.

For to the difference about forms there had been added a difference about doctrine. During the reigns of Edward VI and Elizabeth Calvinistic influences had come in from the Continent, so that at the time of the accession of James almost the whole English Church, including James himself, was Calvinistic. While the hard doctrine of predestination doubtless caused distress to many, it on the whole produced strong men, probably because they thought of themselves not so much as clay in the hands of the potter, but as instruments of God, chosen by Him before the foundation of the world, to do Him service.

But in Holland Arminius, Professor of Divinity at Leyden, was teaching a different doctrine. God had not damned any of His creatures before He made them, Christ died for all, it was for the individual to determine whether he would accept or reject salvation. To the orthodox this seemed a step toward Rome, partly because whatever was not Calvinistic must be Roman, partly because Arminius himself had made a visit to Rome, and had not felt called upon to denounce everything that he saw there, but largely because it was the High Church party in England, the men who were trying to force Roman forms upon the Church, who were inclined to accept it.

These men did not generally call themselves Arminians; indeed Laud, the chief of them, sometimes denied that he was an Arminian, and there was some truth in his denial. He was not so much an Arminian as an anti-Calvinist, he had fought Calvinism at Oxford before he ever heard of Arminius. He was opposed to all religious dogmatism, believed that in such matters the human mind was not capable of arriving at the truth. And while his own doctrines, so far as he had formulated them, probably coincided rather closely with those of Arminius, he had reached them independently, so it was hardly fair to call him by his name.

Of course the fact that men prominent in the High Church either espoused Arminianism, or were indifferent to doctrine, tended to strengthen the Calvinism of the Puritans. So it is sometimes said that while the High Church insisted upon uniformity in worship, the Puritans insisted upon uniformity in doctrine.

But even from the beginning of the struggle, this was not quite true, there were Puritans in England who were not Calvinists, notably the Baptists, and soon there were to be Unitarians and Quakers. Moreover the fundamental principle of Puritanism was such as would put an end to doctrinal uniformity. For as the Puritan acknowledged no authority but the Bible, the Bible was necessarily subject to private interpretation. And with private interpretation would come great variety of doctrine. In his farewell sermon to the Pilgrim Fathers, John Robinson admonished them not to stop with what God had revealed to Luther and Calvin, for if Luther and Calvin were now living, they would be as ready and willing to embrace further light as that they had received. "And the Lord has yet more truth to bring forth out of His Holy Word. Be ready to receive whatever truth shall be made known to you." To different minds different truths would be made known.

But what widened the breach between Arminianism and Calvinism more than anything else, was the fact that in the other struggle that was going on, the struggle against political despotism, Arminianism, strangely enough, became the champion of absolute monarchy, while Calvinism fought for Parliamentary government. To a certain extent this had also happened in Holland.

It was in the attempt to destroy the anarchy following the Reformation, to attain nationalism and religious unity, that absolute monarchy had developed on the Continent. Under the Tudors it had looked a little as though this might also happen in England. In Plantagenet and Lancastrian days whatever opposition there had been to the King had been in the Lords. The Wars of the Roses had destroyed the military power of the feudal baronage, and with it went their power to name ministers or to dictate policy. Because the Tudors had protected them from domestic anarchy and foreign aggression, the Commons had been only too glad to act as the instrument by which they carried out their policy. It was much that they were the instrument, soon they would be more.

Moreover Henry VIII and Elizabeth really represented the people, were in close touch with their wishes and prejudices, so that when the House of Commons fell in with their wishes, they really fell in with the wishes of the people, including their own. The result was that while Continental despotism tended to make the people incapable of self-government, Tudor despotism tended to educate them for it.

But James did not know the English people, came to the throne puffed up with his ideas of Divine Right, and determined to be absolute. Speaking of the Parliament to the Spanish Ambassador in 1614, he said, "I am surprised that my ancestors should have permitted such an institution to come into being." To his first Parliament he said, "The state of monarchy is the supremest thing on Earth, for Kings are not only God's lieutenants upon Earth, and sit upon God's throne, but even by God Himself they are called gods. As to dispute what God may do is blasphemy, so it is seditious in a subject to dispute what a king may do, in the height of his power." As for the House of Commons, it derived all matters of privilege from him, it sat not in its own right, but by his grace.

The challenge thus thrown down was immediately taken up. The Commons hastened to tell the foreign king that he had been misinformed. The result was, that from the time that James came to the throne until 1640, there was no royalist party in the Lower House. The House of Commons formed a perpetual opposition, and this at a time when the Crown was dependent upon it in a sense that it had never been before.

For up to the beginning of the seventeenth century the King had in the main "lived upon his own," that is all ordinary expenses of the government had been paid out of the revenues of the Crown. Only when there were extraordinary expenses had Parliaments been asked to make a special grant, so it had not been necessary to call them together at other times. But when the Stuarts came to the throne, the royal revenue was no longer sufficient for ordinary expenses.

Owing to the fact that during the Tudor period, Crown lands had been given away or sold to favorites at low prices, or in many cases encroached upon, there had been considerable actual diminution. And this had happened at a time when a more highly developed society was constantly calling for more governmental expenditure, and while, largely because of the influx of the precious metals from the Spanish Colonies in America, there was a steady and universal rise in prices.

And while the Crown had been growing poorer, the men likely to be elected to Parliament, owing in great measure to the spoils of the monasteries, had been growing richer, therefore more independent, more eager to grasp at power than ever before.

So the situation of the early Stuarts was this. Not in sympathy with the people, and not understanding Parliament they were dependent upon Parliament, as Kings had never been before, while Parliament was in a position to resist them, as Parliaments had never been before. The Kings thought they were there to carry on the business of government as their predecessors had done, but they were no longer able to carry it on, except as Parliament gave them the money to do so. Parliament refused to give them the money, unless it understood and approved of the way that the business was being carried on. Not that the House of Commons was niggardly for, as Fuller put it, the Englishman cared not how much his purse was let bleed, so it was done by the advice of the physicians of the State. Though not at first clearly recognized, in time that came to mean that if the House of Commons must pay for the government, the House of Commons must be the government.

So there were disputes over taxation, disputes over foreign affairs, disputes over royal favorites, but back of them all was the religious dispute. It was largely for religious reasons that the Commons objected to the King's foreign policy, and the favorites who were supposed to have suggested it; chiefly because of religious disputes that they either failed to grant subsidies, or Parliaments were broken before they had granted them, so that forced loans and free gifts were demanded, and arbitrary imprisonment meted out to those who refused to pay them.

Now it happened that in all these disputes the Ritualists and Arminians, generally though not always the same, took the side of the King. To induce the great majority of Englishmen to drop their favorite doctrine, and make additions to their ritual was a stupendous task, and the more so since the prominent High Churchmen were generally too scholarly and fastidious, lived too much apart from the people to win popular support, perhaps even thought it beneath their dignity to try to do so. So to accomplish their object, they had to rely upon the King. And while most of them did not fully accept the doctrine of Divine Right, they decided that if the King would support them in the affairs of the Church, they would support him in the affairs of the State. "Defend thou me with thy sword, and I will defend thee with my pen," was the concluding sentence of Montague's "Apello Cæsarem." It expressed the common sentiment of his type of churchmen.

And Charles not only defended them, but promoted them almost to the exclusion of all others. Had he confined himself to securing toleration for the minority, it is quite possible that in time they would have become the majority. But when he gave the minority rule over the majority, it could but tend to increase the opposition.

For it came to pass that the Calvinist, denying free will to man, worked for the freedom of the subject, while the Arminian, granting him free will, worked against it. This tended to increase the number of the former. Men who did not understand the difference between Calvinism and Arminianism knew that for them, Calvinism meant freedom from arbitrary taxation, while Arminianism meant submission to it. So that in 1625 Pym said that "under the name Puritan (by that time a derisive synonym for Calvinist), had been collected the greater part of the King's true subjects."

During James' reign the quarrel did not come to a head. If the King had dealt roughly with the Puritan divines, who had signed the millenary petition, and later met him at Hampton Court, it was because he thought that granting their demands was a step toward the establishment of the Presbyterian form of Church government, from which he had suffered so much in Scotland. "No Bishop, no King!" he had cried. As a matter of fact, there was as yet among the Puritans no great opposition to the Bishops. As for doctrine, James was himself a Calvinist, nor does it appear that he had any special fondness for an elaborate ritual. If toward the close of his reign he showed some favor to Arminians and ritualists, it was not because of a preference for their doctrine or ritual, but because they supported his prerogative.

On the whole during the last years of his reign there was peace in the Church. Abbot, a decided Puritan with a fierce hatred of Arminianism and of Rome, was Archbishop of Canterbury, but he had little influence. The man who stood next to Buckingham in the King's favor was John Williams, a distant kinsman of Cromwell. Williams was Bishop of Lincoln, and on Bacon's disgrace had succeeded him as Lord Keeper of the Great Seal. In modern phraseology he would be called a Broad rather than a High or Low Churchman. So far as doctrine went, his leaning, at least in the early part of his career, was toward Calvinism. As for form, his own taste was toward ritualism, but it was taste rather than principle, within fairly wide limits he was inclined to let people do as they pleased. For neither Papist nor Puritan did he have any antipathy. He was statesman rather than churchman, his policy was to bring the King more into harmony with his people.

And yet it was Williams who first recommended Laud for a Bishopric. That was in 1623. Laud was forty-eight years old, but preferment had been slow in coming to him. He had been Archdeacon of Huntingdon—Oliver had probably known him there—President of St. John's College Oxford, chaplain to the King, Dean of Gloucester, and Prebendary at Westminster. But he was not as yet known throughout England, and at Court he was only "parva Laus," physically the smallest man there, and understood by those who cared to inquire into the matter, to be the highest high churchman in England.

Probably it was partly because it was to his private interest to do so, but largely because of his sense of fair play, that Williams, when he recommended the Puritan Davenant for the bishopric of Salisbury, recommended the High Anglican Laud for the poor Welsh bishopric of St. David's. And James was not favorable to the appointment. When Williams insisted he said, "Because I see I shall not be rid of you unless I tell you my unpublished cogitations, the plain truth is that I keep Laud back from all place and authority, because I see he hath a restless spirit and cannot see when matters are well, but loves to toss and change, and bring things to a state of reformation floating in his brain." When Williams still urged the matter, the King said, "Then take him to you, but on my soul you will repent of it."

Williams did repent of it. Laud soon formed an intimacy with Buckingham. Williams himself had risen largely because he had been able to do Buckingham a service. But now Buckingham liked Laud better, he made him his chaplain, corresponded with him during his absence in Spain, and after his return they were constantly together. Williams was crowded out.

When Charles came to the throne Buckingham was even more powerful with him than he had been with his father, and Laud rose with him. From the first day of the new reign, Williams was in disgrace, the Great Seal was taken from him in October, Laud took the place that should have been his at the coronation.

Charles was naturally a High Churchman, his taste inclined him to ritualism. He accepted the High Church standard of orthodoxy from the beginning, nine days after James's death Laud presented Buckingham with a "schedule in which was writ the names of many clergymen," marked O or P, Orthodox or Puritan, that the King might know whom to promote, and whom to keep back.

He indoctrinated the King and Duke not only on religious matters, but on the proper way of resisting Parliament. Whether he believed in the Divine Right of kings or not, he knew that if he was to have his way in the Church, the King must have his way in the State. So when the Commons made their attack upon Buckingham in 1626, it was Laud who advised the King's course of action, and even wrote the speeches which Charles delivered in his behalf. And it was by Laud's advice that tracts in favor of the Forced Loan were circulated, expanding and enforcing the doctrine of the royal prerogative.

But there were High Churchmen who went even further than Laud. Dr. Sibthorpe, a Northamptonshire vicar, preached an assize sermon, in which he declared that "the ruler must be obeyed, whether he rule justly or unjustly, courteously or cruelly." If the prince imposed an immoderate or even an unjust tax, the subject was bound in conscience to submit. Even "if princes command anything which subjects may not perform, because it is contrary to the laws of God or of Nature, or impossible, subjects are bound to undergo punishment, without either resisting or reviling, and so yield passive obedience when they cannot exhibit an active one." When Archbishcop Abbot refused to license this discourse for publication, he was suspended and banished from Court, his archiepiscopal functions vested in four bishops, of whom Laud was one. The sermon was licensed by the Bishop of London, and Sibthorpe was made a royal chaplain.

In the following year Dr. Mainwaring preached in defense of the Forced Loan before Charles himself. He went even further in his adherence to absolutism. "Among all the powers ordained of God, the royal is the most high, strong and large. No power in the world or in the Church can lay restraint upon it. That sublime power which resides in earthly potentates is not a derivation or collection of human power, but a participation of God's own omnipotency." So the payment of taxes, imposed by the King, could be refused only on peril of eternal damnation. Even Laud protested against the printing of this sermon, on the ground that it would be distasteful to the people, but the King insisted, the sermon was published.

So illegal taxation, forced loans, arbitrary imprisonment, and the views of such churchmen as Montague, Sibthorpe and Mainwaring were the matters that were agitating England when the Parliament of 1628, Oliver Cromwell's first Parliament, met.

CHAPTER V

The Parliament of 1628

THE House of Commons in which Oliver Cromwell took his seat on the seventeenth of March 1628, was a notable assembly. "And they say," writes a contemporary, "that it is the most noble, the most magnanimous that ever these walls contained. I heard a lord estimate that they were able to buy the Upper House, (His Majesty alone excepted), thrice over, notwithstanding there be of lords temporal one hundred and eighteen. And what lord in England would be followed by so many freeholders as some of these are?"

Indeed the wealth of this House of Commons has aroused suspicion. Just as modern historians sometimes tell us that the American Civil War was at bottom an economic struggle between the North and the South, and that in order to arouse popular feeling the slavery issue was exaggerated, and purposely exaggerated, so a school of historians has arisen who, perhaps with less evidence, tell us that the English Civil Wars were simply an effort on the part of a wealthy oligarchy to transfer the sovereignty from the Crown to themselves, and that they used the religious dispute to serve their purpose.

Now it is certainly true that by the time parliamentary government was fully established, the House of Commons was a close oligarchy, and it continued to be so for several generations. But when a struggle is prolonged through generations final results seldom correspond to original intentions. It is probable that the Parliaments of the first half of the seventeenth century got no further in their thinking than that the King was exercising certain powers arbitrarily, and while there were precedents both for and against this, they decided that he should not exercise them at all, that they should belong to them. If he should not exercise them, then they should, there was no one else. Possibly the majority of the members would not have cared very much at first who exercised them, provided the things were done which they wished to have done. I think that was true of Cromwell in the early part of his career. But I doubt whether they were consciously working in their own interest, and indeed whether they were really working chiefly in their own interest. They believed that they represented the people,

55

were working in the interest of the people, and in this belief I think that they were almost, if not quite right. For it is only fair to say that the House of Commons of that time, although largely an assembly of wealthy men of aristocratic birth, was much closer to the people than a similar assembly would have been a century later. We must not forget that those were days in which gentlemen mingled freely with yeomen and shopkeepers, knew them and understood them, and it was felt that because of their prestige and experience, they could look after their interests better than could men of their own class.

Of course the actual voters were only a minority of the population, in the counties still the forty-shilling freeholders, that is men who owned at least fifteen or twenty acres of land; while in the boroughs the franchise varied greatly, sometimes only members of the corporation, sometimes all who had burgess rights, occasionally even all the inhabitants of the place were allowed to vote. Yet, however it may have been later, at that time there seems to have been some truth in Selden's contention, that the non-voters were "involved in" the voters. For not only the forty-shilling freeholders, but also the fee-farm holders, who were perhaps half the population, and the populace of the towns were with the Parliament in its opposition to Buckingham, and in its desire to keep taxation down when it did not approve of expenditure. Moreover opposition to Spain, fear of Rome, dislike of High Church innovations, and opposition to Arminianism were very wide spread. Indeed as long as Parliaments occupied themselves chiefly with the redress of grievances, and the punishment of those whom they considered responsible for them, and that was almost up to the Civil War, they may be said to have fairly represented the spirit of the people. Even when two distinct parties were formed in the Long Parliament, they corresponded to a similar division among the people.

And while the House of Commons of 1628 was largely an assembly of squires and country gentlemen, it was also largely a Puritan assembly. For as we have seen, opposition to the Forced Loan, arbitrary imprisonments and the High Churchmen who supported them, had brought over to the Puritan side many who cared little about doctrines and ceremonies. All the gentlemen who had refused to pay the Forced Loan were returned at the polls.

However the minds of others may have been divided on the issues at stake, it is certain that Oliver Cromwell's interest centered in the religious problem. He had many kinsmen and friends in the House, most notable of whom were his cousin John Hampden, and Hampden's close friend Sir John Eliot. Yet all through that first session he sat silent. To the debate that led to the passing of the Petition of Right he contributed nothing. He was not an orator, his interest was in the religious, not the constitutional dispute. And he was never given to talking for the sake of calling attention to himself. Moreover he was still under a cloud, worried about the soul that he felt was not yet right in the sight of God. So far as his depression would allow him to do so, it was better that he should sit still, listen and learn.

The first thing that he heard was Laud's sermon. The conscientious man who, in his effort to force the peace in Church and State, had done so much to destroy it, preached from the text "Endeavour to keep the unity of the Spirit in the bond of peace." That unity was to be kept by a righteous King, to whom Parliament was to supply information.

Next came the King's speech, not quite in harmony with the Bishop's, for he asked not for information, but for money. He told the Houses that he had called them together to provide funds to meet the common danger. If they did not do this, he must use other means which God had put into his hands. This was not to be taken as a threat, for he "scorned to threaten any but his equals." He was ready to forgive and forget the misbehavior of the last Parliament, but he expected this one to do better.

Then Oliver sat through the great speeches which resulted in the Petition of Right, eloquence which at times moved the House to tears, and which was even occasionally interrupted by the sobs of the speaker himself. Evidence, a modern historian thinks, that the members were in a state of hysteria, induced by religious fanaticism. We must put ourselves in their place, realize that when they spoke as they did, they were risking not only liberty, but even life. And they dared to run the risk, because they believed that the rights and privileges that made their fathers free men were at stake, not only at this particular time, and in this particular case, but for all time and in all cases. If the King was willing to forgive and forget the distractions of the last Parliament, he doubtless expected this Parliament to forgive and forget the Forced Loan and illegal imprisonments. But it was not a case of forgiving and forgetting, but of seeing that it did not happen again.

"For this particular," said Sir John Eliot, "admits a power to antiquate the laws. It gives leave to the State," (the King or his ministers), "to annihilate or decline any act of Parliament; and that which is done in one thing, or at one time, may be done in another."

In the same strain Phelips declared that "if they could go back to their countries (counties) leaving our posterities as free as our ancestors left us, this Parliament would be entitled the Parliament of Wonders. To this end he proposed that the House prepare to consider grievances for His Majesty's view, "not to make a law to give us new liberties, but declaration with respective penalties; so that those who violate them, if they will be vile, they shall fear infamy with men, and then we shall think of such a supply as never a Prince received, and with our moneys we shall give him our hearts, and give him a new people, raised from the dead." That was the way to preserve the unity of the Spirit in the bond of peace, not Laud's way, not the King's way.

So the great debate went on, until it resulted in the Petition, reluctantly accepted by the King, on the seventh of June 1628. No longer were Englishmen to be subjected to forced loans, or arbitrary taxation, to arrest or imprisonment save by due process of law, no longer were soldiers or sailors to be quartered on them against their will, nor were they to be at the mercy of tyrannous decrees, called by the name of martial law.

And when it was known that the King had given his assent to this charter of liberties, not asserting new rights, but confirming old ones, Oliver had a chance to witness such manifestations of delight in London, as had not been seen since the day when Charles as Prince of Wales, had returned from Spain without the Infanta. Church bells rang, bonfires blazed, happy crowds gathered everywhere, there were expressions of joy, thankfulness, relief. People breathed freer.

And the Commons were as good as their word. They granted the King five subsidies, more than any House had ever willingly voted before, as much again as the whole national revenue of the Crown. There can be little doubt but that Oliver voted with them.

But they were not satisfied. It was on Saturday that the King gave his formal assent to the Petition of Right. On the previous Tuesday Sir John Eliot had moved, that as they intended to furnish His Majesty with money, they should also supply him with counsel. Therefore he desired that a Declaration be made to the King of the danger wherein the Kingdom stood by the decay and contempt of religion, and by the inefficiency of his ministers.

On Wednesday the King, alarmed for Buckingham, sent a message to the Speaker that, as the session was to end in a week, the House should husband the time, and dispatch old business, without entering upon new. The next day there was another royal message, ordering the House not to cast or lay any aspersion upon any minister of His Majesty.

Notwithstanding these two messages, Sir Edward Coke, eighty years old, and "not knowing whether he should ever speak again in this House, had decided now to do so freely, and to protest That the Author and Cause of all these miseries was the Duke of Buckingham." To this statement "the House had responded with cheerful acclamation, as when one good hound recovers the scent, the rest come in with full cry, and every one came home, and laid the blame where he thought the fault was."

It was in the hope of stopping this Remonstrance that the King had finally given his assent to the Petition of Right. It did not stop it, the Remonstrance went through just the same.

It asked that the penal laws against the Catholics be enforced, and called attention to the fact that while books written by Arminians were readily licensed, those written by Calvinists were not, that Arminianism was the sure way to promotion, since two prominent Arminians, Neille and Laud, were the prelates highest in favor, and thus the religion of the minority was being forced upon the majority.

Then came the crux of the whole matter. The principal cause of all the evils and dangers to which they had been subjected during the last three years, had been the excessive power of the Duke of Buckingham, and his abuse of that power. There was no demand for vengeance, but the King was asked to "take into his princely consideration whether it was safe to continue the said Duke in his great offices, or in his place of nearness and confidence about his sacred person." If, as in modern times, a simple vote of want of confidence had been sufficient to put a minister out, there would have been no danger of impeachment, and no fear of assassination.

How acceptable this Remonstrance was to the King, as he put it, every man might judge; for his part, he was sure no man could justify it. But the Commons had set to work on another Remonstrance, even more unacceptable, this time concerning Tonnage and Poundage, as the customs duties were then called.

"No man was henceforth to be compelled to make or yield any gift, loan, benevolence, tax or such like charge, without common consent, by Act of Parliament." So said the Petition of Right. But since customs duties fell upon goods, either before they entered, or after they left the country, the position of the lawyers then was, and long had been, that they were not to be regarded as taxes. During the whole Tudor period, and occasionally before, they had been granted to the

King for life by the first Parliament of the reign. Owing to the fact that Charles's first two Parliaments had been dissolved before there was time to consider the matter, they had not been granted to him, but he had collected them as usual. In this Parliament there had been a movement to grant them for a single year, and discuss the question at length in the next session. When the King refused to accept them in this way, they proposed to assert what certainly was very doubtful, that the customs duties, like other taxes, were included in the Petition of Right.

Now for Tonnage and Poundage Charles was prepared to fight as for life. For with the expansion of trade the customs were steadily increasing. If only he could continue to collect them, as his predecessors had done, it was just possible that, in spite of the decrease in other sources of the royal revenue, he could, in times of peace, dispense with parliamentary subsidies, and therefore with Parliaments, when they proved annoying to him.

So, hearing that this Remonstrance was in preparation, on the twenty-sixth of June he suddenly prorogued Parliament. He was not willing, he said, to receive another Remonstrance, to which he must give a harsh answer.

Such was the first session of the first Parliament of which Oliver Cromwell was a part. He had learned something of the questions which were before the country, something of the man with whom it had to deal. A pasquinade had been nailed to a post in Coleman Street, "Who rules the Kingdom? The King. Who rules the King? The Duke. Let the Duke look to it." But the King had repeatedly said that the Duke had done nothing except at his command. Was Oliver, in the light of what he had seen and heard, beginning to believe this, to realize that the real struggle must be with the King himself? It may have been so, but it is far more probable that, like most of his fellow members, he believed that the Duke had simply hypnotized the King, and that when he was removed, all would be well.

During the interval of the Prorogation, Charles set to work to prove to himself and his people, that he could get what he wanted while keeping to the letter of the Petition of Right. Tonnage and Poundage were collected as usual, merchants who refused to pay were punished.

As for the Remonstrance in which Laud, Neille and Buckingham had been especially named as objectionable, there was nothing to do about that but to treat it with open contempt. On the fifteenth of July Laud was promoted to the Bishopric of London. There he would rule over the most Puritan and Calvinistic of all dioceses. Neille,

regarded at that time as even more objectionable, had shortly before
been transferred from Durham to the more important see of Win-
chester. For his assertion that the King must be obeyed in spite of
the laws of the land, the Commons had presented charges to the Lords
against Mainwaring. The Lords had condemned him to imprisonment
during the pleasure of the House, to pay a fine of a thousand pounds,
and to be expelled from Court for life. The King pardoned him, and
gave him the rich living of Stamford Rivers. Montague, another High
Church defender of absolutism, who had incurred the displeasure of
Parliament, was made Bishop of Chichester.

As for Buckingham, he was more in favor than ever, and was sent
to Portsmouth to take command of the fleet that was to go to the
relief of Rochelle. There, on the twenty-third of August, Felton's
ten-penny knife did what the King had refused to do, removed him
from all positions of honor and trust. Foolishly and wickedly, we say,
and on the scaffold Felton said so himself. But London and England
rejoiced. After all, when a nation believes that a minister is hurling
it to destruction, and he cannot be removed in any other way, it must
be by death. Perhaps it does not matter very much whether that
comes through a Bill of Attainder or an assassin's knife. The news
reached Laud as he was consecrating Montague as Bishop of Chichester. Charles was at his prayers.

The fleet sailed without the Duke, but refused to go into action.
Rochelle surrendered, England smarted with the disgrace, Charles
hastened to make peace.

No doubt Cromwell kept all these things, and pondered them in his
heart. But perhaps he did more pondering later than at the time.
Just then he may have been more worried about the state of his soul
than about the state of England. It will be remembered that the
register at St. John's gives 1628 as the second date on which he submitted to some form of Church censure. At any rate on September
13th, he was in London to consult the famous physician, Sir Thomas
Mayerne, who found him "valde melancholicus." Of course it is possible that distress over the condition of Church and State had mingled
with concern over his own soul to produce this condition. Perhaps
he found London still rejoicing over Buckingham's death.

When Parliament was prorogued, the understanding had been that
it was to come together again in October. But this was now considered
unsafe until something more was done to secure the peace of the
Church. In November, at Laud's instigation, a Declaration was issued "that in these curious and unhappy dissensions, which have for

so many years in different times and places, exercised the Church of Christ, we will that all further curious search be laid aside, and these disputes shut up in God's providence, as they be generally set forth to us in the Holy Scriptures, and the general meaning of the Articles of the Church of England according to them. And that no man hereafter shall either print or preach to draw the Articles aside any way, but shall submit to it in the plain and full meaning thereof, and shall not put his own sense or comment to be the meaning of the Articles, but shall take it in the literal or grammatical sense."

Peace was to be won by silence. If Arminians as well as Calvinists were silenced, it did not make much difference, the object was not so much to foster Arminianism, as to destroy Calvinism. Before Parliament reassembled, attempts were made to appear impartial. Montague was persuaded to write a letter to Abbot, in which he disclaimed any wish to uphold Arminianism, Abbot himself was invited to Court, and bidden to attend the meeting of the Council. On the 17th of January, 1629, there was a proclamation, calling in "Apello Cæsarem." Three days later, Parliament came together for its second session.

It soon became apparent that these measures had brought not peace, but a sword. There was a debate about Tonnage and Poundage, but religion was the chief business of the session. It was to no avail that Apello Cæsarem had been called in, since its author had been given a Bishopric. As one member put it "if they get Bishoprics by writing such books, we shall have many more that will write books of the same kind." But it was against the Declaration that the main battle was waged, the Declaration that had warned Parliament that it must leave religion alone, and had left the sole interpretation of the Articles to the Prelates, some of whom, as Eliot said, might be the fathers of all ages, but not all, witness Doctors Laud and Neille, witness likewise Montague so lately preferred. "No," said Pym, "it belonged to the duty of a Parliament, to establish true religion and punish false," and they proceeded to do so in such a way as to make it clear that they "rejected the sense of the Jesuits and Arminians." Intolerance had begotten intolerance, the determination of the minority to silence the opinion of the majority had created a determination on the part of the majority to silence the minority.

There were further attacks upon Bishop Neille, stories of how while he had silenced Calvinism, he had refused to silence Popery and Arminianism. And it was then, upon the sixteenth day of February, 1629, that Oliver Cromwell arose, and as one historian says, "stuttered and stammered his maiden speech."

We do not know that he "stuttered and stammered"; it is certain that he spoke in great excitement, but it is not likely that he was conscious that it was a maiden speech, or even a speech at all. He simply had a fact to contribute. It was an old story that Dr. Beard had told him. On the Sunday after Easter it had been the custom to select a preacher to give from an out-door pulpit in Spital Square, a summary of three sermons that had been preached before the Mayor and Aldermen. At least twelve years before Dr. Beard had been appointed to give this summary. One of the three sermons preached by Dr. Alabaster, had contained "tenets of Popery." At least Dr. Beard thought that it had, and intended to dispute them. Neille, at that time Bishop of Lincoln, and Dr. Beard's diocesan, had sent for him, and forbidden him to do so. Beard had persisted in his intention, and Neille had reprimanded him.

What was in Cromwell's mind when he told this story? Doubtless he meant to show that the Neille who had silenced Dr. Beard was the same Neille who now, through the Declaration, would silence everybody. But was he contending that whereas the Declaration would silence both sides, he would grant freedom of speech to both sides? At least he did not say, as other members had, that Calvinists alone should be allowed to preach, did not ask that the Alabasters be silenced, but only that the Beards be allowed to speak.

However it hardly seems possible that at that early date, he had arrived at that degree of toleration. It is almost certain that a few days before he had risen with the rest of the House when the Resolution was read, the Commons' Declaration in answer to the King's Declaration. "We, the Commons in Parliament assembled, do claim, profess, and avow for truth, the sense of the Articles of Religion which were established in Parliament in the reign of our late Queen Elizabeth, which by public Act of the Church of England, and by the general and concurrent exposition of the writers of our Church have been declared to us, and we do reject the sense of the Jesuit and Arminianism."

But there is no evidence that any system of theology ever made any real appeal to him. If he had accepted Calvinism, it was because it was the prevailing creed of the country, especially of that part of the country in which he lived. Moreover it was opposed to ritualism, and opposed to Rome. But to him religion was not a system of theology, it was union and communion with God, the desire to know Him, and to do His will, the God of the Bible, the God speaking in the course of events, the God speaking in his own heart. If he did not especially distinguish between the God of Kings and Chronicles, the God of Hosea, and the God of Jesus, that was hardly to be expected of one of his generation.

The debate on religion was interrupted by one on Tonnage and Poundage. Not so much an interruption as it seemed, for to prevent the King from having his way in the Church, Parliament must meet frequently. To insure this, he must be absolutely dependent upon it for supply. The Petition of Right had forbidden him to levy direct taxation without consent of Parliament. Now the Commons proposed to control indirect taxation, by granting Tonnage and Poundage for a year only. But Charles had continued to collect, and the Judges had upheld him.

On February 26th the religious question was again taken up directly. There were complaints of ceremonies imposed, Popery and Arminianism spreading, the special favors shown Neille and Laud who were discountenancing and hindering the preferment of the orthodox, favoring and preferring such as were contrary. That was the crux of the matter, the King's authority was being used to exalt the religion of the minority over that of the majority. The Commons saw no remedy save that of compulsory conformity to the religion of the majority.

The end is known. How on March 2nd, 1629, the King having sent an order to the House to adjourn, Holles and Valentine held the Speaker down in his chair, while Eliot's three Resolutions were read:

"Whosoever shall bring in innovations in religion or by favour seek to extend or introduce Popery or Arminianism, or other opinions disagreeing from the True and Orthodox Church, shall be reputed a capital enemy to this kingdom and commonwealth."

"Whosoever shall counsel or advise the taxing and levying of the subsidies of tonnage and poundage, not being granted by Parliament, or shall be an actor or instrument therein, shall likewise be reputed an innovator in the government, and a reputed enemy to this kingdom and commonwealth."

"If any merchant or other person whatsoever shall voluntarily yield or pay the said subsidies of Tonnage and Poundage, not being granted by Parliament, he shall likewise be reputed a betrayer of the liberty of England, and an enemy of the cause."

Thus the "great, warm, ruffling Parliament" of 1628 ended.

Oliver saw it all, was a part of it all. With how much of it was he in sympathy? He certainly was determined that forms and ceremonies should not be forced upon an unwilling people, that Popery and Arminianism should not suppress Calvinism. Was he determined that

Calvinism should suppress Arminianism? Was he sure that Parliament should be the sole governing power? Did he even see that it was aiming at that? Probably in the heat of the moment he was carried away, there were years ahead in which he would experiment, and think it out.

Some one else was looking on and thinking it out at the time. No one had been more instrumental in framing and carrying the Petition of Right than Sir Thomas Wentworth. During the recess he had been raised to the House of Lords. At that remove he had had a chance to watch the proceedings of the Commons. He came to the conclusion that he had seen enough of Parliamentary government. Henceforth he was to be known as the Great Apostate.

And yet no apostate to his real convictions. It was one thing to oppose the evil counsellors of the King, another thing to consent to the transfer of the sovereignty from King to Parliament. For he saw more clearly than any one else did, that while the Commons might think they were only maintaining their ancient privileges, they were really aiming at the whole power in Church and State. And was this disorderly mob, ignorant on many subjects, easily swayed by passion, always liable to be working at cross purposes, fitted for that? Was it not, as King James had said, a Body without a Head? Moreover he was no lover of the Puritanism on which they were insisting.

And so he threw himself on the side of absolute monarchy. Had not that been the trend everywhere on the Continent, and had not order and prosperity been increased thereby? And even at best Parliaments could only express the average sense of their generation, while a wise king could sometimes raise his people above their generation. Not that he would do away with Parliaments altogether; there would perhaps be times when it would be well to advise with them, there would certainly be times when it would be necessary to go to them for money. But the real power must be in the hands of a wise King, a true father of his people, surrounded by able ministers. But how make Charles wise, how secure able ministers? To which Strafford would have countered, how make Parliament wise, how secure able leadership? That seemed to him a more difficult problem than the other.

And indeed there was a long way to go before Parliamentary government could be made practicable. No one was fated to realize this more than Cromwell.

He was a very conscientious man, this Wentworth who must now be called Strafford. Indeed they were all conscientious men, the leaders on both sides, Charles, Laud, Strafford, Pym, Hampden and Eliot, all honestly working for what they believed to be England's good. But Strafford seems to have been the only one of them who had a clearly defined theory, who knew exactly where he wanted to go. Charles never showed himself less wise, more blind to his own interests, than when he sent him away from him, first to be President of the Council of the North, afterwards to Ireland.

On the twenty-second of March the King issued a Proclamation. After speaking of Eliot as an outlawed man, desperate in mind and fortune, he said "And whereas for several ill ends the calling again of Parliament is divulged, however we have showed by our frequent meetings with our people our love to the use of Parliaments; yet the late abuse having driven us unwillingly out of that course, we shall account it presumption for any to prescribe any time to us for Parliaments, the calling, continuing and resolving of which is always in our own power. And we shall be more inclinable to meet in Parliament again, when our people shall see more clearly into our interests and actions, when such as have bred this interruption shall have received their condign punishments, and they who are misled by them and by such ill reports as are raised on this occasion, shall have come to a better understanding of us and themselves." That is there were to be no more Parliaments until the Commons had been schooled to obedience, had learned to see that the King was wiser than they.

That was on March 27th. On March 29th Laud recorded in his diary that two papers had been found in the yard of the Dean of St. Paul's. "One concerned the Lord Treasurer Weston, the other concerned myself, and was to this effect: 'Laud, look to thyself, be assured thy life is short. As thou art the fountain of all wickedness, repent thee of thy monstrous sins, before thou art taken out of the world, And assure thyself neither God nor man can endure such a vile counsellor to live.' Lord, I am a grievous sinner, but I beseech Thee deliver my soul from them that hate me without a cause."

CHAPTER VI

Personal Government of Charles I

march 22, 1628

ON the dissolution of Parliament Cromwell returned to Hunting-don, and resumed his ordinary life as a gentleman farmer. His property there had been somewhat increased by land left him by his uncle Richard. No doubt he was in some respects a changed man, he had learned much, there was much for him to think about. And there may have been times when he was so absorbed in his own thoughts that his fellow townsmen found him a little removed from them.

But there is no likelihood that his days or his nights were spent in excited anticipation of future greatness. He had no desire to emulate that far off Uncle Thomas, indeed he would seem not to have admired him, there is even a story that he disclaimed all relationship to him, though he probably only disclaimed him as an ancestor. If he had ever dreamed in childhood that he would some day become the greatest man in England, all that was past now. Perhaps his father had thrashed it out of him. Other men who have achieved greatness have planned for it, and prepared themselves for it, Oliver was to have greatness thrust upon him. He was "by birth a gentleman, living neither in any considerable height, nor yet in obscurity," and in that position he expected always to remain. Of course he might go to Parliament again, if ever there was to be another Parliament, but it was not likely that he would play a great part there, he had given no promise of it in the last Parliament, he had not the gifts of his cousin Hampden. And if there was not to be another Parliament, neither he nor any one else who thought as he did, could play any part at all. So to his neighbors he may have seemed

> "As though his highest plot
> To plant the bergamot."

And perhaps it was his highest plot for his own life. But if he did not think of himself as playing a great part, he must have thought much of the things in which Fate had decreed that he should play a great part.

There were those nine colleagues of his in the late Parliament, who had been arrested because of their conduct in the House. He had supposed that the Petition of Right had made imprisonment without due process of law impossible, but it belonged to the Judges to interpret the law, and they had interpreted it in the King's favor.

There was Sir John Eliot, his cousin Hampden's friend who, when brought before the Court of King's Bench, had refused to plead on the ground that the Court could not take cognizance of words spoken in the House, and so he had been left to languish and die in the Tower. His last extant letter was to Hampden. Perhaps Cromwell read it.

And there was the King, keeping within the letter of the law, and even of the Petition of Right, but able to get a revenue, and so able to dispense with Parliaments. True he had had to go very far back, and enforce laws that had been in disuse since Plantagenet times. But the Judges said he had a right to exact fines of those holding estates by military tenure who had not taken up knighthood; that he had a right to revive old forest laws, so that men had to pay heavily to recover lands held by their fathers for generations; that he also had a right to create monopolies, by which he got a considerable revenue, and the people paid four times what he got.

As for Tonnage and Poundage, he saw it collected as usual. True that for six months the London merchants had given up buying and selling rather than pay it, but that could not be continued indefinitely. Trade was resumed, the customs duties were paid.

Yet he saw that the country was prosperous, that the poor law was well administered, and that while the nobility were grumbling over the revival of the forest laws, the gentry over knighthood fees, and the people generally over monopolies, taxation was not, on the whole, excessive. The main difficulty was that the King was able to govern without a Parliament.

And in 1634 he began to hear men talk about "the fundamental laws of England," a phrase that was soon to be on everybody's lips. No one knew exactly what these laws were, but the men that used the expression meant, as Ludlow afterward put it, that the King was not to be allowed to govern them "as a god by his will" but that the "people should be governed by laws made by themselves" (or at least a part of themselves) "and live under a government devised by their own consent." They were determined to have a voice in controlling their own destiny.

It was in connection with ship money that the phrase came into existence, or at least, became popular. England needed a navy, the King did not wish to summon Parliament. So raking up old precedents, he levied ship money, at first in 1634 only on the maritime counties, in later years on the inland counties as well.

No doubt a navy was needed. Not only to compete with the navies of France and Holland, but also to protect England from the pirates who were seizing her merchant vessels, carrying off her seamen as slaves, ravaging and kidnaping on the coasts of Cornwall and Devon. And no doubt there were historical precedents for the method that Charles had taken to secure it, but historical precedents do not count for much with a generation that has forgotten them. No doubt also that in case of a sudden and unexpected emergency arising when Parliament was not in session, the King might be justified in taking whatever steps were necessary to meet it, trusting Parliament to ratify what he had done later. But no such emergency seemed to exist in 1634, there was plenty of time to call Parliament.

And when ship money was levied, not only once, but year after year, it was evident that it was not done just to meet an emergency, but was to be a permanent policy, that this tax was intended, as Clarendon was later to admit that it was, not only for the support of the navy, but "for a spring and magazine that should have no bottom, and for an everlasting supply of all occasions." Cromwell would hear men say, and would himself realize, that if it were successful, it would be possible never to summon Parliament again, the King would be absolute.

And when his cousin, John Hampden, by refusing to pay the twenty shillings levied upon him, became the most talked about man in England, and the case was brought before the Court of Exchequer, these fears were confirmed. In spite of the able advocacy of St. John, a cousin by marriage of both Cromwell and Hampden, the Court decided in favor of the King.

And one of the Justices, Lord Finch, "by an unnecessary logick," Clarendon says, blurted out all that was implied in the decision, all that Englishmen feared. "Acts of Parliament," he said, "are void which bind the King not to command his subjects, their persons and goods, and no Acts of Parliament make any difference." There they had it, not only would ship money make Parliaments unnecessary, but even when summoned, their Acts would make no difference.

All these things Oliver would observe and ponder in his heart. He probably had many opportunities of talking them over with Hampden and St. John. But he was not moved to active resistance, nor, so far as we know, to public utterance. He paid his fine for not taking up knighthood, and probably paid ship money, at least there is no record that he did not, which is pretty good evidence that he at least was not plotting to transfer the sovereignty from the Crown to a wealthy oligarchy. After all taxation was not excessive, and it is possible that at this time he cared very little about who did the governing, provided that the religion of the minority was not imposed upon the majority. If he wanted Parliament to meet, it was chiefly in order that it might prevent that. For his interest was almost entirely in the religious struggle, in the religious struggle at home and abroad.

For this reason he was probably giving even more excited attention to what Gustavus Adolphus was doing abroad than he was to what was happening at home. Two books, "The Sweedish Intelligencer," and "The Sweedish Soldier," were being widely circulated in England. There is reason to believe that Cromwell not only read them, but studied them carefully.

For like the majority of his countrymen, he was blind to the many complicated issues involved in the Thirty Years' War. To him as to them it was simply a struggle between Catholicism and Protestantism, and it was in Gustavus that the hope of the Protestant cause lay. So he welcomed the news of his success "with tears of joy in his eyes," and when word came that he had fallen at Lützen, he "mourned for him as though he had been a Swede." Twenty-two years later he told the Swedish Ambassador so. By that time he had made practical use of Gustavus' military tactics.

In the religious situation at home there was little to encourage him. He saw that preferment in the Church was constantly given to those who represented the religion of the minority. He had evidence that, even while Abbot lived, Laud was the dispenser of the royal patronage. For during the three years following his appointment as Bishop of London, no less than fifteen Bishops were either appointed or promoted, almost all of them of the Laudian persuasion, Arminians, Ritualists, Absolutists. So that when some one asked what the Arminians held, a wit replied, "All the best livings in England."

And when in 1633, the year that Gustavus fell at Lützen, Laud succeeded Abbot as Archbishop of Canterbury, Cromwell watched him as he proceeded vigorously to "establish an orderly settlement of the worship of God in England." So rigorously that Falkland complained that "the conforming to ceremonies was more exacted than the conforming to Christianity," and that "there was less severity

toward those who damn our Church than toward those who, with
weak consciences, and perhaps as weak reasons, through dislike
of some ceremonial garment, or some commanded posture, abstain
from it."

And Cromwell, what did he think about it? We know, for twenty-
five years later he told his last Parliament. While Falkland objected
simply on the ground that it was a tithing of mint, anise and cummin,
while the weightier matters of the law were neglected, to Cromwell
it was a more vital matter. He saw in the new regulations "a desire
to innovate upon us in matters of religion, and so to innovate as to
eat out the core and power and heart and life of all religion, by
bringing on us a company of poisonous Popish Ceremonies, and imposing them upon those who were accounted the Puritans of the
Nation." So he became, as his kinsman Bishop Williams tells us,
"a common spokesman for the sectaries, and maintained their part
with great stubbornness."

Williams himself took a very common sense view of the matter.
There was a great deal of trouble about the position of the communion
table. According to the Elizabethan Instructions and Canons, it was
to stand at the east end, but was to be moved down into the body
of the Church when required for use. But as it was difficult to move
it had become customary for it to stand in the body at all times.
Now Laud ordered not only that it be placed in the east end, but
used there. To this the Puritans objected strenuously. So when
there was a dispute over it at Grantham in Williams' diocese, he
decided that in accordance with the Elizabethan canon, the table
should stand ordinarily at the east end, but should be moved down
when it was to be used. He even went beyond the canon, and decided that when placed at the east end, it should stand east and
west as a table, not north and south as an altar. This was not his
preference, in his own private chapel the table stood north and south,
altar wise, but to him it was merely a preference, too small a matter
to quarrel over. "Lastly," he wrote to the Vicar, "whichever side
soever, you or your parish, shall first yield to the other in these
needless controversies, shall remain in my judgment, the more dis-
creet, grave and learned men of the two; and by the time you have
gained more experience in the care of souls, you shall find no such
ceremony equal to Christian charity."

But Cromwell could not take such a common sense position. To
him the new ceremonies were popish ceremonies, and like most
of his fellow Puritans he feared that the Archbishop was leading

England back to Rome. And to make the table an altar was to create a sacramental rather than a teaching church, seemed to imply transubstantiation, thereby tending to exalt the priesthood daily becoming more unpopular, was in short a long step toward Rome.

There was really no danger that Laud would go back to Rome, or seek to take England back, but it is small wonder that Cromwell thought that he would. The Pope thought so too, and twice offered him a cardinal's hat.

And there were other things than the forms to arouse Cromwell's fears and the Pope's hopes. For instance, it was evident that Laud did not dislike the Catholics, he enjoyed and even sought their company, while he avoided the Puritans. And with his belief in the apostolic succession, his feeling for historical continuity, he had no difficulty in acknowledging the Church of Rome as a true Church, a position which he refused to accord to the Protestant churches of the continent, the churches from which English Protestantism had drawn so much inspiration. Falkland complained that the Anglican Bishops had "slackened the strictness of that union, which formerly existed between us and those of our religion beyond the sea, an action as unpolitick as ungodly."

But it was not only fear of Rome that aroused Cromwell's opposition to Laud's innovations. He objected to the new forms that were being made compulsory, because he believed that they would "eat out the core and power and heart and life of all true religion," that through them religion might degenerate into mere formalism. Perhaps he did not appreciate the fact that the fight against forms might become as much a substitute for true religion as the fight for them.

And so, as Falkland put it, Laud had brought about the destruction of Unity under the Pretence of Uniformity. Yet it was largely in the interest of unity that he had insisted upon uniformity. Let the fruitless theological controversy rest, it served only to raise questions "not answerable in this life." And let men unite in approaching the True God, Who after all is Unknown and Unknowable, with beautiful forms. Doctrines divide, forms might unite. And only a united Church of England could withstand the assaults of Rome which, notwithstanding reports to the contrary, he did wish her to withstand. On the scaffold he reminded his audience that the Jews had said of Jesus, "If we let Him alone the Romans will come, and take away our place and nation." So they put him to death, and the Romans came, because they had not listened to Him. Now he prayed God that this clamor of "Venient Romani" might not help to bring the Romans in, for "the Pope never had a harvest in England since the Reformation, such as he hath now in the sects and divisions that are amongst us."

Poor Laud! How he had miscalculated! It was his own well-meaning policy that had created not only strife within, but secessions from the Church that had hitherto been almost comprehensive with the nation. Sects had arisen and multiplied. And it was of these sects that Cromwell had become "the common spokesman."

Moreover the opposition to Laud was increasing on other than strictly religious grounds. Falkland complained that he was "unpolitick." That was the trouble with him, he was "unpolitick." He was conscientious, he was well-meaning, in many respects he was liberal, but he was not politic. And because he was not politic (in some ways much to his credit), he gave the Puritans strange allies. Just as the Puritans were to do later, as the Americans have recently done in Prohibition, he made the mistake of making vice crime. In the twelve months immediately preceding the Long Parliament, more than two thousand persons were brought before the Archdeacon's court in London for tippling, Sabbath breaking, and incontinence. And in this matter there was no distinction between rich and poor. Indeed the rich, as the greater, or at any rate the more conspicuous sinners, paid the heavier penalties. The Church, like the God Whom she worshiped, was to be no respecter of persons. So for a time the dissolute rich made common cause with the Puritans.

And then Laud insisted that the clergy should be gentlemen. Such men were likely to hold up their heads in the presence of the Squire, sometimes even to usurp the jurisdiction which he had thought belonged exclusively to him. So the resentful Squire joined the Puritan in opposition to the increasing power of the priesthood.

So Cromwell saw that while the country was peaceful and prosperous, everywhere there was seething discontent, discontent which could find active expression only in a Parliament, and neither he nor any other man knew whether there ever would be a Parliament again. And the discontent became daily more sullen and more hopeless.

This dammed-up feeling did however find a certain outlet in 1637, when Prynne, Bastwick and Burton stood in the pillory. There had not been much excitement in 1634, when Prynne stood there alone for an attack upon the theater. Indeed certain members of the Inns of Court, some of them Puritans, had seized the occasion to give a masque at Whitehall in the presence of the King and Queen, and

Milton had written "Comus." But when in 1637, with Bastwick and Burton, he was again sentenced to the pillory and imprisonment for life, this time for attacks on the new ritual and on the power of the Bishops in Church and State, flowers were strewn in the paths of the victims, and on their way to their distant prisons crowds gathered everywhere to applaud them. It is true that they were all venomous pamphleteers, and it is quite possible that they would have been sued for libel today. But they were not sedition-mongers, and in the main points of their attack the majority of the English people were with them. So Laud had decided in his own favor, against a majority of the people.

During all these years, Andrew Marvell pictures Cromwell as "living reserved and austere." It may well have been so. For things were going wrong in Church and State, and there was nothing that he could do to set them right. That was the great trouble, that feeling of powerlessness that would force him to retreat within himself, make him not only reserved and austere, but perhaps sullen, gloomy, even irritable at times. One fancies that there were occasional flashes of that terrible temper which he had not yet learned to subdue.

And during the whole period the melancholy, the blackness of darkness that would come over him when he thought about his own soul, his heart that was not yet right in the sight of God, continued. He was, a friend tells us, "in a very low and afflicted condition, suffering great troubles of soul, lying a long time under sore troubles and temptations." In his own words, he "dwelt in Meshec which signifies Prolonging, in Kedar which signifies blackness."

So, looking back through the centuries, we see him a despairing man, in despair about his own soul, in despair about the Church of God in England. And no doubt there were times when the two despairs mingled and blended, each reënforcing the other, so that he could not distinguish between them. For, says his friend, "the time of his extreme suffering was when this cause of religion, in which we are now engaged, was at its lowest ebb. He suffered and rose with the Cause, as if he had one life with it."

In the midst of this suffering he found occasional relief in espousing the cause of the poor in his neighborhood. That at least was something that he could do. However a case may be made out that the Parliamentary movement was chiefly an effort on the part of the rich to snatch power from the King, and then use it in their own interests, that liberty to them meant only the monopoly of a class, it certainly

does not apply to Cromwell. All through his life his sympathies
went out to the poor, always his voice was raised against those "who
make many poor, to make a few rich."

Up to 1630 the government of Huntingdon had been very democratic. There had been two bailiffs and a Council of twenty-four
members, elected annually by the whole body of citizens. But it
would seem as though so much democracy had not tended toward
harmony, for the burghers themselves petitioned Charles I for a new
charter, "to prevent popular tumults." This was granted in the summer
of 1630. By it an oligarchy took the place of the democracy; the
government was entrusted to a Mayor and twelve aldermen, the first
Board of Aldermen, nominated by the King for life, to elect the
Mayor, and fill vacancies in their own body as they occurred.

Cromwell, who was named as one of the Justices of the Peace,
seems to have approved the change. He had not as yet espoused
democratic theories of government, in fact he never did fully espouse
them, and probably this seemed to be the only way "to prevent
popular tumults."

The first Mayor under the new arrangement was Mr. Robert
Barnard, a barrister who had been an active promoter of the change.
When its terms were examined it was found that the Mayor and
Aldermen might do as they pleased with the common lands, so many
of the poor were afraid of being deprived of their right in them.
This might cause severe suffering.

Now if Cromwell was not sure that government should be by
the people, he was very sure that government should be for the people,
especially for the poor of the people. So he championed their cause,
and in dealing with Mr. Barnard appears to have lost his temper.
At any rate the corporation complained to the Privy Council "that
Mr. Oliver Cromwell had made disgraceful speeches to Mayor Robert
Barnard."

So on November second 1630, the Council committed Mr. Oliver
Cromwell to custody. On December first the case was referred to
the arbitration of the Earl of Manchester, a Montagu, and brother
of the Montagu who had bought Hinchingbrooke.

So far as the matter in dispute went, Manchester found Cromwell
in the right, and ordered the charter to be amended, so that "the number of men's cattle of all sorts, which they now keep according to
order and usage upon their commons, shall not be abridged or altered."
Nevertheless he thought the language used by Mr. Oliver Cromwell

in speaking of Mr. Robert Barnard blameworthy, and that an apology should be made. To this Cromwell consented. Manchester's report reads:

"For the words spoken of Mr. Mayor and Mr. Barnard by Mr. Cromwell, as they were ill, so they are acknowledged to be spoken in heat and passion, and desired to be forgotten; and I found Mr. Cromwell very willing to hold friendship with Mr. Barnard, who, with a good will, remitting all the unkind passages past, entertained the same. So I left all parties reconciled."

And yet only six months later, in May 1631 we find Cromwell selling all his property in Huntingdon for £1800, and renting grazing lands at St. Ives, five miles eastward, but still on the Ouse. Did he do this because, after his quarrel with Mr. Barnard, he no longer found Huntingdon a pleasant place to live in? Or is it possible that he was anticipating a time when nowhere in England would there be a pleasant place for him to live in? Those were days in which many of his friends "being together in Lincolnshire, were falling into discourse about New England," the days in which men from near-by Boston and its vicinity were going out to found another Boston across the sea. It may have been that he was thinking of following their example. At any rate he put his property into a form in which it could be easily disposed of, rented rather than bought land at St. Ives.

To St. Ives he took his wife and children, there were now six of them. Since Richard's christening feast two had been added, Henry and Elizabeth, the two that were to be most after their father's own heart. In St. Ives two more were born, James who died in infancy, and Mary who lived to a good old age. He took them back to Huntingdon to be christened, perhaps because his mother and sister Elizabeth, who do not seem to have accompanied him to Huntingdon, still lived there. Or it may have been that he no longer cared for the ministrations of his old friend, the Rev. Henry Downhall, Richard's godfather, who had become vicar of St. Ives. In later years he and Cromwell were to go very different ways, perhaps the separation was already apparent. However Cromwell attended his Church "generally with a piece of red flannel around his neck, being subject to inflammation." For though espousing the cause of the sectaries, he was still himself in the Church of England.

Only one letter written by Cromwell during his residence at St. Ives has come down to us. That concerns a lectureship likely to come to an end through lack of financial support. As in many churches there

was very little preaching, individuals or corporations sometimes engaged lecturers to preach, and do nothing else. Since it was the
Puritans who felt the need of preaching, the lecturers and their
supporters were generally Puritans. Laud objected to them, and did
what he could to make their existence impossible.

Somewhere in Huntingdonshire there was a lectureship that had
been founded by certain citizens of London. In 1636 some of these
citizens had failed to renew their subscription. Perhaps Dr. Welles
the lecturer, Dr. Welles "a man of goodness and industry and ability
to do good every way" could not be retained. Cromwell thought that
since so many of the lectureships had been suppressed "with too much
haste and violence by the enemies of God His Truth" (presumably
Laud and his coadjutors), it was no time to let another fall through
failure of support on the part of its friends. So in January 1636 he
wrote to one of the subscribers, his "very loving friend, Mr. Stone,
at the Sign of the Dog in the Royal Exchange, London."

"Among the catalogue of those good works which your fellow-
citizens and our countrymen have done this will not be reckoned
for the least, that they have provided for the feeding of men's souls.
Building of hospitals provides for men's bodies; to build material
temples is judged a work of piety; but they that procure spiritual
food, they that build up spiritual temples, they are the men truly
charitable. Such a work as this was your erecting the lectureship in
our country (county). Now the lecture must not be allowed to fall,
through withdrawal of the pay."

If Cromwell had ever entertained the idea of going to America, he
gave it up in 1636 when his uncle Sir Thomas Steward of Ely died,
leaving him a considerable fortune. He moved to Ely with his family,
became farmer of the tithes as his uncle had been. This time his
mother went with him. For her it was going home, in Ely she had
been born and grown up, in the cathedral there her first husband
and the child she had borne him were buried. Probably the house
to which her son took her there, that set apart for the farmer of
the tithes, was the one in which she had passed her girlhood. It
still stands, next to St. Mary's Church, and is now used as the Vicarage. Not a rich man's house, indeed it is hard to see how Cromwell,
with his wife, mother, and nine children, to say nothing of servants,
could have been accommodated in it, but with its many windows
and narrow branching staircases, it has a rare charm, and a quaint
air of gentility.

At Ely Oliver continued to champion the cause of the poor. In

1634 a company of Adventurers, headed by the Earl of Bedford, had been incorporated to drain the fens around St. Ives and Ely and carry the Ouse direct to the sea. Part of the reclaimed land was to go to the Company, part to the Crown, the remainder was to provide a fund for the upkeep of the drainage works. In 1637 when the work was declared finished, and the Adventurers claimed their reward, many commoners complained that they would lose the rights of pasturage and fishing which they had hitherto enjoyed. Cromwell espoused their cause, promising them that they should enjoy every part of their commons. But in 1638 the King declared that the work had not really been completed as represented, that he would himself see that it was properly finished, and in the meantime the people of the district were to continue in possession of their lands and commons. For Charles I was also in sympathy with the poor.

As for Cromwell, he was to continue his activities in behalf of the common rights, and to win such a following in this way, that in 1643 a royalist news sheet nicknamed him "Lord of the Fens."

It was while he was at Ely that his first great sorrow came to him. His two older sons, Robert and Oliver, perhaps Richard also, were at school in Felsted, near their grandfather Bourchier's country home. There Robert died in May 1639, only eighteen years old. Oliver spoke of this on his death bed. "When my eldest son died, it went to my heart like a dagger, indeed it did." But he found comfort in the words of St. Paul, "Not that I speak in respect of want. I have learned in whatsoever state I am therewith to be content. I know both how to be abased, and how to abound, both to be full, and to be hungry, both to abound and to suffer need. I can do all things through Christ which strengtheneth me." This Scripture, Oliver said, saved his life.

Perhaps it was his spiritual life to which he referred. For by that time he had found relief from his "low and afflicted condition," his "soul had come alive again." This great sorrow must not kill the new life. Seven months before, in October 1638, he had written to his cousin Mrs. St. John.

"Truly then this I find. That He giveth springs in a dry and barren wilderness where no water is. . . . He giveth me to see light in His light—Blessed be His Name for shining in so dark a heart as mine." Now that the worst was over, "if he could honor his God here either by doing or by suffering he would be most glad."

The blackness of darkness was never to return. "Dull care never sits beside a rider whose pace is fast enough," Theodore Roosevelt used to quote from Horace. Cromwell's pace was soon to be very fast indeed.

For the year 1638 marked a turning point in the outward as well as in the inward things that were afflicting him. The opportunity to honor his God by doing was near at hand.

It was in 1637 that Prynne, Bastwick and Burton had suffered Star-Chamber sentences, in 1638 that the Judges had decided against Hampden. The popular indignation in both cases had been sufficient to make a wise King tremble and retrace his steps. Yet it is possible that Charles might have worked his will in England, that there would have been no more Parliament and no civil war, had not Scotland and Ireland entered into the picture. As yet Ireland was quiet. Strafford was there, working out his policy of Thorough, writing to Laud about it, hoping soon to see it established in England also, rejoicing that there the Ship Money decision had "forever vindicated royalty from the conditions and restraints of subjects." It was a good government that he was giving Ireland, a government calculated to bring peace, order and industrial prosperity such as she had never known before. But in bestowing these blessings he was utterly disregarding the wishes and prejudices of the people. There were curses, not loud enough to be heard in England, or to be heeded by the lonely intellectual against whom they were directed, but they were very deep.

It was from Scotland that resistance was to come, Scotland about which Cromwell and most Englishmen knew as little as they did about Cathay. When, in 1623, James told Williams that he objected to promoting Laud because he had a restless spirit, he added that he had been pressing upon him the project of "bringing the Scots to a nearer conjunction with the Liturgy and Commons of the English Church, and this notwithstanding that after the General Assembly of 1610 he had pledged his royal word that he would try their obedience no further "anent ecclesiastical affairs." He had rebuffed him, but "for all that he feared not mine anger, but assaulted me with another ill-fangled platform to make that stubborn kirk stoop more to the English pattern."

In 1637 Laud, now all powerful, and with a King at his back who did not know that stubborn kirk as his father had known it, made a serious attempt to carry out his ill-fangled platform. A prayer-book was to be forced on Scotland, differing from that in use in England mainly in the fact that it was even more opposed to Puritan and Presbyterian ideas. An attempt to read the new service in St. Giles' cathedral, Edinburgh, was met on July 23rd, 1637, with Jenny

Geddes' footstool. Strafford in Ireland was informed that there was in Scotland "horrible ado against the bishops for seeking to bring in our service book." In March 1638 all good Scots were taking the Covenant, in which they bound themselves, by all means lawful, to recover the purity and liberty of the Gospel, as established and professed before the recent innovation. In May Laud was writing to Strafford that he was thoroughly uneasy about the Scotch business. "If God bless it with a good end, it is more than I can hope for. The truth is that snowball hath been suffered to gather too long."

Charles was determined to put an end to this Scotch business, at least to the Covenant. "So long as it is in force," he said, "I have no more power in Scotland than a Duke of Venice, which I will rather die than suffer." Certain concessions were made "to win time that they may not commit public follies till I be ready to suppress them." When these proved useless, there was nothing for him to do but suppress them by force of arms. For that money was necessary, he did not dare to summon Parliament, so the First Bishops' War was financed by a voluntary contribution amounting to only £50,000. With that Charles managed to get to Berwick, where he discovered that his raw recruits would have to meet Alexander Leslie with a force of veterans who had seen service on the Continent, "lusty and full of courage, great cheerfulness in the faces of all." His supplies gave out, he could not keep his army together, so the Treaty of Berwick was signed in which it was agreed that all matters, civil and ecclesiastical, should be settled in a Scotch Assembly and Parliament. There had been no fighting, only one man had been killed, and that by accident. The Scots went home in love with the King.

The King went home to find some way out of the concessions which he had made. He refused to confirm the acts of the Scotch Parliament, and summoned Strafford from Ireland. Strafford came home, determined not to rest, "till he had conformed that kingdom in all, as well for the temporal as ecclesiastical affairs, wholly to the government and laws of England; and Scotland was governed by the King and Council of England."

Money was necessary, so he advised the King to summon Parliament. To refuse to grant supplies in such an emergency seemed to him unthinkable, it would be nothing short of treason. If any one did refuse, he should be "laid by the heels, till he learned to obey and not to dispute."

So on April 13th, 1640, after an interval of eleven years, there was again a Parliament in England, the Parliament that was to be known as the Short Parliament. The borough of Cambridge chose Oliver Cromwell as one of its members, "the greatest part of the burgesses being in the Hall." There was considerable excitement about that election.

This House of Commons was on the whole a moderate body, yet it did not respond to the danger as Strafford had hoped, was not even moved by the statement that the Scots were trying to secure aid from the French. What mattered it, since the Scots, and even the French if they came to their assistance, would only be fighting their battles? Grievances must be redressed before they would grant money for the Scotch war or anything else. "Till the liberties of the kingdom were cleared they knew not whether they had anything to give or no." Charles offered to abolish ship money if they would give him twelve subsidies. The Commons hesitated about giving so much, even Strafford thought the demand too high, but the King refused, or at least his secretary, the elder Vane, possibly with some ulterior motive, said that he refused to consider a lesser grant. Whereupon the Commons demanded that other grievances be first redressed, and were preparing to ask the Lords to join with them in a protest against the war with the Scots, when on May 5th, 1640, the King suddenly dissolved them. They had been in session only three weeks. Cromwell had been a silent member.

The Opposition leaders were not discouraged. There was a "marvelous serenity upon their faces." Oliver's cousin St. John announced "All is well. Things must be worse before they can be better, and this Parliament would never have done what was necessary to be done."

Strafford continued to push the war. "Now," he said to the King, "you are loose, and absolved from all rules of government. In an extreme necessity, you may do all that your power admits. Parliament refusing, you are acquitted towards God and men. You have an army in Ireland you may employ here to reduce this kingdom. One summer well employed will do it."

Somehow an army was gathered, an army that the general of cavalry at Newcastle described as "men fit for Bedlam and Bridewell." As they marched northward they broke into the churches, burned the communion rails, and moved the tables into the body of the church. Neither army nor people wished to beat the Scots. Strafford had been appointed commander-in-chief. He made almost superhuman efforts, he was ill, had to be carried to his army on a litter. But he had to confess that the war was lost before it had begun. "Never came any man to so lost a business," he exclaimed. The Treaty of Ripon was signed. Northumberland and Durham were left in the hands of the Scots, as pledges that, until the terms of a general peace were agreed upon, they would be paid £850 a day for the maintenance of their army. Instead of fighting the Scotch, England was paying them, and did not at first begrudge it, for they had fought her battle, made her Parliament possible.

Charles called a Great Council of Peers to meet with him at York. All that they could do was to advise him to call another Parliament. The Long Parliament was summoned.

CHAPTER VII

The Long Parliament

THE Long Parliament was convened November 3rd, 1640. Lord Morley has noticed that of Englishmen of mature powers, only two famous names were missing from its membership, Milton and Hobbes. Hampden had been riding through the country doing considerable electioneering.

Many of the members of the Short Parliament had been returned, but they were of a different mood from what they had been then. "The same men who six months before," says Clarendon, "were observed to be of very moderate tempers, and to wish that gentle remedies might be applied, talked now in another dialect, both of things and persons, and said they must now be of another temper than they were the last Parliament."

Indeed the sudden dissolution of that Parliament, and the fact that during the interval ship money, coat and conduct money, all the familiar and objectionable expedients for raising a revenue, had been resorted to, had convinced them that half measures would no longer suffice. "They must now," said St. John, "be of another temper, they must not only sweep the house clean before, but must pull down all the cobwebs which hang in the tops and corners." They had little fear of a sudden dissolution this time. The Scotch army was their protection. "No fear," they said, "of raising the Parliament, so long as the lads about Newcastle sit still." And so they set to work to make a thorough job of it, determined not only to redress grievances, but to make such grievances impossible in the future, so that when they separated, there should be no doubt that Parliament, and not the King, was the real sovereign of England.

And no one was more determined than Oliver Cromwell, he had waited so long, now he must act. He had been again returned by the borough of Cambridge. When the House first met no less than seventeen relatives or marriage connections of his and Hampden's were included in it. By 1647 the number had risen to twenty-three. As there was no regularly organized Government or Opposition, the leaders of the popular party met at Sir Richard Manly's house, in a court behind Westminster Hall, to arrange measures and methods of procedure. Of these leaders Pym stood first in the House, Hampden, with even more reputation throughout the country, next to him. As a man of rising ability, cousin of Hampden and St. John, Cromwell probably met with them. He soon found himself serving on no less than eighteen committees.

The accounts that have come down to us of him at this time make the impression of a man full of energy and determination, somewhat crude outwardly and perhaps inwardly, not as yet able to control that terrible temper of his, the fiery passions that had accumulated and been bottled up during those years of forced inaction, yet making his abilities felt even from the beginning.

There is a story that rather early in the history of this Parliament some one asked Hampden, "Pray, Mr. Hampden, who is that gentleman? For I see he is on our side, by his speaking so warmly to-day." To which Hampden replied, "That sloven, whom you see before you, hath no ornament in his speech, but if we should ever come to a break with the King, which God forbid, that sloven will be the greatest man in England."

So far as we know, his first speech in the Long Parliament was on the ninth of November, only six days after the opening of the session, when he rose to deliver the petition of John Lilburn, a victim of the Star Chamber who, at the age of twenty, had been publicly lashed all the way from the City to Westminster, and had since then been imprisoned for three years in the Fleet. Cromwell secured his release. Later he was to meet him many times, both as friend and as foe.

It was while he was delivering this speech, that Sir Philip Warwick saw and heard him, and gave us his unforgettable portrait of him. He tells us how he himself, "very well clad, as became a courtier, came into the House one morning, and perceived a gentleman speaking, very ordinarily apparelled, in a plain cloth coat, made by an ill country tailor, with plain linen, not very clean, and a speck or two of blood upon his little band; his hat without a hatband, his stature of a good size, his sword stuck close to his side, his countenance swollen and reddish! his voice sharp and untuneable, his eloquence full of fervour." And this gentleman was "very much hearkened unto"; a fact which tended much to lower Sir Philip's reverence for the great council of the realm.

It has been suggested that the "speck or two of blood upon his little band" may have been due to an accident in shaving. And it might well have been so. For doubtless Cromwell was very much excited as he made his toilet that morning, and it is small wonder if he failed to guide his razor aright. It was the first time that he had spoken in Parliament for more than eleven years, indeed the first time that he had ever made a real speech at all. And the subject on which he was to speak was exciting, he was excited over it himself, and he wished to excite others. Indeed, Sir Philip tells us "he aggravated the imprisonment of this man by the Council-table, unto that height the very government itself had been in great danger by it." And perhaps his indignation made his voice more "sharp and untuneable" than usual. It certainly helped to make his eloquence "full of fervour."

Another observer goes a little more deeply into the matter, so as to partly explain why he was "very much hearkened unto." "When he delivered his mind in the House," he tells us, "it was with a strong and masculine excellence, more able to persuade than to be persuaded. His expressions were hardy, opinions resolute, asseverations grave and vehement, always intermingled with sentences of Scripture, to give them the greater weight, and the better to insinuate into the affections of the people. He expressed himself with some kind of passion but with such a commanding deportment, till at his pleasure, he governed the House, as he had at most times the leading voice." But this last was to be later, he did not at first take a leading part in debate.

Then there is Clarendon's account of him. "When he appeared first in Parliament, he seemed to have a person in no degree gracious, no ornament of discourse, none of those talents which used to reconcile the affections of the standers by; yet as he grew in place and authority, his parts seemed to be renewed, as if he had concealed faculties, till he had occasion to use them; and when he was to act the part of a great man, he did it without any indecency, through want of custom." Even Sir Philip Warwick, when he saw him later, had to confess that "he was of a great and majestic deportment, and comely presence."

Clarendon has given us another picture of him. In this he appears at his old business, defending the rights of the people in the common lands. Some waste lands at Somersham, near St. Ives, had been enclosed without the consent of the commoners and sold to the Earl of Manchester. As soon as the Long Parliament met, the Commoners petitioned the House of Commons for redress. The Lords intervened, and issued an order in favor of Manchester. Then the dispossessed commoners proceeded "in a riotous and warlike manner," with the beating of drums, to break down the fences. Lord Manchester issued sixty writs against the offenders. Cromwell moved and carried that the matter be referred to a committee of the commons. Of this committee Hyde, afterward Clarendon, was chairman. Let him tell the story.

"Cromwell," he says, "ordered the witnesses and petitioners in the method of the proceedings, and seconded and enlarged upon what they said with great passion, and the witnesses and persons concerned, who were a very rude kind of people, interrupted the counsel and witnesses on the other side with great clamour, when they said anything that did not please them; so that Mr. Hyde was compelled to use some sharp reproofs, and some threats to reduce them to such a temper, that the business might be quietly heard. Cromwell, in great fury, reproached the chairman for being partial, and that he discountenanced the witnesses by threatening them. The other (Hyde) appealed to the committee, which justified him, and declared that he behaved himself as he ought to do; which more inflamed him (Cromwell), who was already too much angry. When upon any mention of matter of fact, or the proceeding before or at the enclosure, the Lord Mandevil (Manchester's son) desired to be heard, and with great modesty, related what had been done or explained what had been said, Mr. Cromwell did answer and reply upon him, with so much indecency and rudeness, and in language so contrary and offensive, that every man would have thought that, as their natures and manners were as opposite as it is possible, so their interest could never have been the same. In the end his whole carriage was so tempestuous, and his behavior so insolent, that the chairman found himself obliged to reprehend him, and tell him that if he (Cromwell) proceeded in the same manner, he (Hyde) would presently adjourn the committee, and next morning complain to the House of him."

Evidently it was the same Mr. Oliver Cromwell with whom Manchester had had to deal before, when he had made "disgraceful speeches to Mr. Robert Barnard." The same fiery temper, the same uncouthness, and the same fierce zeal in the cause of the poor.

In the proceedings against Strafford, Cromwell took no active part, but he was in sympathy with them. Indeed the attempt to impeach Strafford was the action of the House as a whole, there was no dissenting voice. When, in the fear that the charges against him could not be proved, or that if proved, they could not technically be construed, as high treason, the impeachment was turned into a Bill of Attainer, there was some opposition, but it was not on party lines.

There were no parties in those early days of the Long Parliament.

That Strafford was not technically guilty of high treason, that from a judicial point of view the proceedings against him were a hollow mockery, is certain. But the Commons regarded their action as one of self-preservation. That he was planning to subvert what they had recently learned to call "the fundamental laws of England," was beyond a doubt. He had labored to subvert the rights of parliaments, and the ancient course of parliamentary proceedings. Worse, he was making autocracy efficient, and whichever form of government succeeded first in gaining efficiency, would be the one that would prevail. So he suffered not so much for what he had done, as for what they feared that he would do. He could be removed only by death. "Stone dead hath no fellow," said Essex. He had declared the King "loose and absolved from the laws." "Why should he have law himself, that would not that others should have them?" asked St. John.

He was arrested and impeached just as he was about to accuse the parliamentary leaders of high treason, for encouraging and aiding the invasion of the Scots. That Pym got ahead of him was probably due to the indecision and vacillation of the King, that indecision and vacillation of which he had so often complained before. Technically he had a better case against Pym than Pym had against him. But Parliament and the people believed that, whatever the technical case was, he was a traitor to their liberties, while Pym was their savior. So far as he and Pym were concerned, it was not only a case of "My life, or thy life"; it was a case of Strafford's life, or the life of Parliamentary government, this new form of government that was just beginning to evolve in the world.

Yet when Cardinal Richelieu, on hearing of Strafford's death, remarked, "The English were so foolish that they killed their wisest man," there was some truth in his judgment. Strafford was not a wise man, in that he did not understand his generation, yet he was perhaps the only really constructive statesman of that generation. He alone knew what he wanted, the others only knew what they did not want. He fell a martyr to what he honestly believed to be the best government possible for the England of his day. To him the choice was between order and anarchy, and that meant between absolute monarchy and parliamentary rule. He chose absolute monarchy, knowing full well the weakness of the particular monarch whom he had to support. That parliamentary government should have seemed to him anarchy is not surprising. Until the cabinet system was developed, it was almost that, Cromwell was to find it so, and to resort to some of Strafford's measures. Only to him they were always to be desperate expedients, not thought out theories.

There had been a time when Pym and Strafford had been friends. Now each had done his best to do the other to death for England's sake, and Pym had won. On the last day of Strafford's life, Browning makes Pym recall that friendship, and say,

> "Even thus I love him now;
> And look for my chief portion in that world
> Where great hearts led astray are turned again.
> Soon it may be, and certes, will be soon.
> My mission over, I shall not live long.
> Ay, here I know I talk, I dare and must
> Of England, and her great reward, as all
> I look for there: but in my inmost heart
> Believe I think of stealing quite away
> To walk once more with Wentworth, my youth's friend,
> Purged from all error, gloriously renewed,
> And Eliot shall not blame us."

It is not very likely that Pym felt that way then. But who shall say? In the Great Beyond perhaps Pym and Wentworth, Cromwell too, did meet, and each recognized the other's greatness, each knew that whatever the faults and mistakes had been, they had all loved and lived for England, that each in his own way had tried to guide her into the paths of order, peace, righteousness and happiness.

But even before the minister who had counseled and done his best to develop absolute monarchy had been removed, it had been almost unanimously decided that the special courts that made it possible must also be done away. So again the acts abolishing the courts of Star Chamber and High Commission, denying the right to levy ship money, declaring that customs duties, Tonnage and Poundage, were subject to parliamentary grant, were the acts of Parliament as a whole, there was practically no opposition. With these measures we know Cromwell to have been in deep sympathy. We have already noticed that his first speech was in behalf of a victim of the Star Chamber.

The cause of all the evils, it had been frequently declared, was the intermission of Parliament. That must be no longer possible. Of this too Cromwell was certain. So when Strode introduced a bill, reviving a law of Edward III, by which Parliament must be summoned every year, it was Cromwell who moved its second reading, December 30th, 1640. It was referred to a committee of which he was a member. This committee transformed it into a Triennial Act, in accordance with which Parliament was not necessarily to be summoned every year, but at least once in three years.

Then on May 11th, 1641, came an Act which was revolutionary. The existing Parliament was not to be dissolved without its own consent. This really was to make not Parliament in general, but the existing Parliament, the supreme sovereign; not only to deprive the king of all power to make his dissatisfaction effective, but also to deprive the electors, the people of England, of all such power. It was destined to make trouble in the future, and to no one more than to Cromwell. But it was the king who, by quick dissolutions of Parliaments that had not pleased him, and by reigning for more than eleven years without a Parliament, had forced the issue. Cromwell voted for it. So did Hyde and Falkland, as well as Pym and Hampden.

For in dealing with political abuses the House had been all but unanimous. It was in the discussion of religious questions that the division was to arise that was to lead to civil war. And in this Cromwell was to take a prominent part. That was natural, it was in the religious controversy that his real interest lay. In other matters he was not very intelligent, and simply voted with his friends.

Some changes must evidently be made in the Church of England, both as to organization and as to discipline. All along he had been considering what these changes should be. Was the Scotch system desirable? In February 1641 he wrote to his friend Mr. Willingham, at his house in Swithin Lane, asking him to send him the reasons of the Scots, to enforce their desire of uniformity in religion; he "would peruse it, against we fall upon the debate, which will be speedily."

There was plenty of debate on that subject. In December 1640 the Londoners had presented a petition signed by fifteen thousand persons, demanding the total abolition of episcopacy. In January 1641 there was a Petition and Remonstrance from seven hundred ministers of the Church of England, asking not for its abolition, but for its reform, for which the removal of Bishops from secular office and from the House of Lords seemed to be necessary. When these petitions were discussed in the Commons, some one urged their rejection on the ground that the Bishops, the Lords Spiritual, were one of the estates of the realm, therefore a part of the constitution, and moreover that equality, parity he called it, in the Church would lead to parity in the State.

This latter statement excited and bewildered Cromwell, for in dealing with existing circumstances, it was no part of his temperament or intellectual make-up to think very far ahead, or to speculate upon remote consequences, which after all were only possible or probable. So he rose quickly, and began to deny it with such vehemence that "divers interrupted him and called him to the bar." However Pym and Holles insisted that he be allowed to continue, so he went on, and said that he did not see "why the gentleman that last spoke should make an inference of parity from the Church to the State, nor" (such was his excitement that he strayed quickly to another subject), "that there was any necessity of the great revenue of Bishops." He was "more convinced touching the irregularity of Bishops than ever before, because, like the Roman hierarchy, they would not endure to have their condition come to a trial."

That was on February 9th. As his letter to Mr. Willingham is dated only February, we do not know whether it was written before or after that speech.

As a matter of fact everybody was of opinion that something must be done to lessen the power of the Bishops. For it was the exorbitant power of the Bishops (it must always be remembered that they were appointed by the King), that was largely responsible for the evils of which they complained. For the last ten years they had been either directing or upholding the policy of the Crown, not only in ecclesiastical, but also in secular affairs. So in May 1641, the Commons passed a bill excluding clergymen in general from holding secular office, and in particular depriving Bishops of their seats in the House of Lords. In June the Lords threw it out.

It was then that Cromwell took a fatal step, a step which served to divide an almost unanimous House, give the King a party, and make the civil war inevitable. We know how strongly he was feeling against the encroachments of the Bishops. Were they not appointed and paid to preach the Divine Right of Kings, and the Damnable Sin of Resistance and, what was worse in Cromwell's eyes, to introduce Popish ceremonies, such as ate the "core and power and heart and life out of all true Religion," and interfered with the way in which the individual, led by the Spirit, might seek to approach his Maker? Well, if the Lords insisted that these Bishops should have seats in their House, and be permitted to hold secular office, there was only one remedy for the disease, there should be no Bishops at all. So he was largely responsible for the introduction of a more extreme measure into the Commons, the famous Root and Branch Bill.

This Bill was brought in on the 27th of May, even before the Lords had finally rejected the more moderate Bill, but they were that day holding a conference with the Commons on the subject. It demanded the abolition of the Bishops altogether, their government having been "dangerous to church and commonwealth, and the main cause and occasion of many foul evils." It went further, denounced the services of the Church of England, not only Laud's innovations, but even the Liturgy, still dear to many members of the House, and to many Englishmen outside.

It was introduced by Sir Edward Dering, who appears not to have been really in sympathy with it. He later repented of the part that he had taken and gave this account of it. "It was pressed into my hands," he said, "by Sir Arthur Haselrig, being then brought to him by Sir Henry Vane (the younger), and Mr. Oliver Cromwell."

It never got further than the committee stage, but it served to divide the House which, had it continued to be all but unanimous, might possibly have forced its will upon the King without civil war. Possibly, but not probably. For the character of Charles I must be taken into account. He was just as conscientious as were his opponents, just as ready to fight for, and to die for what he believed to be fundamentally right. But in order to obtain it, his conscience did not forbid him to make equivocal promises, and then get out of them. So the division would probably have come, even if Cromwell and Vane had not precipitated it. But they did precipitate it.

The new King's party was led by Hyde and Falkland. The latter at least separated himself reluctantly from his former friends. For he had admired Hampden, had made a powerful speech against ship money, had joined in the prosecution of Strafford, and had spoken vigorously for the Bill to remove the Bishops from the House of Lords.

Indeed it was on the expulsion of the Bishops that the only serious difference of opinion had arisen between Hyde and Falkland. Hyde had objected to their exclusion on the ground that "it was changing the whole frame and constitution of the kingdom, that there never had been a time when the Bishops were not part of the Parliament, that they were one of the estates of the realm." But when he had done speaking "the Lord Falkland, who always sat next to him (which was so much taken notice of, that if they came not into the house together, as usually they did, everybody left the place for him who was absent), suddenly stood up, and declared himself to be of another opinion; and that, as he thought the thing itself to be absolutely necessary for the benefit of the church, which was in so great danger, so he had never heard the constitution of the kingdom would be violated by passing that Act; and that he had heard many of the clergy protest that they could not acknowledge that they were represented by the bishops—And so with some facetiousness, answering some other particulars, he concluded for the passing the Act."

But when it came to abolishing the episcopacy altogether, Falkland drew back. No one ever drew up a more severe indictment against the existing bishops than he. "He is a great stranger in Israel," he began, "who does not know that this kingdom hath long laboured under many and great oppressions, both in religion and liberty, and his acquaintance here is not great, or his ingenuity less, who doth not know and acknowledge, that a great, if not a principal cause of both these, hath been some Bishops and their adherents."

After enumerating the religious grievances in language as strong as Cromwell himself would have used, (and it must be remembered that Falkland was not a Puritan), he addressed himself to the civil grievances. The Bishops had had great influence with the King, had they used a little freedom of speech at Whitehall they might have saved the Commons the use of it in the Parliament House. Having all power in ecclesiastical matters, they had labored for equal power in temporal matters, had endeavored to dispose of every office as well as of every benefice, had stirred up the trouble in Scotland, had been almost the sole abettors of Strafford, when he was "practicing upon another kingdom that manner of government which he intended to settle upon this."

Nevertheless there were some good Bishops even now. And they must not forget that the principal martyrs of Mary's reign had been Bishops, and that "we owe the light of the Gospel we now enjoy, to the Fire that they then endured for it."

And—and this was the most important point—was it well to abolish, in a few days' debate, an order which had lasted in most churches sixteen hundred years, and in all churches from Christ to Calvin? He did not believe bishops to be jure divino, in fact he believed them not to be jure divino, but simply convenient or inconvenient. But all great innovations in government were dangerous, "even when what is introduced by that mutation is such as would have been profitable upon a primary foundation." The greatest danger of "Mutations" was that all the dangers and inconveniences which they might bring could not be foreseen. As no man would undergo great danger, but for great necessity, his opinion was that they should not root up the ancient tree, dead as it appeared, but try lopping the branches. Therefore he would not abolish the Episcopate, but he would deprive the Bishops of their seats in the House of Lords, of all temporal power, and perhaps of part of their revenues, leaving them only so much as was necessary for the dignity of learning. These measures, combined with the Triennial Act, already passed, would probably be a sufficient protection. And he added, "when it is not necessary to change, it is necessary not to change."

That was one of the wisest statements ever made in a legislative body. It would have been well if Cromwell had heeded it. But his blood was up, he was going to see this thing through. Perhaps the principal thing that he could have said against Falkland's last argument was that the present Bishops, so long as they continued in office, would be sure to be the principal advisers of Charles. And in case of their death or deposition, if deposition were possible, Charles would appoint their successors.

To another argument of Falkland's he could have made no reply. "We have not," said Falkland, "done what we should doe first, and others have not done what they should doe first. That which we should doe first, is to agree to a succeeding forme of government, that every man, when he gives his vote to the destruction of this, may be sure that he destroys not that which he likes better than that which shall succeed it." Cromwell knew that he did not want Bishops, but he himself said that he did not know what he did want, he had no plan for a succeeding form of government.

It is not probable that he ever looked back upon, and regretted the position that he took at this time. He was not given to looking back and regretting, pretty fair evidence that he was not, as some have maintained, a neurotic. "It is the voice of fear," he once said, "that suggests to us, 'If I had done this, if I had avoided that, how well it would be with us,' but that is vain reasoning." And yet it is possible that when he had had more experience, when he had learned how much easier it is to destroy than it is to build up, he would not have been so strong for Root and Branch.

Compromises were proposed, but feeling ran high, it was not a time for compromise. Even the abolition of Bishops was not enough for the extreme Puritan party. There were further attacks upon the Prayer Book in which Cromwell joined. It was resolved, not only that communion tables be removed from the east end of chancels, but also that the chancels themselves be leveled, that pictures of any persons of the Trinity be removed, that pictures and images of the Virgin be destroyed. Forced to choose between one set of zealots and the other, Hyde and Falkland entered into communication with the King. The division in Parliament was reflected in the country, Episcopalians became Royalists.

From August until October there was a recess of Parliament. The King went to Scotland, in the hope of stirring up a party there in his favor. Thence he wrote to the Secretary of State, "I command you to assure all my servants that I am constant to the doctrine and discipline of the Church of England, established by Queen Elizabeth and my father, and that I resolve by the grace of God to die in the maintenance of it." He was to be true to his word.

He proceeded to fill five vacant bishoprics, four of them with divines displeasing to the majority in the Commons. Again Cromwell blazed up, moved for a conference with the Lords on the subject. Hampden was in Scotland, watching the King's movements.

It was a divided House that came together in October. Moreover, the Scotch army had been withdrawn, and in the absence of the protection which it afforded, the Parliamentary leaders feared a coup d'état on the part of the king. Then in November came the news of the Irish rebellion and massacre.

Of course that was not what it seemed to Englishmen of the time. Generations of misgovernment and misunderstanding, of barbarities and confiscations, had simply maddened the Irish people. From a material point of view Strafford's government had been successful. He had given Ireland prosperity such as she had not known before, he had also given her impartial justice and equal laws. But he had not succeeded in conciliating a single section of the population. Indeed his very impartiality, his readiness, like Laud in England, to punish rich and powerful transgressors, had alienated even the old English settlers. The Northern Presbyterians resented the uniformity which he had tried to enforce. The native Irish had been outraged by his contempt for their old tribal organization. While he had treated the Catholics with fairness and moderation, they believed that he was only biding his time. And there was the proposed plantation of Connaught. Yet his removal brought no relief. For it meant that the Puritan influence prevailed in England, and from that they had even more to fear than from Strafford. There was just one ray of hope. The disbanding of his army had filled the country with men trained to arms. It was possible to strike.

So a rebellion broke out, first in the six counties of Ulster, in which there had been English plantations under James I, then in Wicklow, the most recent plantation. The object was simply to drive out the colonists, and recover the lands from which the native Irish had been expelled. Many were murdered, more were plundered. It is impossible to estimate the number who perished, the best authorities think perhaps four thousand were killed, and twice as many more died from hardships and destitution. But it was reported in England that from fifty to a hundred and fifty thousand had been murdered in cold blood. It was believed to be a Papist rising, the Queen was a Papist, she had instigated it, perhaps the King had been her accomplice. Indeed Sir Phelan O'Neill, the Ulster rebel leader, declared that he had a commission from the King.

When we remember the critical time at which the news of the massacre reached England, and the general English ignorance of Irish history, it could hardly be expected that a sane view would be taken of it. We who remember the excitement over German atrocities can understand. Parliament resolved that it would never tolerate Popery in Ireland, or in any other of His Majesty's dominions, and decided that Ireland must be reconquered by more confiscations of Irish land. Two and a half million acres there would be set aside to re-pay those who advanced money for that purpose. On this matter there was no party division, it was again a unanimous Parliament. There was a general subscription, and Master Oliver Cromwell, as ignorant of Irish history as were most of his countrymen, subscribed five hundred pounds. It was a whole year's income, but his property was in such a form that he could realize money easily.

How little he knew about Irish history at the time, and he never knew any more, is shown by the speech that he delivered to the Irish clergy eight years later.

"Ireland" he said, "was once united to England. Englishmen had good inheritances which many of them had purchased with their money; they and their ancestors, from you and your ancestors. They had good leases from Irishmen for long times to come; great stocks thereupon, houses and plantations erected at their own cost and charge. They lived peaceably and honestly among you. You had generally equal benefit of the protection of England with them; and equal justice from the laws, saving what was necessary for the State, out of reasons of state, to put upon some people apt to rebel upon the instigation of such as you. You broke this union. You unprovoked, put the English to the most unheard of and barbarous massacre (without respect to sex or age), that ever the sun beheld. And at a time when Ireland was in perfect peace."

An army must be raised to reconquer Ireland, but who should control it? The Parliamentary leaders dared not trust the King. They remembered that while the proceedings against Strafford were pending, he had plotted to bring up an army to overawe them. Later, in Scotland he had been tampering with army officers in the hope that he might gain support against Parliament. Therefore who could doubt that if an army raised to conquer Ireland, were under his control, it might later be turned against the liberties of England? So on November 6th Pym brought forward an address, saying that, unless the King would employ ministers approved by Parliament "they would take such a course for the securing of Ireland, as might likewise secure themselves." On that very same day, Cromwell went a step further, and moved and carried the motion that the two Houses "should appoint the Earl of Essex commander of all the trained bands south of the Trent, to continue in this position until Parliament took further notice." Then in December came Haselrig's militia bill, giving supreme command of all the trained bands in England to a general approved by Parliament.

For these measures it was necessary to gain the support of the nation. It was with that end in view that the Grand Remonstrance was drawn up, not intended as an appeal to the King to mend his ways, (that seemed hopeless), but as a justification to the people of the course that Parliament was taking. There was first a long catalogue, naturally somewhat exaggerated, of the evils from which the nation had suffered during the reign. Then came a statement of what Parliament had done, and hoped to do to remedy them. Having set forth that the root of all the evil was a malignant design to subvert the fundamental laws and principles upon which the religion and justice of the kingdom were based, it proceeded to make two demands; first, that the King would employ only such counselors and ministers as the Parliament could confide in; second that care should be taken "to reduce within bounds that exorbitant power, which the prelates have assumed to themselves, whilst maintaining the golden reins of discipline," and that for this purpose "a general synod of the most grave, pious, learned and judicious divines" be called "to consider all things necessary for the peace and good government of the Church."

With this Cromwell was in the fullest sympathy, and because the extreme position of Root and Branch had been abandoned, and episcopacy was not to be abolished but limited, he hoped and believed that it would meet with little opposition. So, when owing to the pressure of Falkland and his friends, the final debate was postponed two days, he asked Falkland, as they left the House together, "why he would have it put off, for that day would have quickly determined it." Falkland replied, "There would not have been time enough, for sure it would take some debate." To which Cromwell, in some surprise, retorted "A very sorry one."

He had had little experience in politics, and so intense was he in his own feeling that he had failed to realize the change in public opinion that the last few months had brought about, he had not taken in that that the King had now a strong party, more willing even to trust him, if necessary, with the government of the State, than to trust Parliament with the government of the Church. So his mind was not prepared for the long and bitter debate that came off on November 22nd, chiefly on the ecclesiastical clauses of the Remonstrance. It did not pass until two o'clock the following morning, and then only by eleven votes. And when the majority proposed that it should be printed, "I thought," wrote one who was present, "we had all sat in the Valley of the Shadow of Death; for we like Joab's and Abner's young men, had catched at each other's locks, and sheathed our swords in each other's bowels." And Cromwell said to Falkland "I will take your word for it another time. But if it had been rejected, I would have sold all that I have the next morning, and never seen England more; and I know that there are many other honest men of the same resolution."

On the twenty-fifth of November, just two days later, the King returned to Whitehall, determined now to do what Strafford had meant to do, put an end to his troubles, by arresting the parliamentary leaders. For he honestly believed, as Strafford had, that their negotiations with the Scots during the late war, and the changes they had sought to make in the constitution, could be construed as high treason.

So he made friends with the city magnates, removed the guards around the House, and put a man whom he could trust in charge of the Tower. And when the Commons petitioned that their guard be restored, he assured them that they were perfectly safe without it, and that their security should be as much his care as the protection of his own children.

But the very next day, January 3rd, he sent his attorney general to impeach five members, Pym, Hampden, Holles, Haselrig and Strode, of high treason, and a sergeant-at-arms to arrest them. The Commons refused to give them up. So the following day he came himself, with four hundred armed men at his back. The birds had flown, the House adjourned to the City, where they had taken refuge. For the good will that the City had recently had for the King had flown also; like the House, it refused to give the members up.

And the whole nation was roused. Petitions supporting the House came in from all over the country. "I remember," wrote a Lancashire man some years afterwards, "upon the occasion of King Charles I demanding the five members of the House of Commons. Such a night of tears, prayers and groans, I was never present at in all my life; the case was extraordinary, and the work was extraordinary." A few days later the five members returned in triumph to Westminster. Charles had quitted Whitehall, never to see it again until he came back to die.

There was instant preparation for war. Pym moved that the House go into committee on the state of the nation, Cromwell that they should consider means for putting the kingdom in a state of defense, Hampden introduced a motion to put the Tower of London and the militia in such hands as Parliament could confide in. "By God!" was Charles' answer, "not for an hour. You have asked that of me in this which was never asked of a king, and with which I will not trust my wife and children."

The King got to York and attempted to get possession of Hull, a great arsenal and convenient port for landing succors from Holland and Denmark. The Governor, Sir John Hotham, drew up the draw-bridge, and refused to admit him. Parliament submitted nineteen propositions to him, in which it virtually claimed the whole sovereignty, Government to be carried on by persons chosen by Parliament rather than by persons chosen by the King. Charles refused to be "but the outside, but the picture, but the sign of a King." Hyde was with him, sending out able manifestoes, attracting many to his side. Early in July Parliament appointed a Committee of Safety, resolved to raise an army of ten thousand men, and appointed Essex as their general. On August 22nd, 1642, the King set up his standard at Nottingham. Civil war had begun. Scotland had made it necessary to call a Parliament, Ireland had brought on the war.

All through this Parliament Cromwell makes the impression of being in a very excited condition. Not only in his controversy with Manchester, but in his defense of Lilburn, in his attack upon the Bishops, in his action with respect to Ireland, in his intense feeling on the subject of the Grand Remonstrance, and in his haste in preparing for war. He had not been able to do anything for so many years. Now his opportunity had come, and he was letting himself go, excitedly and vehemently, perhaps not always wisely. Evidently he had not yet become, like his cousin Hampden, "supreme governor over all his passions and affections." Something of that would come in time. Meanwhile it is to be noticed that while he had a hot temper there is no instance on record in which it was aroused by a personal affront to himself, it flared up in behalf of the Church, in behalf of the poor. For he thought always of "the public," not of his "own private."

CHAPTER VIII

The War

"I was a person that from my first employment was suddenly preferred and lifted up from lesser trusts to greater, from my first being a Captain of a Troop of Horse, and I did labour as well as I could, to discharge my trust, and God blessed me therein as it pleased Him."

—OLIVER CROMWELL.

IT has often been noted that the English civil wars of the seventeenth century were brought about by a combination of two movements that had no necessary connection, Puritanism and Parliamentarism, and that as a result of the conflict Parliamentary Government was saved, but Puritanism did not for any length of time get the upper hand, for after all it did not represent the underlying temperament of the English people, it was simply the form which resistance to absolutism took at the time.

Yet the underlying motive of Puritanism does represent that temperament. For insistence upon the supreme importance of the individual was the core of the whole movement. And while this at first took the form of resistance to any authority imposed between the individual and his God, it soon came to mean the right of free and independent inquiry in every department of thought and life. The principle of the power of the people in the government of the Church carried with it the principle of the sovereignty of the people in the government of the State. "Political liberty as a fact in the modern world," says Figgis, "is the result of the struggle of religious organisms to live."

And perhaps it is fair to say that Puritanism was the principal cause of the struggle. For it was fear of Puritanism that had led Charles I to govern so long without a Parliament. And later it is possible that the Long Parliament, practically unanimous on the constitutional question, might have settled it without a war, (certainly might have done so under a different King), had not Puritanism given the King a party.

The better men on the King's side were actuated by personal loyalty, respect for time-honored institutions, dislike of Puritanism, and fear of anarchy. But for the most part they did not wish to fight, for the majority of them were no more in love with absolutism, than were their opponents. To them it was a choice of evils.

The better men on the other side were actuated by a desire to destroy absolutism, and to save Puritanism. They did wish to fight, they did not as yet perceive the danger of anarchy. A time was coming when they would realize it to the full, when Cromwell would say "Misrule is better than no rule, and an ill government, a bad government, is better than none."

But although Puritanism was the underlying cause of the difficulties, at the outbreak of hostilities, even in the minds of many ardent Puritans, the political motives were strongest. Baxter thought it "a wonder if so many humble, honest Christians, fearful of sinning and praying for direction, should be all mistaken in so weighty a cause, and so many Damn Mes in the right." (The common soldiers of the King had a reputation for swearing, and so were called Damn-Mes.) "But yet," he adds, "this was not the rule I went by. I had a great reason to believe that if the King had conquered the Parliament, the Nation had lost all security of their liberties, and been at his mercy." Mrs. Hutchinson tells us that although her husband was "satisfied of the endeavour to bring back Popery, and subvert the true Protestant religion, he did not think that so clear a ground for the war as the defence of English liberties." Ludlow has already been quoted as saying that the question in dispute was as to "whether the king should govern as a god by his will, or whether the people should live under a government devised by their own consent."

As for Cromwell, we have seen that he had always been zealous for religion, and so little interested in constitutional matters, that during the eleven years that Charles had governed without a Parliament, he had submitted without a protest. Yet there is evidence that at this time even he put the constitutional motive first. In 1644 he wrote to a friend of "the honour and liberty of the Parliament, for which we unanimously fight," and added "I profess I could never satisfy myself of the justness of this war, but from the authority of the Parliament to maintain itself in its rights." Later he wrote "Religion was not the thing that was at first contended for."

All through his life he was a man who hesitated long before he decided upon a course of action which involved a violent break with the past, and then, when he had once made up his mind, he threw himself into it with all his might, it was impossible to shake him. But he did not hesitate about going into the war, perhaps because he did not realize that it was a violent break with the past, and it seemed to him that it had been forced upon him. And he went in to win.

Therefore he lost no time about it, what was to be done must be done quickly. It was not until August 22nd, 1642, that the King set up his standard at Nottingham, but he did not wait for that. It was on January 14th, only ten days after the attack on the Five Members, that he moved that a committee be appointed to put the kingdom in a state of defense. Money was needed, so although far from wealthy, he subscribed £500 to the fund for raising an army. His immediate responsibility was for his own constituents, so on July 15th, still before the King's standard had been raised, he moved to make an order to allow the townsmen of Cambridge to raise two companies of volunteers and to appoint captains over them. He had already sent to Cambridge £100 worth of arms at his own expense, and on that day the Commons sanctioned his action, and voted that he be reimbursed.

It has commonly been said that the North and West were loyal to the King, the South and East to the Parliament. This is only roughly true, in every county there was division. Everywhere there were both Royalists and Parliamentarians. And everywhere families were divided; Oliver's own uncle, Sir Oliver and his sons, were on the King's side, while his daughters and their husbands were with the Parliament. The new owner of Hinchingbrooke was a Royalist, but his son, young Edward Montagu, later to become the great Admiral Montagu and first Earl of Sandwich, ran away to join the Parliamentary forces.

And everywhere perhaps the neutrals were in the majority. There were a few intellectuals who, seeing the right and wrong on both sides, found it difficult to decide between them. But in the main the indifference arose from the fact that it was a war of ideas, and in no country do the majority care for ideas. Only in London was there any general willingness to take up arms. So in August the House of Commons sent its more zealous members into their own shires to keep the Royalists from arming, and if possible, to win the neutrals to their cause.

Cromwell went down into Cambridgeshire. There his energy and ubiquitousness were amazing. It was in the blood. With the same energy and ubiquitousness had his great-grandfather Richard suppressed monasteries, converted Abbots, put down Pilgrimages of Grace.

Even before he appeared in person he had had his eye on Cambridge. Although the University was not quite so loyal as was Oxford, the King knew that he could count upon it. So in July he sent for its money and plate, (there was a great melting down of beautiful plate at that time, to be used as money, on both sides). Cromwell got ahead of him. With the help of his brothers-in-law, Valentine Walton and John Desborough, he intercepted the messengers, thus preventing their getting to Cambridge. In August, armed with parliamentary authority, he seized the magazine in the castle of Cambridge, and got possession of the plate, valued at £20,000 to be used in the Parliamentary service. And when the heads of some of the colleges and the Bishop of Ely tried to put in force the King's commission of array, "down came Mr. Oliver Cromwell in a terrible manner, with what force he could gather together, and surrounded divers colleges, while we were at devotions in our various chapels, taking away several doctors of divinity, heads of colleges, and these he carried away with him to London in triumph."

On a Sunday morning in this same August, the sons of Judge Bramston, one of the Ship Money judges, were returning from York, where they had had an interview with the King. As they were between Huntingdon and Cambridge, certain musketeers started out of the corn, commanded them to stand, and told them they must go before Mr. Cromwell, who was four miles off, to be searched. By giving one of the musketeers twelve pence, they managed to get away, but they saw plainly that it would not be possible for their father to get to the King. "Neither did he go at all, but stayed at him till he died."

Cromwell was among his old neighbors, he knew them well, so knew who would bear watching. One of them was that Mr. Robert Barnard of Huntingdon, with whom he had had an altercation twelve years before. Yes, he writes to him, evidently in reply to a letter that he had received, it is most true that his lieutenant and soldiers from his troop were at Mr. Barnard's house to inquire after him, the reason being that he had heard him reported active against the proceedings of the Parliament, and for those that were disturbing the peace of the county and of the Kingdom, and that he had been with those of the county who had had meetings, not a few "to intents and purposes too-too full of suspect." With all his heart Mr. Cromwell desires that Mr. Barnard's judgment and practice may alter. As for himself, he must be pardoned for doing what his relation to the public calls for.

Later Mr. Barnard appears to have gone to London to prove to Manchester that he was not a disaffected man. Cromwell writes again to tell him that he knows certainly that he is disaffected toward the Parliament, however he has protected him in his absence, and if he chooses to return, he may "go freely into the country about his occasions." Presumably his private occasions, if there were any more meetings "too-too full of suspect," he was known and watched.

Another man to be looked after was his own uncle, Sir Oliver. Since he had been forced to sell Hinchingbrooke that gentleman had been living at Ramsey Mere. He and his son Henry were Royalists, it would be well to be on the look-out for arms and ammunition and anything else that he might be planning to send to the King at York. So his nephew with his dragoons came to the house. The story goes that while the dragoons made their search, the younger Oliver, standing with his head uncovered, conversed respectfully with the older, and that when he parted from him, he craved his blessing, whether upon himself or upon his mission, the record does not say. The whole tale may be apocryphal, but as Oliver was in military charge of the county it is probable that he visited his Royalist uncle more than once.

But it was not enough to put down malignants. He must train himself and his neighbors for active service. In 1657 he told his Parliament that he knew his calling from the first. That calling was, as he conceived it, to be a commander of cavalry. He got a Dutch officer to teach him drill, and set to work at once to raise a troop of horse in his own county, and to train them for action.

"Infinite great," says a horseman of the time, "are the considerations which dependeth upon a man, to teach and govern a troop of horse. To bring ignorant man and more ignorant horse, wild man and wild horse, to those rules of obedience, which may crown every motion and action with comely, orderly and profitable proceeding, hic labor, hoc opus est." It was indeed labor, but we can fancy that it was also sport to Cromwell. He loved men, and he loved horses; he was realizing his power, feeling that he was growing.

And the men in that first little company of his, there were only sixty of them, were neither wild nor ignorant, they were men whom he had known for long, his neighbors and his friends, men like-minded with himself, men to whom religion was not just a battle-cry, but as it was with him, the passion of life. His brother-in-law, John Desborough, was his Quartermaster-General. Another brother-in-law, Valentine Walton, was in command of a similar company in the same district.

The Earl of Essex was appointed "Lord General for King and Parliament," for the fiction was still kept up that the Parliamentary army was fighting for the King, to deliver him from evil counselors. The Earl of Bedford was in command of the horse, seventy-five troops of sixty each. Of the sixty-seventh troop Oliver Cromwell was captain.

On the twenty-third of October, 1642, Edgehill was fought, and Cromwell was there. "These persons underwritten," says an eye-witness, "never stirred from their troops, but they and their troops fought to the last minute." Cromwell was one of those whose names were underwritten. When the rest of the cavalry was swept away by Rupert and Wilmot, his troop with two others found shelter behind the unbroken portion of the Parliamentary infantry, and thus were enabled to do good service to the end.

At the beginning of every war men believe that it will be short; if it were otherwise, they would hesitate longer before entering upon it. In 1642 it was commonly thought that a single decisive victory for either side would end it. Edgehill had not been decisive, therefore there must be another battle, but probably only one. Cromwell saw more clearly. He realized that Edgehill had proved that neither army was sufficiently trained or disciplined to win a decisive victory. What advantage there was had fallen to the King, and this was owing to his superiority in cavalry. Some of Essex's foot regiments were excellent, but in the main the ranks of the cavalry had been recruited from men attracted by pay and plunder. Cromwell had realized from the first that it was the cavalry who would win the war, this battle confirmed his opinion. He must continue the work that he had begun, and on a larger scale.

So about this time, (whether before or after Edgehill we cannot be sure), "in a manner of foolish simplicity," he talked the matter over with Hampden. "Your troopers," he said, "are most of them old decayed serving men, and such kind of fellows; and their troopers are gentlemen's sons, younger sons, and persons of quality. Do you think the spirits of such mean and base fellows will ever be able to encounter gentlemen that have honour and courage and resolution in them? You must get men of a spirit, and take it not ill what I say, I know that you will not, of a spirit that is likely to go as far as gentlemen will go; or else I am sure that you will be beaten still."

Hampden thought that "he talked a good notion," but that it was impracticable. Cromwell could never see that what was necessary was impracticable. "It's necessary," he wrote, on one occasion, "therefore to be done." He told Hampden that he thought that he could do "somewhat" in the matter, and he set to work to do this "somewhat." He got leave of absence, went down into the eastern counties, and set to work to raise and train more men.

His success was phenomenal, almost like a fairy tale. By March

1643 instead of one troop he had five, in September ten. When the New Model was formed in 1645 he had no less than eleven hundred troopers of his own choosing. And he had proved that he knew how to choose. "In nothing," says a contemporary, "was his good understanding better discovered." He had taken care to "raise such men as had the fear of God before them and made some conscience of what they did." "He had a special care," says Baxter, "to get religious men into his troop; these men were of greater understanding than common soldiers, and, making not money, but what they took to be public felicity to be their end, they were the more engaged to be valiant; for he that maketh money his end, doth esteem his life above his pay, and therefore is like enough to save it by flight, if he possibly can; but he that maketh the felicity of Church and State the end esteemeth it above his life, and therefore will the sooner lay down his life for it." So Oliver reasoned. "A few honest men," he said, "are better than numbers." He got the honest men, but he got the numbers too.

He fairly gloated over them. In September 1643 he wrote, "My troops increase, I have a lovely company. You would respect them, did you know them." Again, "Indeed we find our men never so cheerful as when there is work to do." The spirit that animated him animated them also. For himself he says, "I hope to God to desire to venture my skin," and he adds, "So do mine." When the war was over he could say "I must say to you that they never were beaten, and whenever they were engaged against the enemy, they beat continually." "Truly, they were never beaten, no not once."

He did not quite stick to his rule of having only gentlemen as officers, or rather his definition of a gentleman changed. "I had rather," he said, "have a plain russet captain who knows what he fights for, and loves what he knows, than what you call a gentleman and that is nothing else. I honour a gentleman that is so indeed." "It may be it provokes some spirits to have such plain men made captins of horse. It had been well that men of honour and of birth had entered into these employments, but why do they not appear? Seeing that it was necessary that the work must go on, better plain men than none, but best to have men patient of want, faithful and conscientious in their employment." However he preferred gentlemen when he could get them, and it is not true that the officers who served under him were mainly men of low birth. Later in the New Model army, out of thirty-seven general officers and colonels, twenty-one were commoners of good families, nine members of noble families, only seven not gentlemen by birth.

His discipline was strict, there was to be no plundering, no wenching, no drunkenness, even no swearing. We smile a little when we read "No man swears but he pays his twelvepence; if he is drunk he is set in the stocks or worse." But after all this was not peculiarly Puritan legislation. Five years later a decree of the Parlement of Paris punished blasphemy by cutting off the lips and piercing the tongue. And Philip II of Spain had decreed ten years in the galleys to profane swearers. Cromwell's discipline was much milder, and while it was to fail later when there was an attempt to apply it to the nation as a whole, with his own soldiers there was little difficulty; they were men like minded with himself, felt as he did about these things.

He was very popular with them. They had known him as the man who had at various times protected the poor against the rich, and who had so recently resisted the attempt of the Earl of Manchester to enclose lands in defiance of common rights. Now his "familiar rustic carriage," the fact that "he was as full of vivacity, hilarity and alacrity as another man is when he hath drunken a cup of wine too much" endeared him to them. Even his love of horse-play, (one of his officers remembered long afterward that Oliver loved an innocent jest), his occasional buffooneries, his quick flashes of temper, made them feel that he was one of them, not so much their commander as their leader and their friend. "They are honest sober Christians," he said, "they expect to be used as men." He used them so. Above all, he made them feel that he sought "not theirs, but them and their welfare, and to stand with them for the liberty of the gospel and the laws of the land."

It was probably not necessary for him to impart to them his love of horses, for that too they shared with him. Most of them were freeholders, many rode their own horses, taking a special pride and interest in them. But Cromwell required them "daily to look after, feed and dress their horses and when it was needful, to lie together on the ground with them." He also taught them to clean and keep their arms bright, and have them always ready for service. He and they must be prepared for any emergency. There is no reason to suppose that he ever uttered the words so often attributed to him, "Trust in God and keep your armour bright," but perhaps more than any words that he did utter, they express the heart and mind of Cromwell.

He taught them things on a larger scale, things which Rupert was also teaching his men, things which perhaps both he and Cromwell had learned from Gustavus Adolphus. But he also taught them things which Rupert did not teach: not to pursue a fleeing foe when the day was still in doubt, but to wheel to the support of other troops, and whether they won or lost in the first charge, to rally quickly for another. Because he was successful in teaching them these things the war was won. "This difference was observed shortly from the beginning of the war," says Clarendon, "that though the King's troops prevailed in the charge, and routed those they charged, they never rallied themselves again in order, nor could be brought to make a second charge on the same day, whereas Cromwell's troops if they prevailed, or if they were beaten and routed, presently rallied again, and stood in good order, until they received new orders."

Toward the close of 1642, Parliament passed an ordinance associating Norfolk, Suffolk, Essex, Cambridgeshire, and Hertfordshire for purposes of common defense. This was called the Eastern Association, there were several such associations, but this was the only one that amounted to anything. Later Huntingdonshire and Lincolnshire were added to it. Cambridge was its headquarters. Of the army of this association, Manchester was commander. He was a Montagu, nephew of the Montagu who had bought Hinchingbrooke, son of the Manchester whom Cromwell had opposed in the matter of the enclosures, himself the Mandeville who, in the affair of the enclosures, had "with great modesty, related what had been done," and whom Cromwell had answered with "indecency and rudeness." That does not seem to have affected the relations between them now. Cromwell had a share in Manchester's appointment, served at first as a colonel under him, soon rose to be Lieutenant General, that is commander of the horse, next to Manchester himself. And Manchester, whom the Scotch Baillie characterizes as "a sweet meek man," recognized the superior military ability of his Lieutenant General, and allowed him "to guide the army at his pleasure." So most of the soldiers who "loved new ways" put themselves under his command, and Cromwell was able on a large scale to maintain the principles on which his own troops had been formed and disciplined. By March 1644 Manchester's army numbered fifteen thousand men, and the Parliamentary cause, losing everywhere else, was triumphing in the Eastern Association.

The Royalists soon recognized Cromwell as the outstanding cavalry officer with whom they must reckon. "Is Cromwell there?" Rupert asked a prisoner before Marston Moor. On being answered in the affirmative he asked "And will they fight? If they will, they shall have fighting enough," and sent the prisoner back with this message. To which Cromwell replied, "If it please God, so shall he."

Both sides saw fighting enough, but it was Cromwell who won Marston Moor for the Parliament. It was he who, after his superiors in command had fled from the field, was able to rout Rupert's horse, and hasten to the Scotch infantry, still holding its own, and thus turn defeat into victory. There was to be a dispute about it later, but Rupert never had any doubt as to who had won that victory. "Ironsides!" he exclaimed when he saw Cromwell's action, and the name was to stick for all time both to Cromwell himself and to the force which he commanded.

All the time his religious faith and confidence were growing. He was constantly renewing that faith by mystical communion with the Most High. On the eve of Marston Moor he was found in a disused room with his Bible before him, wrestling in prayer. Before Basing House he spent hours on his knees. All his victories he ascribed to the right hand of his God upon him. It is true that the Soldiers' Pocket Bible, (not a Bible, but a little pamphlet published in 1648 for the use of the army in Scotland), contained the statement "A soldier must concede that sometimes God's people have the worst in battle, as well as God's enemies," but to Cromwell the worst never came in this First Civil War; he conquered always, was never defeated, no, not once. Dr. Beard's pupil took this as evidence that God approved his cause and fought for him. To him God was always saying, "Up, and be doing, and I will stand by you." Whatever one's theological views may be, it is certain that this confidence was a main source of Cromwell's strength. "In the high places of the field his faith worked at a more than ordinary rate. Insomuch that success and victory was in his eye, when fears and despondencies did oppress the hearts of others, and some good men too."

And it was not only Dr. Beard's teaching that gave him this abounding, inspiring confidence. Consider what had happened to the man himself. He was forty-three years old, had had no military training, had never seen a battle, and he suddenly found that he was a military genius. Is it any wonder that, brought up as he had been, he should have felt that it was God Who had taught his hands to war and his fingers to fight? "Not unto us, not unto us, but unto Thy Name give glory." That was his song after every victory, and he meant it.

And what had happened to him, had also happened to his men. It is true that the Parliamentary forces often, notably at Naseby, outnumbered the King's army, so that a Napoleon might have said "God was on the side of the greater battalions." But the New Model Army that won Naseby was made up of raw and inexperienced men, the Royalists called it "the New Noddle," and for its "brutish general" Fairfax, they had the greatest contempt. "I can say this of Naseby," Oliver wrote, "that when I saw the enemy draw up, and march in gallant order toward us, and we a company of poor ignorant men, I could not, riding about my business, but smile out to God in prayer, in assurance of victory, because God would, by things that are not, bring to naught things that are."

And so all through the war he was a happy man, happy perhaps in a sense in which he had never been happy before, and was never to be again. He was fighting on the Lord's side, that had been proved by the unexpected, almost miraculous powers that had been given him. Like the Psalmists of old he believed that his enemies were the enemies of God, could quote with approval the regret of his dying nephew that God had suffered him no more to be the executioner of his enemies. Yet even in the midst of this joyous excitement he could be tender to a fallen foe. There is a story that while they were stripping and burying the dead of Marston Moor, the wife of a royalist, who had come upon the field to search for her husband's body, was accosted by a general officer who asked her what she was about, listened to her tale with deep sympathy, besought her to leave that terrible place, himself called for a trooper, and set her upon the horse. Later she inquired his name, and learned that he was Lieutenant General Cromwell. And when, in the midst of his excitement, he had time to reflect, he always realized the misery that even this humane war was bringing upon his country, and longed for it to end.

He was no longer worrying about his own soul, but he was doing considerable thinking on religious lines, or perhaps he was jumping to conclusions without much thinking. It was the larger aspect of the matter that he was revolving in his mind, the question of religious toleration.

In June and July 1643 the Parliamentary armies were suffering great reverses. Pym decided to appeal to the Scots for help. Fearful lest Charles, if victorious in England, would fall upon them next, they were only too ready to give it, and yet they demanded a price. That price was the Solemn League and Covenant. Perhaps to most of the Parliamentary leaders this did not seem much of a price. Already an Assembly of Divines had been convened at Westminster to decide upon ecclesiastical alterations in the English Church, and since it was not to be Episcopalian, it probably would be Presbyterian, differing from Scotch Presbyterianism only in the fact that it would be under Parliamentary control. That is final decisions in Church matters would be vested in Parliament, not in an assembly of clergy and lay elders.

Yet Cromwell's friend, young Sir Harry Vane, who had fought for toleration unsuccessfully in New England, and had come back to fight for it in Old England, had his doubts in the matter. So when the Scotch demanded that the English promise to reform their church "according to the example of the best reformed churches," meaning of course the Presbyterian Church, he insisted upon adding the phrase "and according to the Word of God." The Scots could hardly refuse to accept this, but it left a loophole, as Vane intended that it should, for those who interpreted the Word of God in different ways.

Now of all the Protestant churches of the day, the Presbyterian Church of Scotland was the most rigid, both as to doctrine and as to discipline. But with their zeal for education, the followers of Calvin had so instructed their people that in Scotland there was very little heresy, therefore very little persecution. What persecution there was was reserved for witches, of which there were plenty.

But when the Scotch came to England, they found such a different state of things that they reported, "The humour of this people (the English) is very variable, and inclined to singularity, to differ from all the world, and from one another, and shortly, from themselves; no people had ever such need of a Presbytery."

The reason for this was to be found in the history of the last few years. As we have seen up to the time of Laud, with the exception of the Catholics, the Church of England had been almost synonymous with the nation. Considerable variety in ceremony had been allowed within it, and there had been no strenuous nation-wide insistence upon doctrinal orthodoxy. But resistance to Laud, accompanied by an intensive study of the Bible, (made possible by the cheap pocket Bibles), had brought about a great ferment of religious thinking and consequently great differences of opinion. Though the Long Parliament had been as firm for doctrinal uniformity as Laud had been for ceremonial uniformity, it would have been impossible to enforce it. Sects had arisen, and with the outbreak of the war they declared themselves more openly.

Outsiders sometimes called them all Independents, but strictly speaking the Independents were what we now call Congregationalists, most of them differing from the Presbyterians only in the matter of church government. They would have neither Bishop nor Presbytery, each congregation was to be free to settle its own affairs, though most of them were willing to allow Parliament a certain authority over the Church as a whole.

Nevertheless it was not altogether illogical to huddle all the sects together as Independents. For if a church is simply a collection of like-minded individuals, these different congregations will naturally evolve different opinions and doctrines, there will be sects. There were many of them, Independents, Baptists, Antinomians, Socinians, Familists, Seekers. There were to be more. All of them stood for some sort of toleration, some for a limited toleration, some for a broad toleration, some for no National Church at all. The Presbyterians stood for a National Church, their own, and no toleration.

On the twenty-fifth of September, 1643, the members of the House of Commons were required to sign the Covenant, soon afterwards to be sworn to by every Englishman. As many members were not present on that day, they could not sign then, but most of them did so afterward. Cromwell was with the army, and was one of the last to sign. He did so on the fifth of February, 1644. One cannot help wondering whether the delay was altogether owing to absence from Westminster.

It is just possible that from his first entrance into public life he had inclined toward toleration. It has been noticed that, in his first speech in Parliament, in 1628, he did not ask that Dr. Alabaster be silenced, but only that Dr. Beard be heard. It is also just possible that he deliberately thought the matter out, but as he was not given to that kind of thinking, it is more probable that the necessity of practicing toleration led him to the theory of it.

For, as was natural, the number of sectarians in the army, especially in Manchester's army, where the religious sentiment was dominant, was out of proportion to the number in the nation at large. Cromwell could not get on without them, they made the best officers and the best soldiers, and above all, they were the most determined to fight the war to a finish. Indeed in a moment of irritation he had said to Manchester, "I will not deny that I desire to have no man in my army, but such as are of the Independent judgment." When Manchester asked why, he replied "That in case there shall be propositions for peace that might not stand with the end that men aim at, the army might prevent such a mischief."

So although he was not interested in their doctrinal disputes, it was not strange that he came to feel that the men who had done most to win the war, must at least be allowed freedom of conscience for themselves. And associating with them constantly, it was natural that he should love them, and wish to protect them. Thus what had been at first a struggle against innovations gradually became to him a battle for "liberty for all species of Protestants to worship according to their own light and conscience." For the rest of his life this was to be his passion, and the main cause of his tragedy.

With such views it may well be imagined that there was not much love lost between him and the Scots. For even earlier than Milton he came to realize that "new presbyter was but old priest writ large." To Manchester he once said "In the way that they (the Scots) now carry themselves, pressing for their discipline, I could as soon draw my sword against them, as against any in the King's service." As for the Assembly of Divines, mostly Presbyterian and intolerant, he said that they were persecutors of honester men than themselves.

There was one Scot with whom he particularly did not get along, Crawford, the Major General in Manchester's army, commander of the foot as Cromwell was commander of the horse. He had on various occasions found it necessary to advise him "to bear with men of different minds from himself." Crawford had not taken the advice, and therefore had had "many stumbling blocks in his way." Finally, when he was on the point of dismissing a lieutenant colonel on the ground that he was an Anabaptist, Cromwell wrote to him, March 10th, 1644 (notice that he himself had taken the covenant only a little more than a month before):

"Surely, you are not well advised to turn off one so faithful to the cause, and so able to serve you, as this man is. Ay, but the man is an Anabaptist! Admit that he be, shall that make him incapable to serve the Public? . . . Sir, the State in choosing men to serve it, takes no notice of their opinions, if they be willing faithfully to serve, that satisfies— Take heed of being sharp, or too easily sharpened by others, against those to whom you can object little but that they square not with you in every opinion concerning matters of religion."

But although Cromwell was constantly becoming more tolerant, there is a story that would indicate that he was not yet prepared to go so far as to tolerate the Laudian forms. In August 1643 Parliament had passed an act against them; they were to be abolished at once; as to what forms of worship were to be adopted, the Westminster Assembly would soon decide that. If church authorities failed to comply with the order, military men were to see that it was executed.

At Ely Cathedral there was a Rev. Mr. Hitch, who failed to comply. Oliver was Governor of Ely, his home was there, and he was there for a time with his family. On the 10th of January, 1644, he wrote to Mr. Hitch, "Lest the soldiers should in any tumultuous or disorderly way attempt the reformation of your cathedral church, I require you to forbear altogether your choir service." He advised him to catechize, read and expound the Scriptures, to preach as beforetime, but more frequently. The Parliament with the Assembly of Divines, would in due time give him further directions.

To this letter, Mr. Hitch paid no attention. He too had a conscience in the matter, and continued to worship his God as aforetime. Whereupon Cromwell entered the cathedral, with soldiers at his back, walked up the choir, and announced "I am a man under authority, and commanded to dismiss this assembly." He then drew back a little that the congregation might pass out. But they did not pass out. Mr. Hitch continued the service. Thereupon Oliver exclaimed "Leave off your fooling, and come down, Sir!" At which Mr. Hitch did leave off, and he and the congregation passed out.

To the modern mind this has an ugly sound, and it is even probable that it is not exactly what Cromwell himself would have done at a later date. We must however bear in mind that he had announced himself as a man under authority, he had come simply to execute the orders of Parliament. Nor is it quite clear whether he meant to designate the service itself as fooling, or simply to indicate that he thought that Mr. Hitch was fooling with those parliamentary orders which must eventually be obeyed. And while the "harsh untuneable voice" may have been more harsh and untunable than usual, it is at least possible that it was playful. Cromwell probably knew Mr. Hitch well, they had lived together in Ely, and Ely was and is a very small place. It is noticeable that he signs his letter to him "Your loving friend."

And yet the question arises, had Parliament passed an order forbidding Baptist or other sectarian services, would Oliver have been so ready to execute it? The answer is that the House of Commons, though perhaps it would have liked to pass such an order, would not have dared to do so. It would have deprived them of their best soldiers, without whom the war could not have been won. For a similar reason Cromwell would not have executed the order, had it been passed. It was on January 10th, 1644, that he wrote his letter to Mr. Hitch, on March 10th that he wrote to Major General Crawford, "Sir, the State in choosing men to serve them, takes no notice of their opinions. If they be willing faithfully to serve, that satisfies." That was the key to the whole matter, the various sects were eager to serve his cause, the Laudian ceremonies were preëminently the badge of the enemy. To prevent Royalist uprisings within the bounds of the Eastern Association was his great care. These ceremonies might indicate sympathy with such uprisings. His toleration was as yet practical, not theoretical. However there can be no doubt that he still hated the Laudian innovations, (again we must bear in mind that they were innovations), and was still smarting over the fact that they had been made compulsory.

But there were other things besides religious differences to trouble Cromwell. When was the war going to end, how long must the bloodshed and misery go on? Instead of one battle ending it, there had been two years of indecisive fighting. He saw that while he and others could win battles, a successful battle seemed to mean nothing, permanent victory and peace were as far off as ever. The conviction was being borne in upon him that, as one member of Parliament put it, these victories "seemed to have been put into a bag with holes," that what was won one time was lost another, that the blood that was being shed appeared "only to manure the ground for a new crop of contention." It was just all to no purpose, or to worse than no purpose.

So the problem that he set himself to solve was how to win a victory that would put Parliament in a position to dictate terms of peace. For he knew that the country was sick of a war that seemed to be meaningless, and that there might be a peace from sheer weariness, a peace from which nothing would be gained.

He saw that there were three main difficulties, that the forces were largely local forces, not directly subject to Parliament, that the pay was irregular and inadequate, and that the commanders did not really wish to win.

The existence of local forces, those of counties and associations, made it impossible to properly supply and recruit the main army under Essex. In 1643-44 there were four large armies, commanded respectively by Essex, Manchester, Waller and Hopton. Men who were dissatisfied by conditions in one, or had perhaps been cashiered or punished, ran away and enlisted in another. Massey, governor of Gloucester, complained "There is such a liberty given that all comers are entertained by every association without enquiry. The consequence is that in some armies it is presumably more advantageous to be cowards and runagates than to be faithful, resolute and constant soldiers."

As local forces were raised and paid, when they were paid, by their own localities, they were largely under the impression that their business was simply to protect those localities so "when the enemy had left their own particular quarter, they thanked God that they were rid of him, and returned to their usual avocations." They saw no reason why they should obey the orders either of Essex or of Parliament. We find Manchester making the assertion "My army was raised by the Association, and for the guard of the Association. It cannot be commanded by Parliament without their consent." Manchester's army was larger than that of Essex.

It followed that when such armies thought that their own localities were in danger, they were particularly unwilling to go out of them. Thus when in May 1643 Essex ordered the forces of the East Midlands to unite to relieve Lincolnshire, Cromwell, who was anxious to obey, found to his distress that the local commanders were unwilling. "Believe it," he wrote to the committee of Lincoln, "it were better in my poor opinion that Leicester were not, than that there should not be an immediate taking of the field by your forces to accomplish the common end." No wonder that Speaker Lenthall wrote to him, "The House hath commanded me to let you know that nothing is more repugnant to the sense of this House, and dangerous to this kingdom, than the unwillingness of the forces to march out of their respective counties." In June 1644 Sir William Waller struck at the root of the matter, when he told the Commons that an army composed of local levies would never do the business. "Till you have an army merely your own that you can command, it is impossible to do any thing of importance." Indeed had it not been for the fact that the King's army was even worse organized, they would have been beaten long ago.

Then there was the constant difficulty about pay. No army could be expected to fight that was not properly clothed and fed. Cromwell's letters are full of this. "The money I brought with me is so poor a pittance when it came to be distributed among my troop that, considering the necessity, it will not half clothe them, they were so far behind. If we have not more money speedily, they will be exceedingly discouraged. I am sorry you put it to me to write thus often.— Gentlemen, make them able to live and subsist that are willing to spend their blood for you." "Forget not money, I press not hard, though I do so need that I do assure you, the foot and dragooners are

ready to mutiny. Lay not too much upon the back of a poor gentleman who desires without much noise, to lay down his life, and bleed
his last drop, to save the Cause and you." "I assure you that we
need exceedingly.—There is no care taken how to maintain that force
raised and a raising by my Lord of Manchester. The force will fail,
if some help not." "I desire not to seek myself, but I have little
money of my own to help my soldiers. My estate is little. I tell you
the business of Ireland and of England hath had of me in money
between eleven and twelve hundred pounds; therefore my private can
do little to help the public."

But perhaps the thing that irked Cromwell most was the knowledge,
daily borne in upon him, that the commanders did not really wish
to win. Perhaps the majority on both sides did not really wish to
win. It is to be remembered that this was a civil war, and not even
like the American Civil War, a war between different sections with
widely different traditions and interests. It was more as it was in
the American border states, neighbor was fighting against neighbor,
brother against brother, friend against friend. All through the conflict there were often friendly relations and intermarriages between
those on opposing sides. Moreover what were they really fighting
for? and what would they do in case of victory? Perhaps that was
not quite clear to any of them. Few, if any, on the King's side, wished
to restore him to absolute power. Few, if any, on the Parliament's
side, were prepared to say what limitations should be imposed.

Cromwell seems to have had no more idea than any one else as to
what the terms of victory should be, but he was sure that the King
should be beaten sufficiently for the Parliament to be able to impose
what terms it would. When Manchester said to him, "If we beat the
King ninety and nine times, yet is he King still, and so will his
posterity be after him; but if the King beat us once, we shall all be
hanged, and our posterity made slaves," he had replied "My Lord, if
this be so, why did we take up arms at first? This is against fighting
ever hereafter, so let us make peace, be it never so base." And when
Manchester was afraid they might beat the King too much, Cromwell
said that if he met the King in battle, he would fire his pistol at him
as at another man.

By degrees Cromwell and young Sir Harry Vane seem to have become fairly sure, that if the King was to be restored, he must be
deprived of all authority, that is put in the position in which the
King of England finds himself today. In June 1644 Vane set out on
a secret mission to the elder Fairfax and Manchester at York, to urge

them to make provision for the government on such terms. The
generals would not listen. Among other things, they urged that the
nobility would not endure such an arrangement. Cromwell, in a temper, declared that he hoped to live to see the day when there was
never a nobleman in England, that he loved certain persons better
than others, because they did not love lords and that it would be
better when Manchester himself was but plain Mr. Montagu.

As a matter of fact, Cromwell and Manchester were no longer on
the good terms that they had been. Baillie, the Scotchman, the same
who had characterized Manchester as "a sweet meek man," and had
regretted that he was allowing his Lieutenant General to "guide the
army as he pleased," was now rejoicing that Cromwell was no longer
the guiding spirit, that his countryman Crawford was getting the
upper hand with Manchester. This Crawford was the Major General
whom Cromwell had rebuked for dismissing an Anabaptist. He had
sent a copy of Cromwell's letter to Manchester, and had pointed out
to him that a complete victory would be a victory of the sects, and
that would mean anarchy. As a lay member of the Westminster Assembly, Manchester had not been particularly zealous for rigid Presbyterian discipline, but this seemed alarming. So he was hoping that
it would not be necessary to fight the war to a finish.

Marston Moor was fought and won July 2nd, 1644, such a decisive
victory that it seemed as though the struggle might soon be ended.
So when Essex was being hard pressed by the King, and the Committee of Both Kingdoms ordered the army of the Eastern Association
to go to his assistance, Cromwell wrote to his brother-in-law Walton,
"That business hath our hearts in it, and truly had we wings, we
would fly thither—for indeed all other considerations are to be laid
aside, and to give place to it as being of far more importance." And
his men felt as he did, indeed he found them "never so cheerful as
when there was work to do." But alas! there were "some amongst
them," that is amongst the commanders, "much slow in action."

Manchester was of the "much slow." He never stirred from Lincoln
until news came that Essex had been defeated in Cornwall. Then,
although ordered by Parliament to prevent the King's march on London, he allowed him to reach Newbury. There he did attack him,
gained a somewhat doubtful victory, but allowed him to get back to
Oxford.

The truth was Marston Moor was plainly a victory of Cromwell
and the sects. They must not be allowed to win more such victories,
for it was commonly reported, Cromwell complains to Walton, "that

they were seeking to maintain their opinions in religion by force," so it gave him "a little ease, to pour his mind, in the midst of calumnies, into the bosom of a friend."

Evidently something must be done about it. For the country was sick of the war, and there might have to be a peace without victory. So on November 23rd a committee was appointed by Parliament "to consider of a frame or model for the whole militia." On the 25th Cromwell appeared at Westminster.

His first move was to bring charges against Manchester, that he had shown himself "indisposed to the ending of the war by the sword," and "always for such a peace, to which a victory would be a disadvantage." This is he had declared "by principles express to that purpose, and by a series of carriages and actions answerable to it." He had "declined whatsoever tended to full advantage upon the enemy, and studiously shifted off opportunities to that purpose, as if he thought the King too low and Parliament too high."

From his place in the House of Lords, Manchester did not so much answer these charges, as bring counter charges against his Lieutenant General. He had at first found him very exemplary, but of late he had been a disgruntled and factious subordinate. At least in one instance the hesitation and failure to act promptly during the Newbury campaign, had been due to Cromwell himself. When he had ordered him to a rendezvous with the horse, he had come to him, and "in a discontented manner, expressed himself, asking me whether I intended to flay my horses; for if I called them to a rendezvous, I might have their skins, but no service from them." Again Cromwell's care for his horses!

Then he brought other charges well calculated to arouse fears and enmity. The House of Lords was informed that Cromwell hoped to live to see the day when there was never a nobleman in England, the Scots that he would as soon turn his sword against them as against any one, the Presbyterians that if he had his way he would have none but Independents in the army, the Assembly of Divines that he had characterized them as persecutors of men more honest than themselves, all who looked forward to the restoration of the King (that meant almost every one), that if Cromwell met the King in battle he would fire his pistol at him as at another man. Thus for one reason or another Manchester thought he could turn almost all England and Scotland against Cromwell. He had been clever about it, probably he had been sincere.

He succeeded with the Scots and with some of the Presbyterians.

Very late one evening the two great lawyers, Whitelocke and Maynard, were summoned to Essex House. There they found the commander-in-chief with the Scotch commissioners, Holles, Stapleton, and other Presbyterian leaders. The Scotch made the charges, and asked the question. Ever since their army came into England, they said, Cromwell had used underhand and cunning means to detract from their credit. He was no friend to their Church, nor was he a well-wisher to the lord general. Under Scotch law they thought he might be tried as an incendiary, "one who kindles coals of contention, and raises differences in the State to the public damage." Would English law permit of this?

To which the English lawyers replied that English law was a little vague on the subject. At any rate there must be absolute proofs— such prominent men as Essex and the Scots must not compromise themselves by taking a position which they could not maintain. And then was it good policy? Let them remember that, although Cromwell had enemies, he was still very popular in some quarters. "I take Lieutenant-General Cromwell," said Whitelocke, "to be a gentleman of quick and subtle parts, and one who hath, especially of late, gained no small influence in the House of Commons; nor is he wanting of friends in the House of Peers, or of abilities in himself to manage his own defence to the best advantage."

The canny Scots listened, weighed the matter, decided that it was a losing game, they would better not play it. It was harder to call off their English allies; Holles and Stapleton thought that they had sufficient evidence, and a strong enough party in the House of Commons, to carry their point. But at two o'clock in the morning, the meeting broke up, having decided to do nothing. Some one, perhaps Whitelocke himself, told Cromwell about it.

Cromwell too was canny. He saw that he might carry his point in the House of Commons, but that it would be at the expense of creating further differences between Presbyterians and Independents, Scots and English, perhaps between Lords and Commons. Moreover was anything really to be gained by simply removing Manchester? The whole army must be reorganized. That was what he was really aiming at, he had only used Manchester to call attention to a general state of affairs.

A committee had been appointed to consider the differences between the two generals. On the morning of December 9th, Zouch Tate, a member of this committee, reported "that the chief causes of our division are pride and covetousness." Although Tate was a Presbyterian, he may have had an understanding with Cromwell. At any rate, Cromwell took advantage of his report. We read that "there was a general silence for a good space of time, one looking upon the other, to see who would break the ice." Then Lieutenant-General Cromwell stood up, and said, (it is his first recorded real speech):

"It is now a time to speak, or forever hold the tongue. The important occasion now is no less than To save a Nation out of a bleeding, almost dying condition, which the long continuance of this war hath already brought it into; so that without a more speedy, vigorous and effectual prosecution of the war, casting off all lingering proceedings, like those of soldiers of fortune beyond seas, to spin out a war, we shall make the kingdom weary of us, and hate the name of Parliament.

"For what do the enemy say? Nay, what do many say that were friends at the beginning of Parliament? Even this, That the Members of Both Houses have got great places and commands; and what by interest in the Parliament, what by power in the Army, will perpetually continue themselves in grandeur, and not allow the war speedily to end, lest their own power should determine with it. This that I speak here to our faces is but what others do utter abroad behind our backs. I am far from reflecting on you, I know the worth of those commanders, members of both Houses, who are yet in power; but if I may speak my conscience without reflection upon any, I do conceive that if the Army be not put into another method, and the War more vigorously prosecuted, the People can bear the war no longer, and will enforce you to a dishonourable peace.

"But this I would recommend to your prudence. Not to insist upon any complaint or oversight of any commander-in-chief upon any occasion whatsoever; for as I must acknowledge myself guilty of oversight, so I know they can rarely be avoided, in military matters. Therefore waiving a strict enquiry into the causes of these things, let us apply ourselves to the remedy, which is most necessary, And I hope we have such true English hearts and zealous affection toward the general weal of our mother country, as no member of either house will scruple to deny themselves and their own private interests, for the public good; nor account it to be a dishonour done to them, whatever the Parliament shall decide upon in this weighty matter."

The Cromwell who made this speech had traveled a long way from the Cromwell who five years before had answered Manchester "with indecency and rudeness." He was getting control of his temper, he was gaining in dignity, in sense of proportion, and in tact. He knew how to manage soldiers, this time at least he knew how to manage a Parliament.

When he had finished, Tate moved that so long as the war lasted, no member of either house should hold any command, military or civil, conferred upon him by Parliament. That would get rid of Essex and Manchester who had proved incompetent, and it would also get rid of Cromwell, competent enough, but distrusted by Scots and Presbyterians. Therefore it seemed a way out of the difficulty. Cromwell himself approved and supported it.

In the light of all that followed, his sincerity at this time was naturally called in question. And we may well ask whether he really thought that his military life was at an end, and whether he was willing that it should be? It seems to me that the only answer to this question is that he felt that the war must be won, and he saw that the war could not be won without the reorganization of the army. If in order to secure that reorganization his resignation was necessary, perhaps the war could be won better without him than with him. In that case he was willing to resign. In any case the war must be won. Of course it is not improbable that, knowing all possible successors as he did, he feared that it could not be won without him, and hoped that some loophole would be found that would render his resignation unnecessary. That does not imply insincerity and trickery. If he wished to get rid of other commanders, it was simply on the ground that they could not win the war. If he wished to be retained himself, it was on the ground that he could win it. He was bent on winning the war, not on his own aggrandizement.

As a result of it all, a Self-Denying Ordinance passed the Commons, by which no member of either House was to be allowed to hold command in the army, or be eligible for any office of state.

But at that time the Committee of Both Kingdoms of which Cromwell was a member, realizing that the difficulty lay not only with the commanders, but with the whole army, were at work on a plan by which Parliament should have, as Waller had said, an army of its own which it could command, and the army could have some assurance of regular pay.

The House of Lords was more interested in what this committee was doing than it was in the Self-Denying Ordinance. That could wait. So they threw out that Ordinance with the statement that "till a New Model be propounded to succeed, they cannot but think the present frame better than such a confusion, as is like to follow it."

It was on the 9th of January 1645, four days before the Lords threw out the Self-Denying Ordinance, that a scheme for the New Model was reported to the Lower House, and on the 11th of January, two days before it was thrown out, the outline of this scheme was voted upon. Parliament was to have an army of its own, numbering 22,000 men, and regular pay was to be provided by regular assessments of specified districts.

Sir Thomas Fairfax, son of the Fairfax to whom Vane had gone at York, was appointed commander in chief. He had made a good military reputation in the North, and though he was religious, it rather counted in his favor that no one knew whether he was a Presbyterian or an Independent. Skippon was made Major General, and commander of the foot. The post of Lieutenant General, commander of the horse, was significantly left vacant. Was it because the House of Commons saw that the only man competent to fill the position was Lieutenant General Cromwell, and hoped, in spite of the fact that he was one of its members, to get him in time? Did Cromwell himself see that?

The Ordinance establishing the New Model passed the Commons January 27th, the Lords February 15th. Then the Lords were willing to consider a Self-Denying Ordinance. On April 3rd such an ordinance was passed, but it was not like the one that they had rejected. It simply provided that all members of either House, holding civil or military positions, were to lay them down within forty days. There was nothing to prevent reappointment.

This second Self-Denying Ordinance contained a clause that was passed after much opposition. By this men might serve in the new army without taking the Covenant. It was simply impossible to dispense with the Independents, the most zealous and efficient of all the soldiers.

Cromwell had had his share in introducing the first Self-Denying Ordinance, which would certainly have ended his military career. When the second was introduced he was not present. Whether he was to retire from the army in forty days or not, he certainly could not do so now. In the west Weymouth and Taunton were being threatened by the royalists. Waller was sent to relieve them, Cromwell's regiment was ordered to assist him.

When, on December 9th the First Self-Denying Ordinance was being considered in the Commons, and the question arose as to whether men attached to their present officers would follow others, Cromwell had answered "Mr. Speaker, I am not of the mind that the calling of the members to sit in Parliament will break or scatter our armies. I can speak this for my own soldiers, that they look not upon me, but upon you; for you they will fight, and live and die in your cause—You may lay upon them what commands you please, they will obey your commands in that cause they fight for."

He was probably carried away by the enthusiasm of the moment, but there is no reason to doubt his sincerity. He had constantly exulted in the belief that his men were actuated by the same zeal for the cause that he himself felt. And perhaps they were, but if so they decided that it could not be won without their commander. On January 12th, Sir Samuel Luke, Deputy at Newport Pagnell, wrote to the Governor, then in London, "I heard there was a great mutiny at Cambridge, by Colonel Cromwell's regiment, who was to be put under another Colonel, which is a Scotchman; but they are resolved to lay down their arms till, as they say, they have vindicated Colonel Cromwell." Perhaps they did not think that the other Colonel, "which was a Scotchman," was really fighting for the same cause that they were. Now again on being ordered to duty without Cromwell, they refused to go. So on March 3rd, a whole month before the Second Self-Denying Ordinance, the House ordered him to go with them. Then all murmurs ceased, where he led, they followed.

It is to be noticed that Cromwell went as a subordinate, but he made no objection to being put under Waller's command. And Waller himself testifies that he gave no evidence at this time that he was conscious of extraordinary abilities. Indeed Waller thought that he did not even know that he possessed them, "for although he was blunt, he did not bear himself with pride or disdain. As an officer he was obedient, and did never dispute any orders, or argue upon them." (Notice that Manchester had just charged him with being factious and disobedient.) Waller also observed that though a man of few words, Cromwell had a way of making others talk, a singular capacity in judging their characters, and guessing their secrets.

Yes, that was Cromwell. He never tried to show off, to make others see how well he could talk, perhaps he couldn't talk very well. But he wanted to accomplish something. What he should aim at, and what it was possible to accomplish, he could decide upon, only as he knew what those under and about him thought, and how they were feeling. So what they thought and how they felt was of real importance to him. That was one reason why they loved him.

The expedition was successful. At the end of April Cromwell returned to Westminster to lay down his commission, a few days before the ordinance required him to do so.

But it was not to be. The King was about to take the field, the New Model was not as yet ready to fight. So Cromwell and his cavalry were sent at once to Oxfordshire to prevent a junction between the King and Prince Rupert. In the words of Sprigge, one of Fairfax's chaplains, "The charge of this service they recommended particularly to Lieutenant General Cromwell who, looking upon himself now as discharged from military employment by the new ordinance, which was to take effect within a few days, and to have no longer opportunity to serve his country in that way, was the night before come to Windsor from his service in the West, to kiss the general's hand and to take his leave of him; when on the morning, ere he was come forth out of his chamber, these commands, of which he thought nothing less in the world, came to him from the Committee of Both Kingdoms."

Perhaps it was not quite such a surprise to Cromwell as Sprigge thought. Yet it does not appear that he had been guilty of any double dealing. He had supported the first Self-Denying Ordinance, which would certainly have put an end to his military career. He had had nothing to do with the forming of the second, he was in the field at the time. That the position of Lieutenant General had been left vacant only goes to show that many members of the House thought that it would probably be necessary to re-appoint him, that no one else could fill the place, it does not appear that he had anything to do with it. There was of course now no legal reason why he should not be re-appointed. And probably events had shown him that he was not unlikely to be.

As it was, in spite of some opposition in the Lords, his command was extended forty days more, until June 22nd. He plunged into Oxfordshire, and accomplished the work assigned to him. On May 26th the Commons "having great testimonies of the gallant, zealous and valiant services performed by Lieutenant-General Cromwell," ordered him to go down into the Isle of Ely. This was no sooner noised abroad than "the courage of the Association began to be high with hope, and the City to be full of joy." But by June 12th he was with Fairfax, who had decided that he needed him. "To speak truth," said one of the news-letters, "it were to be wished that he were in the army, for it's conceived by some that the King will fight, and fighting he might put courage into his friends." That was what Cromwell did, he put courage into his friends. It was becoming more and more evident that he could not be dispensed with.

So on June 10th Fairfax and the Council of War petitioned Parliament to appoint him Lieutenant General of the New Model. It was evident that a battle was pending, there was a great body of horse, it must have a commander. Cromwell was the only man who had proved that he could fill the place, it was not a time to try experiments. "The general esteem and affection which he hath with the officers and soldiers of the whole army," so ran Fairfax's petition, "his own personal worth and ability for the employment, his great care, diligence and faithfulness in the services you have already employed him in, with the constant presence and blessing of God that have accompanied him, make us look upon it as the duty which we owe to you and the public, to make it our suit." To this the Lords vouchsafed no reply, but the Commons consented to the appointment for as long a time as his services seemed to be needed.

When on June 13th he rode into Fairfax's camp, the soldiers were glad. They "raised a mighty shout." "Ironsides," they cried, "is come to lead us!" It was the day before Naseby.

And Naseby was decisive. The morale of the Royalists was weakened, that of the Parliamentarians was strengthened, not only by the victory but by the letters taken after the battle, which proved that the king was negotiating to bring foreign forces into England. Those comparatively indifferent to the cause, but weary of the war, saw that their best hope lay on the Parliamentary side. Cromwell pushed on with the full assurance of final victory. Soon "Langport mercy" was added to "Naseby mercy." There remained a few fortified towns to be taken, but when Oxford, the Royalist headquarters, fell on the twenty-fourth of June 1646, the Parliamentary cause was won. And it was Cromwell who had done it, it was his sword that had determined that England should not go the way of the continental countries, and become an absolute monarchy. So, as Professor Trevelyan puts it, it is well that his statue should stand on guard, outside the doors of the Parliament which he saved.

He had a little time now to attend to domestic affairs. He moved his family, including the old mother, from Ely to a house in Drury Lane, London. And he gave two of his daughters in marriage, Bridget to his Commissary General Henry Ireton, and Elizabeth, said to be his favorite, to John Claypole, a Northamptonshire squire.

CHAPTER IX

Army and Parliament

"I profess I could never satisfy myself of the justness of this war, but from the authority of Parliament to maintain itself in its rights."—OLIVER CROMWELL.

"That which you have by force, I look upon it as nothing."
—OLIVER CROMWELL.

WITH the close of the first Civil War the real tragedy of Oliver Cromwell begins. Henceforth his life was to be nothing but struggle, struggle without and struggle within, a struggle akin to that which broke Woodrow Wilson, and from which an assassin's bullet mercifully freed Abraham Lincoln.

"You have done your work," old Jacob Astley had said to his conquerors, "and you may now go play, unless you fall out among yourselves." It was inevitable that they should fall out among themselves. For Parliament had entered upon the war to secure Parliamentary government, but the men who had done most to win the war were those who demanded religious toleration. It soon became evident that Parliament did not care for religious toleration, and that if it was to be obtained, the army, not Parliament, must rule. Hence the inevitable conflict.

And for Cromwell it was to be internal as well as external conflict. For he could never bring himself to accept the alternative. In 1644 he had complained that there were those who accused the army of seeking to maintain their opinion by force, which he, and he believed they, detested and abhorred. He was always to detest and abhor it, always to fight against it, yet often to yield to it. For Parliament must rule, yet there must be religious toleration, at least for those who had made it possible for Parliament to rule, and were willing to live peaceably under it. So for the rest of his life he was to contend for two ideals, incompatible in his day and generation, sometimes sacrificing one, sometimes the other, never really attaining either. Herein lies his tragedy. What was tragedy to the Greeks but a conflict of ideals in a noble soul, resulting in the apparent defeat of one or all of them?

So it was to be with Oliver. Henceforth he was to be at peace neither with other men nor with himself. There were times when even his God seemed to withdraw Himself from him, and he must walk in darkness. There had been no such experience during the war, then his duty had been clear to him, and he had been able to perform it, he had been at peace with himself, at peace with his God.

As the war had gone on, the religious differences in the army had increased and multiplied. Partly because of the lack of chaplains, and partly because their zeal had stirred them up to do so, many of the officers and men had taken to preaching. And they preached almost every conceivable doctrine. There was only one tenet that they held in common, Toleration.

And in this Cromwell was with them, increasingly with them as time went on. Some of their opinions might be foolish, some of their preaching in bad taste, but he believed that most of them were zealous and sincere in their search after God, and he knew that they had won the war. It had been necessary to tolerate them in order to win the war, and now, even if for no other reason, they must be tolerated because they had won the war. Moreover, the practice of toleration, which necessity had forced upon him, had made him more tolerant in spirit. So while he "joined himself to no sect, and did not openly profess of what opinion he was," he became known as an Independent, even as "the Great Independent." For in toleration of religious differences alone was he definite and explicit. He rejoiced that, while the religious men in the army were of all shades of opinion, they were "held together by the point of Liberty of Conscience, which was the common interest in which they did unite."

This explains his treatment of the saintly Baxter to whom the great evil of the time was sectarianism, the visible unity of the Church his passionate desire, his motto "In things necessary Unity, in things doubtful Liberty, in all things Charity." There might be great variety in the Church, but it must be one Church; the things about which men differed were of too small account to justify schism in the Body of Christ. If any man's conscience required him to be re-baptized, by all means let him be, but let him not on that account cut himself off from those who did not recognize such a necessity. Some Bishops had been oppressive, but neither Episcopacy nor Presbytery was of Divine origin, it was for the government to decide which was the more expedient, for the Church to submit. The Prayer Book was not perfect, yet on the whole an acceptable form of worship; if Government ordained either that it should or should not be used, let the Church obey. The one thing to be avoided was schism.

So it was in the hope of combating this great evil that after Naseby he joined the army as a chaplain. But he tells us that although Oliver Cromwell coldly bade him welcome, he never spake one word more to him while he was with the army, neither did he once invite him to Headquarters, where the councils and meetings of the officers were "so that most of his design was thereby frustrated." It is quite possible that the things that separated the dissenting sects were as unimportant to Cromwell as they were to Baxter, but he knew that to the disputants themselves they were important, so the only thing to do was to tolerate them. Baxter was a broad-minded man, he knew that, but why could he not be sufficiently broad-minded to tolerate the narrow-minded? Especially since the narrow-minded were sufficiently broad-minded to tolerate each other, and happened to be practically useful? Perhaps he also thought that preaching against schism served only to increase it, that Baxter would have had more success if he had preached less against the divisions, more about the things on which they could unite. "He who preaches with love," says St. Francis of Sales, "preaches enough against the heretics, although he does not utter one word of controversy."

Even before the war was over, Cromwell had addressed Parliament repeatedly on the subject of toleration. To the official dispatch that he sent to the Speaker after Naseby he had added, "He that ventures his life for the liberty of his country, I wish that he trust God for the liberty of his conscience, and you for the liberty that he fights for." After Bristol he wrote, "Presbyterians, Independents, Baptists, all have the same spirit of faith and prayer, they agree here, know no names of difference. All that believe here have the real unity, because inward and spiritual" (the only unity that was worth while to Cromwell). "As for being united in forms, commonly called Uniformity, every Christian will, for peace sake, study to do as far as conscience will permit; and from brethren, in things of the mind, we look for no compulsion, but that of light and reason." The House of Commons suppressed these passages in both dispatches.

For in the heat of victory, the Commons were preparing to throw away their opportunity, as victors generally do. If they had listened to Cromwell's plea for toleration, if they had gone further, as the army was afterwards to show itself willing to do, and extended that toleration to the Prayer Book, their victory might have been complete.

There would have been no struggle between Army and Parliament, no military despotism, no tragedy of Oliver Cromwell. Well satisfied with what he had accomplished, or with what he believed that his God had accomplished through him, he might have returned to the life of a simple gentleman farmer.

But it was not to be. Even in putting forth the Grand Remonstrance, the Commons had declared that they had no desire to relax the golden reins of discipline, for no opportunity must be given to their foes to say that in curtailing the exorbitant power of the Bishops, they were willing to open the floodgates to anarchy. They stood for order, there must be a limit to innovations. And as they had stood for order then, they must stand for order now. And since it was not to be the Episcopal order, it must be the Presbyterian order. Not, let it be understood, that they had any great devotion to the Presbyterian order in itself. The Covenant was the price that they had paid for Scotch assistance, they had not been enthusiastic about it. And now it was not Religion but Fear that was making them Presbyterians, even intolerant Presbyterians, Fear lest anarchy in the Church might lead to anarchy in the State, and that in the confusion that would follow, power might pass into the hands of the sectarian army. Pym and Hampden were dead. How much vision they would have had in this crisis can only be conjectured, it is certain that Holles and Stapleton, the second rate politicians who had succeeded them, had none at all.

As for the sects, so long as hostilities lasted, there was practical toleration, for it would have been impossible to win the war without them. Only against lay preachers in the army had the Presbyterian House raised its voice. There was a report that some of these preachers had even denied the necessity of a regular ministry, as John Milton was afterwards to do, and looked down upon the Levites, as they called the professional preachers. That was hardly to be endured by the Church whose motto was, "Let all things be done decently and in order," the Church upon which John Calvin had impressed the necessity of an educated ministry. So in April 1645 Parliament had passed an order that none but ordained ministers be allowed to preach.

Fairfax had not enforced it in the army. To have done so would have been to deprive himself of his best officers. As the Rev. Mr. Edwards, after delivering a sermon in favor of it, came down from the pulpit, a young gentleman in scarlet accosted him thus, "Sir, you speak against the preaching of soldiers in the army, but I assure you if they have not leave to preach they will not fight, and if they fight not, we must all fly the land and begone." That was putting the whole thing in a nutshell.

But Cromwell knew too well that as soon as the war was over, this practical toleration must cease. Complete victory, he could never forget, had been dreaded, because it might mean a victory of the sects. Now that it had been won that was the danger that would be fought against. He had seen, that although in April 1646, while the army was still needed, the Commons had promised due regard for tender consciences, provided there was no difference in fundamentals of religion, in September the second reading of a bill had been passed, punishing with death those denying the Trinity and Incarnation, probably regarded as fundamentals, while those who opposed infant baptism were liable to imprisonment for life. In December he had been present in the House, and had fought with all his might, a Bill prohibiting laymen from expounding the Scriptures. It had passed in spite of him, he had been able to muster only fifty-seven opposing votes. And he knew that, now that the swords of the preaching officers were no longer needed, it would probably be enforced.

He knew too that London was strongly Presbyterian, that the city corporation was planning for the suppression of heresy, that the clergy were crying out for Presbyterianism and Anti-Toleration, asserting that Toleration was "the Devil's masterpiece, could he effect it, he would think that he had profited by the Reformation." He knew that the Rev. Thomas Edwards had been given a lectureship at Christ Church in the heart of the city, "that he might handle these questions and nothing else before all that would come to hear." That gentleman had made a collection of the various opinions and heresies to be found in the army. It is curious reading, scarcely a form of twentieth century belief or disbelief is absent. It was the seventeenth century, no wonder that good Presbyterians were alarmed. Perhaps some of us who are today advocating freedom of speech for those who profess social and economic doctrines that we abhor, find it easier to do so, because at bottom we do not believe that they will prevail. The Presbyterians of the seventeenth century feared that these religious heresies would prevail.

Seeing these things, it is small wonder that Cromwell, who was at the time in a low physical condition, "carried himself with much weariness," and wondered "what the great birth of Providence would bring forth." In this weariness he wrote to a gentleman in Norfolk, "Sir, this is a quarrelsome age, and the anger seems to me to be the worse, when the ground is difference of opinion." In the midst of bitter disputes as to doctrines and ceremonies, he seems to have been attracted by the men who called themselves Seekers, men who took no part in these disputes, men who knew that, not having attained Truth themselves, they could not enforce it upon others, therefore they contented themselves with a patient waiting upon God, in the hope that they might find Him. To his daughter Bridget Ireton he wrote, "To be a Seeker is to be of the best sect next to a Finder, and such an one shall every faithful and humble seeker be at the end." But perhaps it was only the name that attracted him. After all, men can be as fanatical in denouncing all doctrines and ceremonies, as in upholding particular doctrines and ceremonies.

Seeing what was happening while the army was still in existence, he knew that he could not possibly hope for toleration after it was disbanded. And to disbandment *per se* he could not object; he knew that the army was expensive, and that it was no longer needed. But he knew too that Parliament had another motive, it could not possibly carry out its policy of intolerance while there was an armed body of sectaries in the country. And there was a further consideration, perhaps the weightiest of all, which he, believing it to be ground-less, probably did not fully appreciate. Parliament was afraid of the army and of him. What if the army should get ahead of Parlia-ment, take things into its own hands, and impose upon King, Parlia-ment and nation its own terms of peace? Had not Baxter found in that army men who "thought God's providence would cast the trust of religion and the kingdom upon them as conquerors?" And if they undertook this trust, could not Cromwell, the darling of the sectaries, be counted upon to lead them? Had he not said that he desired to have no man in the army but such as were of independent judgment, "that in case there should be propositions for peace that might not stand with the ends honest men aimed at, the army might prevent such a mischief?" Better get rid of the army and its dangerous Lieutenant General as soon as possible.

In February Oliver was ill nigh unto death. It was while he was thus absent from Parliament that a scheme for disbandment was voted upon. No force of foot, beyond what was necessary for garrisons, was to be retained in England. A small force of cavalry was still to be kept up. In March it was decided that Fairfax was to be com-mander in chief of the retained army. Even to that there was great opposition. Later resolutions were carried without a division, to the effect that no member of the House should hold a military com-mand, and that no officer under Fairfax should hold a rank higher than that of Colonel. This was largely in order that Cromwell, the great Independent, might be eliminated. Lesser Independents were debarred by resolutions that all officers should take the covenant, and conform to the Presbyterian church government.

But inasmuch as an army was needed to reconquer Ireland where Ormond, the King's lord lieutenant, having found it necessary to submit to either the English or the Irish rebels had chosen the English, as many as possible of the existing army were asked to volunteer for Ireland. That would get them safely out of England. Of this force Skippon was to be the commander.

Cromwell rose from his sick bed to find himself dismissed, the army that he loved an object of fear and hatred. He did not bear himself less heavily. "There want not in all places," he writes to Fairfax, "men who have so much malice against the army as besots them. Never were the spirits of men more embittered than now. Surely the Devil hath but a short time." To him there seemed to be no danger from either soldiers or sectaries. How could there be danger from men who asked for nothing save freedom to worship God in their own way? He was amazed and indignant to find that there were those who were actually afraid of them. "Upon the Fast Day," he wrote, "soldiers were raised as I hear, both horse and foot, in Covent Garden to prevent the soldiers (or sectaries, the reading is uncertain) from cutting the Presbyterians' throats. These are fine tricks to mock God with." It may have been it was at this time that he said to Ludlow, "It is a miserable thing to serve a Parliament, to which, let a man be never so faithful, if one pragmatical fellow among them rise and asperse him, he shall never wipe it off. Whereas, when one serves a general, he may do as much service and yet be free from all blame and enmity."

For himself there was no need to worry. He could get out of England. If his country did not want or need him, there was another place in which he might fight for both God and Protestantism, a place too in which he would serve a general, not a Parliament. After all, he was a soldier, not a statesman, and the Elector Palatine had offered him a command in Germany. Toward the end of March he had a long conference with him. No doubt it appealed to him to be offered a part in the struggle for which Gustavus Adolphus had given his life. And if the cause of toleration had been lost in England, it might be won in Germany. Did it never occur to him that although it might be possible to win a war in Germany, as it had been in England, it might be just as difficult to make a satisfactory peace?

As for the army his agony was not that it was to be disbanded, but that it was to be disbanded "in envy and malice," that the men who had fought for Parliament were hated by Parliament, that the men who had won liberty and supremacy for the Presbyterian conscience had so little chance for even liberty for their own conscience.

But disappointed and discouraged though he was, he still stood by Parliament. He turned it all over in his troubled mind, but he did not hesitate. Had not the "justness of this war," as he had said in 1644, been "from the authority of Parliament to maintain itself in its rights?" Did he not still "detest and abhor the idea of men seeking to maintain their opinions in religion by force?" And was it not for the present even more important to guard against anarchy than to secure religious liberty? And could that be done in any way except by submitting to Parliament, the only constituted authority that could settle the country peaceably? He abhorred military rule, he had believed that the army should fight until it was possible for Parliament to dictate terms of peace, but Parliament, not the army, should dictate those terms. So he did not resist disbandment nor did he think that the army would resist. "In the presence of Almighty God, before Whom I stand," he said in the House of Commons, "I know that the army will disband, and lay down their arms at your door, whenever you shall command them."

He had believed what he said, and it is probable that it would have been true, had not Parliament been almost incredibly foolish. For the New Model Army was not like Cromwell's "own handful," a "gathered church." It was composed largely of pressed men, chosen for their strong bodies rather than their religious zeal. The soldiers who cared about religious toleration were in a minority, though a very strong minority, those who had any idea of seizing political control were in a very small minority, probably there was no one who had more than a hazy idea on that subject. But all wanted their pay, and all wanted to be sure that when they laid down their arms, they would not be treated as criminals for acts done during the war. The pay of the foot was eighteen weeks in arrears, that of the horse forty-three weeks. But money was scarce, the Scotch must be paid, the English army could wait. So no pay was offered them. Moreover, with the restoration of the King, and Parliament in the temper in which it then was, it was quite possible that many of the things that they had done as soldiers would be reckoned against them as murder and robbery. Parliament gave them no assurance that this would not be the case.

Under these circumstances it is small wonder that the army, deprived by the men whom they had saved of both the spiritual and the material things for which they had fought, fell more and more under the control of the Godly Party, or that the number increased among them who were asking, "What were the Lords of England but William the Conqueror's colonels? Or the Barons but his Majors? Or the Knights but his Captains?"

So when the order for disbandment reached Saffron Walden in Essex, where the bulk of the army was quartered, there were murmurs and consultations. As a result Fairfax was asked to present a petition to Parliament that, before they disbanded or enlisted for Ireland, back pay be guaranteed, and indemnity granted against legal proceedings for acts done in the late war. Alas! of what avail to address such a petition to an assembly that had "so much malice against the army as besotted them?" That assembly not only ordered the petition to be suppressed, but declared that those who persisted in presenting it were to be accounted disturbers of the public peace, and enemies to the State. When we consider how fair and reasonable the demands were, Parliament can hardly be excused on the ground that it was afraid. For there was nothing in them about religious toleration.

New Commissioners were sent to Saffron Walden to urge enlistment for Ireland, and to announce the appointment of Skippon as commander-in-chief there. They were met with cries of "Fairfax and Cromwell, and we all go!" As enlistments were slow, toward the end of April six weeks' pay was offered those to whom forty-three weeks was due. It was too late, and the offer was not enough.

The Army decided upon more vigorous action. In eight of the cavalry regiments two agitators were chosen (the word was at that time synonymous with agents) to negotiate for their rights. Three of these agitators were dispatched to London with a letter which they asked Cromwell to present to the House. In this letter the hand of the Godly Party was evident. It dealt with other matters than pay and indemnity, complained of "scandalous and false suggestions," which were being circulated against the army, of a "plot contrived by some men who had lately tasted of sovereignty," and declared that the soldiers would "neither be employed for the service of Ireland, nor suffer themselves to be disbanded till their desires were granted, and the rights and liberties of the subjects vindicated and maintained."

Amazed and alarmed, the House asked that the three agitators be brought in. They were but common troopers, gave their names as Edward Sexby, William Allen, and Thomas Shepard. Holles, the

Presbyterian leader, was for committing them to prison. He had a
following. But Skippon certified that they were "very honest men,"
whereupon an Independent member suggested that if they were committed, it should be "to the best inn of the town, and sack and
sugar provided for them." Then as Holles himself put it "the House
flatted." It was decided that Skippon, Cromwell, Ireton and Fleetwood should be sent to Saffron Walden, to act as mediators between
the army and Parliament. They were empowered to offer eight
weeks' pay and full indemnity.

What had Cromwell been doing and thinking all this time? He
had not been doing much, and what he had been thinking we can
only conjecture from a knowledge of what his general principles were,
and of what he did afterward. No doubt he still "bore himself
heavily." If he did little it was because he did not know what to do.
He did want the army to have its pay and indemnity, he did want
religious toleration, but he did not want the army to become a political
force. The Government must do the army justice, but the army
must not dictate to the Government, or become the Government.
During the latter part of April he and his friend Vane generally
absented themselves from Parliament. What was the use in going?
He could accomplish nothing, and whatever he said or did would be
looked upon with suspicion.

For both sides distrusted him. The House feared that at any
moment he might put himself at the head of a military revolt. On
the other hand John Lilburn, who had adored him, and in whose
behalf he had intervened a number of times (it will be remembered
that it was on his behalf that he was speaking when Sir Philip Warwick first saw him, and gave us his famous pen portrait of him), now
wrote him that his actions during the last few months had filled him
with grief and amazement. "I am informed this day, by an officer
out of the army, that you and your agents are like to dash to pieces
the hope of our outward preservation, and will not suffer them to
petition, till they have laid down their arms; because forsooth you
have engaged to the House that they shall lay down their arms,
whenever it shall command them." Let Cromwell pick up resolution,
"like a man that will persevere to be a man of God," to risk his life
to deliver his fellow soldiers from ruin. Seeing that he apparently
availed nothing, perhaps Oliver had not yet given up the idea of
getting out of it altogether, and taking service in Germany. He could
at least do something there.

But now it appeared that there was something in England that he could do. However much the House was inclined to distrust him, it was forced to trust him now; for he, and he only, could if he would, do something to heal the breach between army and Parliament, and in any case he could hardly make matters worse.

So it must have been with a sense of relief that he set out to Saffron Walden, though he knew as he wrote to Speaker Lenthall, that he and his brother officers had a task there, "in comparison whereof, nothing that we ever yet undertook was, at least in our apprehension, equal."

For consider what his task was. He knew that the army was enraged, and he knew that it was justly enraged. He loved the army, he did not love Parliament. Yet he must preserve England from anarchy and civil war, and the only way to do it was to preserve the authority of an unjust and unloved Parliament against an, in this case just, and much loved army. He set out resolved, as he told representatives of the army, "to deal very faithfully, through the grace of God both with those who have employed us hither, and with you." But he knew that the only way to deal faithfully with them, was to persuade them to submit to those who had employed him thither, the just to the unjust, for the larger good.

But it must be done. So when he met two hundred officers and a certain number of private soldiers in Saffron Walden Church, he did not talk to them about their grievances, but simply pointed out the fact that Parliament was beginning to be fair to them, and in any case it was their only protection from anarchy. Some of them would be needed there, but the majority were requested to return to their charges, and to impress upon them the concessions that Parliament had made; to wit, the addition of a fortnight's pay, eight weeks instead of six, both to those who went to Ireland, and to those who did not go, and a very full Act of Indemnity. And, above all, they must make the very best use they could of the interest which all, or any of them, might have in their respective regiments, "TO WORK IN THEM A GOOD OPINION OF THAT AUTHORITY WHICH IS OVER BOTH US AND THEM. FOR IF THAT AUTHORITY FALLS TO NOTHING, NOTHING CAN FOLLOW BUT CONFUSION." They had "fought to DEFEND that Authority, so now they must extend their industry and interest to PRESERVE it."

Later Cromwell was to say that he was not wedded or glued to any form of government, but at that time and even to the end, he was unable to conceive of any government for England other than that of a Parliament. Hence his strong plea for it.

The commissioners had ordered the officers to ascertain and let them know just what the temper of the army was. As the infantry had followed the example of the cavalry, and a body of agitators had been chosen to represent the whole army, these regimental agitators reported the opinions and demands of the regiments severally, and they were put into one draft on the principle of including only such demands as were made unanimously by all the regiments.

And the Declaration thus drawn up was such as to make Cromwell thank God and take courage. He had succeeded as well as he could have hoped, he had gained his principal point. The soldiers made no claim to political influence, they insisted only on the redress of practical grievances. And while they felt that they had been misrepresented and ill treated, they denounced only one person by name, the Rev. Mr. Edwards. So on May 21st, after an absence of three weeks, he reported at Westminster, that while he had found little disposition among the soldiers to go to Ireland, he thought that they would disband quietly. The House thanked him for what he had done. And he probably felt that Parliamentary government had been preserved, the danger of army rule had been averted.

That was on May 21st. Less than three weeks later, he had placed himself at the head of the army, and was marching on London! No wonder that those who had suspected and feared him felt that their suspicions and fears had been justified! Was it any wonder that a man who could change as quickly as that was distrusted? Had he indeed changed? Had he not rather been playing a deep game, meaning to do this all the time?

But Cromwell had been perfectly sincere. If he had given a shock, it was because he had received a shock. He had dealt faithfully with Parliament and the army, he had come back to find that during his absence Parliament had not dealt faithfully with the army or with him. He had gone away to deal with one situation, he had come back to find quite another situation. Doubtless the Presbyterian leaders had felt that while he might quiet the army temporarily, he neither could nor would do anything to free England from sectarianism. That must be attended to during his absence, and the temporary respite from fear of the army that he was giving them. On May 12th Charles had announced that he was ready to concede the control of the army for ten years, and the Presbyterian establishment, with no toleration! for three, during which the clergy were to discuss a permanent settlement. And on the 18th, three days before he made his report, the English Presbyterians and Scotch commissioners had expressed their willingness to accept these terms, as a basis of negotiation with the King! Moreover, Parliament, fearing that the army would not accept such an arrangement, was making every preparation to treat it as an enemy! Secret negotiations had been entered into with the French ambassador, and the commissioners of the Scotch Parliament, with the idea of bringing a Scotch force into England if necessary! And every independent officer of the city militia had been dismissed, and its training had been handed over to the common council of London, a strong Presbyterian body! In short it seemed as though while Cromwell had been laboring with the army to prevent another civil war, Parliament had been laboring to bring it on, preparing and training a new army to fight the army that had won the first one!

At any rate the intention was to get rid of that army as soon as possible. On the 27th of May, just six days after Cromwell had made his report and been thanked by the House, it was voted that the entire army be disbanded. To prevent concerted action, the disbandment was to be regiment by regiment, each on a specified day in a specified place. Skippon was to be present to enlist such disbanded men as would go to Ireland.

When news reached the army of what was being done, there was at first a great uproar. One contemporary says that Parliament might just as well have sent its commissioners among so many bears to take away their whelps. The commissioners however did not feel that the army as a whole was even yet politically minded. "Many of the soldiers," they wrote, "being dealt with, profess that money is the only thing that they insist upon, and that five months' pay would have given satisfaction."

Had this been offered at first it probably would have done so, but it was too late now, the Godly and political factions had gained the upper hand. The agitators advised the army to refuse to disband, and made it evident that it was more than a question of pay. "Be active," wrote one, "the good of all the kingdom is in your hands." The uproar was followed by an ominous calm. On May 29th the agitators drew up a petition to Fairfax, asking for a rendezvous of the whole army to determine a plan of action. Two hundred officers, Cromwell's son-in-law Ireton among them, advised Fairfax to grant the petition, for if he did not, the men themselves would have a rendezvous sure to result in a tumult. "I am forced," Fairfax said, "to yield something out of order, to keep the army from disorder, or more inconvenience."

And then on the 3rd of June Cromwell took the most momentous step of his life, the one from which everything else was to follow. He left London to throw in his lot with the army! That meant, though he could not foresee it at the time, that he had delivered himself and England over to the military rule that he hated, and from which he was never to be able to free either himself or his country.

. And yet he whose nature it was, when he had time, always to hesitate, sometimes to hesitate too long before making an important decision, took this step quickly, and apparently without hesitation. He did not have time to hesitate, there was nothing else for him to do, except to let things take their course without him. And that course would certainly be anarchy, and military violence, probably civil war. So his decision was as quick as it would have been on the battlefield.

For he had done his best to persuade the army to submit to Parliament as the only possible government, even though he thereby risked toleration, and though it was "a task in comparison thereof nothing that he had ever yet undertaken had been equal." And as matters then stood, he had hoped that he had succeeded. But now he faced a different situation. Parliament seemed determined with foreign aid to bring on a second civil war, in order to restore the King on terms that would utterly suppress the liberty of the sects, that liberty being dearer to him than anything else. It was plainly impossible for him to continue to support such a Parliament, or to ask the army to do so. And he could do nothing by remaining in London, he had no authority in Parliament; there was no hope that he could induce it to adopt a more conciliatory attitude, indeed he was in danger of arrest.

On the other hand he might do something with the army. He might check the disorganization that was threatening it, and so prevent military violence and anarchy. He might, with its aid, crush the parliamentary intrigues with the Scots, and so prevent civil war. For various reasons he was being urged to come to them. "If he would not forthwith come and lead them," the agitators wrote him, "they would go their own way without him." "Provocation and exasperation," Ireton wrote, "make men think of what they never intended— It shall be my endeavour to keep things as right as I can, but how long I shall be able, I know not." So Oliver made his decision.

That day something else happened. The king, who before the fall of Oxford, had fled to the Scots, had been given up by them, and now lay in the power of the Parliament at Holmby in Northamptonshire.

It was certain that he liked the terms to which he had seemed to consent no better than the army did. So the possession of his person appeared to be the key to the situation. There was a rumor that Parliament intended to remove him from Holmby to a place where he would be more exclusively under its influence. In the present crisis this must be prevented. So on May 31st, a meeting was held at Cromwell's house in Drury Lane, at which there was present a certain Cornet Joyce, apparently already authorized by the agitators to proceed to Holmby to prevent the removal of the king, and to carry him off himself if necessary. But the agitators had no military authority, so Cromwell, who certainly had not originated the plan, was induced to give the required instructions to Joyce.

The story is well known. Joyce reached Holmby on the third of July, the day that Cromwell left London. He told the garrison, who made friends with him and his men, that he had come to hinder a plot to carry the king to London, which might lead to a second civil war. This was perfectly true. Probably at that time he was not definitely planning to take the king away. But during the day there were rumors of an approaching attack. That decided him. He went to the king's bedroom, awakened him, and told him of his plan. Charles, who seems to have taken a fancy to him, fell in with it willingly. When Joyce told him that he had no commission except the five hundred soldiers at his back, he said pleasantly, "It is a fair commission, and as well written as any that I have seen in my life, a company of as handsome proper gentlemen as I have seen in a great while." He himself chose Newmarket as his destination, and when Fairfax and Cromwell decided that his removal had been unnecessary, and declared themselves in favor of his return, he insisted that he preferred to go to Newmarket. So to Newmarket he went.

For his game was to play off Parliament against the army, and the army against Parliament. Even before he left Oxford, he had written to Derby that he was "endeavouring to get to London, not without hope that I shall be able to draw either the Presbyterians or the Independent party to side with me, for extirpating one another, that I may really be King again." That was the hope that he was to cherish, the game that he was to play until the end. This sharp division increased his hope. "Men," he said, "will begin to perceive that without my establishment there can be no peace." But in the game that he was playing, it would not do to let Parliament get too strong. Besides the Army was more courteous to him, they did not interfere with his private devotions, were less zealous enemies of the Prayer Book.

Meanwhile Cromwell had arrived at Kentford Heath, and found the general rendezvous of the Army in session. The agitators had already presented their petition to Fairfax, stating that certain Parliamentary leaders were to blame, and binding themselves not to disband until their wrongs were righted.

Cromwell saw that the agitators must not get control. That way lay the anarchy that he had come to prevent. If he could associate the general officers with the representatives of the regiment, perhaps a certain amount of order and unity might be maintained. So at his suggestion a Council of the Army was chosen, to negotiate with Parliament. It consisted of the general officers, two officers and two privates chosen from each regiment. As a matter of fact, the real direction of affairs soon passed into the hands of the Council of War, consisting only of general officers. The army council became little more than a debating society, working off steam by expressing its opinions. This again was Cromwell's doing. And again Lilburn raised his voice against him: "You have robbed," he wrote him in July, "by your unjust subtlety and shifty tricks, the honest agitators of all their power and authority, and solely put it in a thing called a Council of War."

But it was not only to prevent anarchy in the army that Cromwell had come. He was seeking very earnestly to save England from the rule of the sword, to prevent the army from becoming a political power. So it was under his influence that a statement was published, in which the officers declared that they harbored no wild schemes, "such as the overthrow of the magistracy, the suppression or hindering of Presbytery, the establishment of Independent government, or the upholding of a general licentiousness in religion, under pretence of liberty of conscience."

If the Presbyterian leaders had only understood, it was not yet too late. But it is small wonder that in that state of excitement, they did not understand. In time of war each side thinks that it is acting in self-defense, and each can make out a fairly good case to prove it. So now the army knew that it was acting in self-defense, Parliament believed that it was. For it believed that the removal of the King had been plotted long before, that the Army, actuated by a desire to destroy the Church, was planning a military despotism. So preparations were made for resistance, a fresh army at Worcester was planned, the City was asked to raise both cavalry and infantry. It is true that commissioners were sent to the Army to offer more money in case of disbandment. But it was too late for that now, more than

money was demanded. The army decided that there was nothing
for them to do but to march on London.

From Royston a letter was sent to the Lord Mayor, Common Council and Aldermen of the City of London, the chief supporters of the
new Presbyterian military organization. It was signed by all the
officers, including Fairfax, but was probably written by Cromwell. In
this letter the officers stated that they demanded reparation upon those,
who have to the utmost, improved all opportunities and advantages,
by false suggestions, misrepresentations and otherwise, "for the destruction of the Army, with a perpetual blot of ignominy upon it."
They would not have taken the step they were taking, had it concerned
themselves alone, but under this pretense, they found no less involved
than the overthrow of the privileges of both Parliament and people.
For the Presbyterian leaders, rather than fail in their designs, were
willing to engage the Kingdom in a new war, to put the kingdom into
blood under pretense of the honor of, and of their love to Parliament,
surely not dearer to them than to the army who had given such great
proofs of their faithfulness to it. To carry out their design, they were
relying upon the city of London, whom the officers besought not to
prefer a few self-seeking men beyond the welfare of the public. The
fear was that they might engage many therein upon mistakes, easily
swallowed in a time of such prejudice. All that they desired as
Englishmen, and surely their being soldiers had not stripped them
of that interest, was a settlement of the peace of the kingdom and
the liberties of the subject, according to the votes and declarations
of Parliament before they took up arms. And they found the "ingenious (ingenuous) honest people, in almost all parts of the kingdom,
full of the sense of ruin and misery, if the army should be disbanded,
before the peace of the kingdom had a full and perfect settlement."

They again disclaimed all desire to alter the civil government, or
to intermeddle with the settling of a Presbyterial government, or to
obtain a way to licentious liberty, under pretense of obtaining ease
for tender consciences. "Only we could wish that every good citizen,
and every man that walks peaceably in a blameless conversation,
and is beneficial to the commonwealth, may have liberty and encouragement," that being according to justice itself.

Beyond these things, they would not go, but for the obtaining of
these, they were drawing near to the city, professing that they intended no evil toward it; if the citizens appeared not in arms against
them, they would not give them the least offense. Nor did they come

to do any act that might prejudice the being of Parliament. "We seek the good of all." And they would wait or remove to a further distance, if once they were assured that a speedy settlement was at hand. When that was accomplished, they would disband, or go to Ireland.

If they entered the city, there should be no plunder. "If not provoked by you, rather than any such evil shall fall out, the soldiers shall make their way through blood to effect it. But if after all this, the citizens took up arms in opposition to, or hindrance of the just undertakings of the army, the officers had, by this brotherly premonition, freed themselves from the ruin that might befall that great and populous city, and hereby washed their hands thereof."

But the city did not understand. How could it? Less than three weeks before Cromwell had said that the army would disband at the command of Parliament, but had he not now made himself leader of the army to resist that command? The soldiers said that they were making their demands as Englishmen, rather than as soldiers, but was it not as soldiers that they were now marching upon the city to enforce those demands? So the attitude of the citizens was one of bewilderment and fright. They simply did not know what to believe or think. "Things here are in the most saddest condition that even mortals beheld," wrote Mrs. John Moore to her husband in Ireland. "Every day we look for Sir Thomas Fairfax, his army, whether in love or with force is not yet known.—We are in less safety than you, for there you know your enemies, and here we do not."

Perhaps they would not have understood anyhow, in an atmosphere of fear and suspicion people rarely are in a condition to understand even the clearest statement. But Cromwell had not tried hard enough to make them understand, he had written that letter to the city in haste, "not in haste of the pen merely," Carlyle says, "but in haste before the matter had matured itself for him, and the real kernel of it got parted from the husks." He should have made it very plain that the situation had changed, and that for that change the Parliamentary leaders, not the army, were responsible. That while it was true that not long since he had advocated obedience to Parliament, and believed that the army was with him, he had learned now what he did not know then, that Parliament was preparing for civil war, and was calling in a foreign army to assist it. But his was a slow mind, it was always hard for him to make a clear statement of a complicated matter, he had to chew the cud before he could do it, and there had not been time for that. Events had moved so rapidly, he had been forced to act so quickly, that he probably did not realize himself how completely he had shifted his position.

A few days later came a Declaration announcing the political pro-gram of the army, formulated chiefly by Ireton. Parliament must rule, but by this time the danger that Parliament might become a close oligarchy, had become evident. So long as it was engaged mainly in redressing grievances, a Parliament, chosen as Parliaments had been chosen up to this time, might fairly carry out the wishes of the people. But when it undertook really to rule, there was danger that the rule might be just as tyrannical as that of an absolute monarch. Therefore there was a demand for a speedy dissolution of the existing Parliament, for the equalization of constituencies and for the right to petition. Eleven of the most prominent Presbyterian leaders, Holles and Stapleton the chief of them, were accused of treason, the House was asked to put them on trial and in the meantime to see that they did not vote. To such radical demands, there was at first no reply. For a short time the accused persons redoubled their efforts to raise English forces, and gain the assistance of the Scots against the army of Fairfax and Cromwell.

Then came the alarming news that the northern army under Poyntz, which Parliament had more or less counted upon to resist the army of Fairfax, was on the verge of mutiny, and prepared to join it. The House was frightened, the eleven members withdrew, negotiations were opened with the army, negotiations which dragged on fruitlessly for a fortnight, and then the agitators urged that the march on London be resumed.

Cromwell was troubled. When he left London to throw in his lot with the army, it had seemed as though there was nothing else for him to do, yet he was becoming more and more conscious that, in doing so, he had taken a long step toward military rule. So he deter-mined with all his heart and soul, mind and strength, to fight against it. The root of all the evil, Ireton had said in his Declaration, was arbi-trary power, and this was just as dangerous when exercised by a Parliament not representative of the people, as when exercised by a monarch. Was it not even more dangerous when exercised by an army?

On July 16th a Council of War was held at Reading, to decide whether the army should march on London. With reason and fervor Oliver pleaded with them to wait a little longer, until negotiations could be carried through. The things that he said have often been repeated. "Whatsoever we get by a Treaty, whatsoever comes to be settled upon us that way, will be firm and durable, and will be conveyed over to posterity. That will be the greatest honour to us that ever poor creatures had.—We shall avoid the great objection that will be against us, that we have got things of the Parliament by force.—Things though never so good, obtained in that way, it will exceedingly weaken the things, both to us and to all.—Really, really, have it what you will, *that which you have by force, I look upon it as nothing."*—"I do not know that force is to be used, except we cannot get what is good for the kingdom without it.—That which we seek to avoid is the having a second war, and the defeating of those things that are so dear to us, whose interest ought to be above our lives to us."

When some one objected that while a Treaty might be the desirable thing, they had waited so long that patience was exhausted, he replied: "Give me leave to offer one thing to your consideration. We are very swift in our affections and desires, and truly I am very often judged for one that goes too fast that way, and that is the property of men that are as I am, to be full of apprehension, not so much real as imaginary, to be always making haste, and more so sometimes than good speed." (Is it possible that, seeing how things were going, he was turning over in his mind whether he had not been too full of apprehension, and had not made too much haste, when he joined the army?)

He confessed that he himself had few extravagant or overweening thoughts of obtaining good things from this Parliament, but it might sometime be a reformed or purged Parliament. Even now they must remember there was a party in it, that had been faithful from their first sitting, unto this very day. For them, the holding of their heads above water had been their common work, and every day's work. "That which we desire to-day is that which they have struggled for as for life." He thought "that part of the Parliament on the gaining hand, and that the work that we are now upon tends to make them gain more; and again I wish that we might remember this always, that what we and they gain in a free way is better than twice so much in a forced, and will be more truly ours and our posterities."

When the Council broke up at midnight, then and not till then, had Cromwell carried the day. It was decided to present four demands to Parliament, to wit that no foreign force should be brought into England, that the reformados should be put out of the line, the eleven most obnoxious Presbyterian members suspended from Parliament, and that the London militia be put back into the same hands as before.

And Parliament accepted these terms, even appointed Fairfax Commander in Chief of the whole army, so that there could no longer be any force to resist him. But London would not acquiesce, many citizens signed an engagement in favor of maintaining the Covenant, and restoring the King on his own terms. Bands of apprentices besieged the House, and threatened violence unless the recent votes were repealed. So Parliament yielded, first the Lords, then the Commons, and adjourned until July 30th. Both speakers, eight peers and fifty-seven members of the Lower House took refuge with the army, declaring that Parliament was not free. The army again marched on London. With both speakers and so many members of Parliament with them, they had now as much legal right as the Parliament, and perhaps more moral right. The city prepared to fight, the eleven expelled members took their places in Parliament to direct the resistance.

But one gathers that it was nothing but bluff, the citizens and their Parliamentary leaders alike knew that they had no chance against the army of Fairfax and Cromwell. They probably hoped that a show of resistance would make fighting unnecessary. So when the scouts announced that the army had made a halt, the crowds outside Guildhall cried: "One and all!" when word came that it was advancing, they cried, "Treat, treat!" On the fourth of August London surrendered unconditionally. The army conducted the speakers and the members who had taken refuge with them back to Westminster. The eleven members withdrew permanently, some of them fled to the continent. "These men," Cromwell had said, "will never leave until the army pull them out by the ears." The army had done so now. As there was still a Presbyterian majority, some of the agitators were for a thorough purge of the House. This Cromwell, probably influenced by Fairfax, opposed, it seemed more army rule than was necessary, but he forced a vote, declaring the proceedings of the Houses, during the absence of the speakers, null and void.

And all that Parliament had feared was rapidly coming to pass. The army that had fought to preserve Parliament in its rights against the king, now had both king and Parliament under its control, and was in a position to enforce its own terms of peace upon the nation. But for this Parliament, not the army, was chiefly responsible. Because it feared, it had brought upon itself the thing that it feared.

"That which you have by force, I look upon it as nothing." And Cromwell knew that all that he had so far, he had by force. Would he ever be able to get anything in any other way? At any rate he would try.

CHAPTER X

Army, Parliament, and King

"The army thought that no man could enjoy his life and estates quietly, until the King had his rights."
—OLIVER CROMWELL.

"That which you have by force, I look upon it as nothing."
—OLIVER CROMWELL.

FOR although Cromwell had gained his immediate end, he was not happy. He was fully aware that against his will, and against the will of the majority of the officers, things were drifting toward military despotism. That must be prevented. Major Tulidah had suggested that it was desirable to use force this once that there might be no more force. Cromwell had not wished to use it even this once. He had been driven to it. Now the problem was to prevent its being used again.

The one ray of hope was the King. He must be restored as quickly as possible. That was the only way out of anarchy on the one hand, and military despotism on the other. "The army," Cromwell said, "thought that no man could enjoy his life and estates quietly, until the King had his rights."

Parliament thought so too, and had tried to restore him, but in proscribing his religion, they had offered him terms which his conscience could not accept. Might not the army, in whose possession he was, offer him more acceptable terms, restore him and then retire, leaving King and Parliament to govern the country? The soldiers were not disposed to proscribe his religion. Those who were "held together by the point of Liberty of Conscience, the common interest in which they did unite" would not make an exception of the King's conscience.

So the army chiefs had been negotiating with Charles for some time. Ever since his removal from Holmby he had been treated with the utmost consideration. He had been moved as the army moved, but so long as he kept near army headquarters, he had been allowed to choose his own place of residence, and visit any friends who might happen to be in the vicinity. On the twenty-fourth of August, he had settled down quietly at Hampton Court. There any one might visit him who chose, even noted Royalists. Best of all he was allowed to worship in his own way, his favorite chaplains, Doctors Hammond and Sheldon, were with him.

Fairfax, Cromwell and Ireton were also frequently with him, studying him, weighing him, considering within themselves what manner of man he was, and whether it would be possible to make satisfactory terms with him. They were most respectful in their manner toward him, although it was noticed that Cromwell and Ireton did not kiss his hand, as Fairfax did. As for the King, he was often "very pleasant in his discourse with them."

It was on July 4th, when Charles was at Caversham, that Cromwell had his first long interview with him. He was very hopeful, the charm of the King's manner enchanted him, he even began to feel for him something of the affection with which the Stuarts were wont to inspire those who came into personal contact with them. He realized that he was as sincere in his devotion to his religion as he was to his. And on the subject of Presbyterian intolerance they were agreed.

And he was completely won over when for the first time since the war began, Charles was allowed to see the three of his children who were in England, the Duke of York, the Princess Elizabeth, and the Duke of Gloucester. It was an affecting scene. Cromwell, who loved his own children dearly, was impressed by the way in which the King loved his. Surely so sincere a Christian and so tender a father must be a good man, would make a good King. He told Berkeley that "the King was the uprightest and most conscientious man of his three kingdoms."

So it seemed worth while to make proposals to him. And Ireton had them ready, he had been working on them for some time. On the 23rd of July, two weeks before the army entered London, having been passed by the Army Council, they were submitted to the King.

By this document, known as the Heads of Proposals, the present Parliament was to dissolve itself within a year. In the future there were to be biennial Parliaments, and that they might better represent the people, there was to be a reformed franchise and equal electoral districts. For the next ten years Parliament was to appoint the great officers of State; after that when there was a vacancy, to nominate three from whom the King was to choose one. To take the place of the modern cabinet there was to be a Council of State, the manner of the nomination of which was to be agreed upon, to sit for not more than seven years. Such as had borne arms against the Parliament were to be debarred from the first two biennial Parliaments, and from holding offices of state for five years, but even during that time Parliament might make exceptions in individual cases. Royalists who had been forced to compound for their estates were to be more leniently treated.

So much for constitutional matters. But to Cromwell the articles concerning religion must have seemed more important, and in these the army was true to its principle of toleration. No mention was made of an Established Church, it was neither advised nor opposed, nor was any preference expressed for either Presbytery or Episcopacy. The important thing was that, whether there was an Established Church or no Established Church, whether Presbytery or Episcopacy prevailed, there was to be complete religious toleration. No one was to be obliged to take the Covenant. Neither Prayer Book nor Bishops were proscribed, but if the Prayer Book was used, it was not to be enforced upon any one; if there were Bishops, they were to have no coercive power. Attendance at church was not to be enforced. If for any reason it was necessary to discover Papists or Jesuits, it must be done by other means than enforced church attendance. Meetings for worship apart from regular church services were not to be prohibited. These terms were for England alone, Scotland might make her own arrangements.

It was with this plan for a settlement that the army marched upon London. A noble plan, by far the best that was ever offered during this troubled period, and it should have conciliated all parties, "with charity toward all, with malice toward none." Had it been offered by Parliament at first, it is possible that it would have done so, but it was too late now; the passions of all were too much inflamed. And in a crisis it is generally passion, not reason, that determines the result.

Of course these proposals must be accepted by Parliament as well as by the King, so after a week of consultation between the King and the army chiefs, they were put into final form, and a copy of them given to the Parliamentary commissioners, at that time with the army. Just as soon as the Houses were reconstituted, the plan was presented to the Commons by Sir Harry Vane. Denzil Holles was amazed, spoke of it as "a new platform of government, a Utopia of their own." Probably the House was equally amazed.

Cromwell must have been well satisfied with the Proposals, they were all and more than all that he had hoped for. And while he knew that it was not at all likely that Parliament would consent to such extreme toleration, that did not worry him much. The main thing was to get the King's consent. That being secured, the Army, then on its way to London, was in a position to coerce Parliament, "once for all," it was hoped. And this Cromwell was willing to do, he even told the King that if he accepted, and Parliament refused to do so, he would see to it that the House was purged of opponents. Ireton declared that "the Army would purge, and purge, and never leave purging the Houses, till they had made them of such a temper as to do His Majesty's business." We cannot blame Cromwell and Ireton. For it was the one hope of a peaceful settlement. The purging of the House, had it been necessary, would probably have been "once for all," there would have been no scaffold outside White-hall, no military despotism, Oliver would not have "passed the latter years of his life in the fire, in the midst of trouble." There can be little doubt but that the nation would have acquiesced.

But when Cromwell told Berkeley that the King was conscientious, it was true. Charles was conscientious. And since he honestly be-lieved in both the Divine Right of Bishops and the Divine Right of Kings, he could not conscientiously consent either to tolerate any church other than his own, or to take the position of a constitutional monarch, one who reigned but did not rule.

But although conscientious in his aim, he was not frank about stating it. And Cromwell was puzzled by the devious and round-about way in which he pursued it. He knew of course what he wanted, but a defeated king cannot have all that he wants. The choice was between the terms offered by the army, and those offered by Parlia-ment. Those offered by the army were better, why could he not take them? He was himself a man of compromise, he could not understand the man who would make no compromise, and believed that he could wriggle himself out of the necessity of doing so, the man who had set himself to play off the army against Parliament, Parliament against the army, Scotland against England, England against Scotland. For his hope was in the divisions among the men with whom he had to deal, so he strove to increase them that he might profit by them. "I shall see them glad ere long," he told Berkeley, "to accept more equal terms." "Men will see that without my establishing there can be no peace," he said in one of his letters, "without pretending to prophecy, I will foretell their ruin, unless they can agree with me." Even when most under his charm Cromwell said that he could wish the King would be more frank.

But now it was Ireton who saw through him more quickly than did Cromwell. When the proposals were first presented to him, Charles had said, "You cannot do without me, you will fall to ruin if I do not sustain you." That gave Ireton his clue. "Sir," he replied, "you have an intention to be the arbitrator between Parliament and us, and we mean to be it between your majesty and Parliament." On another occasion the King had exclaimed, "I shall play my game as well as I can." To which Ireton responded, "If your majesty have a game to play, you must give us also liberty to play ours."

So for two long dreary months the game went on, the King at Hampton Court, Parliament twelve miles away at Westminster, the army at Putney, halfway between, Scotland in the distance, playing her part. And nothing was coming of it.

And Oliver was watching the game anxiously, and growing more and more impatient. It was time that counted, what was to be done must be done quickly, or it could not be done at all, the delay was breeding divisions that might end in revolution and anarchy. It was bad enough that there was a division between army and Parliament, but now, more alarming to him even than that, a division was arising in the army itself. And, worst of all, this time it was not so much the Godly as the political party that was gaining ground, the anti-monarchical democratic faction that was beginning to be known as Levelers, a faction of "desperate men as hot as fire." This party, supported outside the army by Lilburn, Wildman and their followers, was clamoring for manhood suffrage, and preaching that they "should think no more of the King, but proceed as though there was no such thing in the world." Cromwell had to stop speeches of men who spoke of the king as Ahab.

He was thoroughly alarmed. There must be no more delay, the King must be restored, and speedily. In such a situation it was possible to proceed only by the method of trial and failure. He had tried to unite King and army to force terms upon Parliament, and had failed. Now he would try to unite army and Parliament to force terms upon the King. Might it not be possible to persuade Parliament to offer such terms as he could persuade the army to accept?

It was not very hopeful, for Parliament was growing more hostile to the King. Toward the end of September the Parliamentary leaders had given evidence that they saw through him as clearly as Ireton had done. The statement was made in the House that the "King's drift was to put a difference between Parliament and the army, and between the English and Scotch nations," and "that he was always an impediment to good resolutions." Whereupon a sharp debate arose as to "whether they should forthwith proceed to the settlement of these kingdoms," communicating their decisions to him, not as propositions, but as ordinances.

All this did not tend to relieve Cromwell. For although by this time he had reason to know, even better than Parliament did, that their analysis of the King's conduct and motives was correct, he was a typical Englishman, clinging to the traditions and institutions of England, desiring as little change as possible. And he believed, and this was really the important point, that the majority of his countrymen were with him in this, therefore no marked change could safely be made. So he "spoke much in the King's behalf." And he spoke plainly, emphatically, urgently. Very frankly and without reserve he told the House that there were two parties in the army, the one was laboring earnestly for the King, the other "little dreamt of, was endeavouring to have no power to rule but the sword." The course that they proposed was not pleasing to the former, and if they did not make common cause with it, the latter would gain the upper hand.

He had done his part, if England was to fall into the power of the army, it was certainly not because its great leader had not warned them. It would be well for those who decry the military rule that came later to remember that.

So Parliament renewed negotiations with the King, but could be persuaded to offer nothing better than the terms which he had already rejected. There was no hope that he would accept them now. He replied that the army proposals would constitute a better basis for lasting peace. Yet he would not accept them either. The truth was he was in high spirits, the more his opponents were divided among themselves the more likely he was to be restored on his own terms. And this latest division had raised his hopes. He told the French ambassador that the factions in the army would be sure to drive one or the other of the disputants to his side. Moreover he was looking hopefully towards Scotland.

Meanwhile Cromwell saw that his own position was becoming more difficult. All the time he had been working for all sides, for the King that he might be restored, for Parliament that it might become the supreme power in the land, for the army that it might have the toleration so dear to their hearts and his. And all the time all sides were becoming more suspicious of him. It was natural. The King could not believe that this simple country gentleman, so suddenly come into great power, was disinterested, he was not used to disinterested men.

Cromwell had asked no favors for himself, therefore he must be playing a deep game. Some of the members of Parliament believed that he had asked such favors, that he was to be Earl of Essex as his kinsman had been, and Knight of the Garter. Some even went further, and suspected that he was scheming to get all power into his own hands, that he had got possession of the King in order to overthrow Parliament, and that when that was accomplished, he would overthrow the King. Care was taken to disseminate these suspicions among the soldiers, in the hope of sowing dissension between them and their chief.

The plan was in a measure successful. Many of his admirers were losing faith in him. "His civilities to the King were visible, but the reality of their intentions was not fully disclosed." The Republicans and Levelers of course turned against him. Even if "the reality of his intentions" had been fully disclosed to them, they would have opposed him; their intentions were different from his. Lilburn wrote to him, "I have much honoured you, and my good thoughts of you are not wholly gone, but I confess that they are much weakened." He offered him a chance to redeem himself, but otherwise threatened to "pull him down from all his present greatness, before he was three months older."

So far as it concerned himself alone, Cromwell was too busy, too intent upon what he was doing to pay much attention to what men were saying about him. "If any man say that we seek ourselves in doing this," he said, "much good may it do him with his thought. It shall not put me out of my way." Some years before, as he was passing into the House of Commons, Major-General Crawford, standing within ear-shot of him, had told Denzil Holles that he was a coward. "And I am very sure," he said, "that he did hear it." But he gave no sign that he had done so, it did not put him out of his way. So the growing distrust of him now did not put him out of his way, but it did trouble him, for it might injure his cause. To a friend he wrote, "Though it be for the present that a cloud be over our actions, yet we doubt not that God will clear our integrity and innocence from any other ends that we aim at, but His glory and the general good."

He was daily becoming more alarmed about the army, less certain that he would be able to control it. For as its political power had developed, there had been more volunteers, and they were political thinkers. So the "faction of desperate men as hot as fire" was increasing in numbers and influence. In October five regiments deposed their agitators, chose new ones, and drew up a manifesto, which they presented to Fairfax. It was entitled "The Case of the Army Fully Stated." It demanded that religious freedom be secured by a permanent law unalterable by Parliament, that the existing Parliament terminate within a year, that future Parliaments be elected by manhood suffrage, and have full power to call ministers to account. There was no mention of King or Lords, but it was tacitly assumed that they were to be abolished.

This paper was at least a credit to the army chiefs, in that it showed them willing even eager, to abdicate in favor of the people. If England was to be ruled by the sword, it was not to be by their wish.

But it was none the less disquieting to Cromwell. He was not entirely unprepared for it, he had known what the army was talking about. Had it come to him while the war was on, it would have come as a thunderbolt or an earthquake, he might even have been inclined to throw up his job. For this was not what he was fighting for, he had never thought that it could come to this, he had taken up arms to defend and restore, not to destroy "the things for which England had been known for hundreds of years." And he believed as firmly as Falkland had, that "when it was not necessary to change, it was necessary not to change." He had differed with him only in the fact that he had thought it necessary to change some things which Falkland had not thought necessary. But this meant a complete overturning of everything, and even if some of the things demanded were good in themselves, this was not the time for them. To press them now would serve only to complicate an already over-complicated situation, to multiply factions where factions were already too numerous, and so lead not to settlement but to anarchy. There was only one thing for him to do, to nip the thing in the bud by restoring the King as soon as possible. So on October 20th he made a three-hour speech in the Commons in praise of monarchy, urging the House to restore Charles before it was too late.

And the fury of the Levelers waxed hotter against him. They made this fact known to him as well as to others. Wildman made an effort "to awaken his conscience from the dead." "O my once honoured Cromwell," he wrote to him, "can that heart of yours, the guardian palace of freedom, harbour such a monster of wickedness as this regal principle?" It was said that some of the extreme Republicans were planning to murder him in his bed.

The soldiers had rechristened their plan the Agreement of the People. To make it a real agreement of the people it must be submitted to the people rather than to Parliament for approval. On October 28th, there was a meeting of the Army Council in Putney Church to consider the matter. Several civilian Levelers were asked to join them, of these the most important was Wildman. Fairfax was ill, so Cromwell took the chair.

It is in these debates, debates that extended over three weeks, that we come closest to the workings of his mind. It is a mind that moves slowly, he has difficulty in separating the kernel from the husks, and in trying to do so he thinks aloud, so we see the whole process. Once when after many words he succeeds in his endeavors, it even seems to him a matter for surprise and gratitude. "Truly," he says, "I think it hath pleased God to lead me to a true and clear stating of our agreement and our difference." And it is not a constructive mind, he has comparatively few suggestions to make, his attitude throughout is that of a listener, of a judge rather than an advocate. He is a patient listener, "no one" it has been said "tolerated fools more gladly than did Cromwell." His power consisted in this habit of patient sympathetic listening, listening until he understood all sides, and was able to sum up the average sense of all. He had a mind capacious enough to understand other men's hobbies, and unless religious toleration be considered a hobby, he had no particular hobby of his own.

And it is very noticeable that he does not lose his temper. On the contrary his courtesy to Rainsborough, Wildman and others, who show him scant courtesy, is very marked. There is no trace of the Mr. Oliver Cromwell who in 1630 had made "disgraceful and unseemly speeches" to Mayor Robert Barnard, or of the Mr. Cromwell who in 1640 had replied to Lord Mandevil with "such indecency and rudeness," and whose "whole carriage was so tempestuous, and his behavior so insolent" that Mr. Hyde had found himself obliged to reprimand him. He had become more of a man of the world, more master of himself.

But it is also true that the case seemed different to him. On those earlier occasions he was dealing with men whom, rightly or wrongly, he regarded as self-seeking oppressors of the poor. Now he believed that he had to do with those who, however they might differ in opinion, had come together "with the same integrity to the public," and that the "foundation of the actions" of all of them was "to do the will of God." "For that's in all our hearts, and to profess above any thing that's worldly the public good of the people." Therefore "in such an assembly he did not know the meaning of any hateful word."

But the strongest reason for avoiding hateful words was that he saw clearly that his main task was to unite them. That was the urgent necessity now. He must defeat the Agreement of the People, but in such a way as to unite, not to further divide them. To the divisions between King, Army, and Parliament, there must not be added this other and most dangerous division in the army itself. No angry word from him must increase that. For if they were bent on going two different ways, "the kingdom will see that it is such a real actual division as admits of no reconcilation, and all that are enemies to us, and friends to our enemies, will have the clearer advantage over us, and put us to inconveniency." While one party was going one way, and the other the other, they would both be destroyed. But he "doubted not but if in sincerity they were all willing to submit to the light that God should cast in among them, God would unite them and make them of one heart and one mind."

So he said to the Agitators "if your hearts be as honest as ours, you do not bring this paper with peremptoriness of mind, but to receive amendments, to have anything taken from it, that may be made apparent, by clear reason, to be inconvenient or dishonest." For they "must not meet as two contending parties, but as some desirous to satisfy or convince each other." There must be liberal and free debate, "that we may understand really and before God the bottom of our desires, and that we may seek God together, and see if God will give us a uniting spirit." The design was to "seek the guidance of God and recover the presence of God that seems to be withdrawn from us." Alas! how far withdrawn it must have sometimes seemed to him in those troubled days! So different from what it had been during the war, then it had always been with him.

For himself he said, "I shall speak nothing but that, as before the Lord, I think in my heart and conscience tends to unite us— And really before I would have this kingdom break in pieces before some company of men be united together for settlement, I will withdraw myself from the army to-morrow, and lay down my commission. I will perish before I hinder it." He was "ready to convince, or be convinced, as God shall please."

The case was stated by Sexby, in a way that Oliver knew to be only too true. "We sought to satisfy all men, and it was well, but in going to do it, we have dissatisfied all men. We have laboured to please the King and I think unless we go about to cut all our throats, we shall not please him; and we have gone to support a House, which will prove but rotten studs. I mean the Parliament, which consists of a company of rotten members." He went on to say that the credit of the Lieutenant General Cromwell and the Commissary General Ireton had been much blasted in these two matters. That is they had tried too much to please King and Parliament. Failure had discredited their efforts. He now prayed them to consider these things that should be offered them. So the plan was put before them.

And Ireton, who was something of a doctrinaire, declared that he would not concur with any one who was not willing to attempt all ways to preserve the King and Parliament. But Cromwell was more conciliatory. He was not, he said, wedded or glued to any form of government, he was willing to consent to anything that the spirits and temper of the nation would go along with. Whatever really commanded the affections of the people was right, "for in the government of nations that which is to be looked after is the affection of the people." And in his despair he thought perhaps hardly anything could be worse than their present condition.

But he did not himself desire radical changes, and he believed that the majority of Englishmen did not. And his line of argument was practically the same as that which Falkland had used against him, in the one radical change that he had advocated, the abolition of the episcopacy. Such great changes, great alterations in the government of the kingdom, alterations from the government it had been under ever since it was a nation, should not be attempted without serious consideration. If they could leap at once out of one condition into another, which had such specious things in it as this plan had, it might be well to do it. But it was necessary to consider not only whether the plan was good, but whether the people of the nation were prepared to go along with it, that is, not so much whether it was right to do it, as whether it was possible to do it. "I know," he said, "that a man may answer all difficulties with faith and faith will answer all difficulties really where it is, but we are very apt, all of us, to call that faith, that perhaps may be but carnal imaginings and carnal reason. Give me leave to say there will be very great mountains in the way of this."

Even among the radicals who desired great changes, (altogether they were in a minority), would there not be splits, would they not desire different changes? While they were disputing over this plan, might not another company of men put out another plausible plan, "and not only another and another, but many of their kind?" So there would be confusion, anarchy, perhaps civil war. "The question is whether these propositions will save us, or whether they will destroy us."

Long afterward Bolingbroke was to say that when the civil wars began, the question was not whether the constitution was to be changed, that would be changed whichever side won, but whether it was to be changed in favor of despotism, or in favor of anarchy. It looked now as though it would be changed in favor of anarchy. To prevent this Cromwell was fighting with all his might. All other ends must be subordinated to that now.

And to achieve it, he knew that the most important thing was that they "should not meet as two contending parties, but as men desirous to satisfy or convince each other." So when it came to the question of manhood suffrage, and Ireton opposed it in principle, and also as tending to anarchy, while Rainsborough argued for it, declaring that Ireton not only believed that the proposers of it were for anarchy, but wished to make all the world believe it, he interposed gently, "Really, Sir, this is not right as it should be. No man says you have a mind to anarchy, but the consequences of this rule tend to anarchy, must lead to anarchy." If unorganized Parliamentary government tended to anarchy as Strafford had feared that it would, and Cromwell was afterwards to find that it did, how much more at that time of excitement and overturning would manhood suffrage do it!

But when the debate became theoretical, as to whether men had a natural right to vote or not, Rainsborough and Sexby arguing in the affirmative, Ireton in the negative, he became impatient, insisting upon leaving abstract considerations, and getting back to what was practical and necessary now. He was a practical man, and the troubled times required a practical solution. Not what was ideally right, as to which there was room for a difference of opinion, but what was practical and necessary *now*, to ward off anarchy and military despotism. He said there was no doubt but that there should be an amendment of the electorate, the Heads of Proposals had already provided for equalizing the electoral districts and amending the suffrage, but it was of course possible that they had not gone far enough. That should be looked into. In this Ireton agreed with him.

But aside from both ideal and practical considerations, were they really free to begin at the beginning, and propose entirely new things? That must be looked into. Very earnestly he reminded the Council that the army had certain engagements to Parliament in the various demands and proposals that they had already made, and he suggested that a committee, in which the various parties were represented, put these into formal shape. This was done, and the result was more like the Heads of Proposals than the Agreement of the People, the most noticeable thing about it being that the new constitution was to be based upon an agreement with the King, (who was therefore not to be discarded), rather than upon a direct vote of the people. And there could be no doubt but that the people wanted the King.

Yet in all this discussion Cromwell had said nothing in his favor. The feeling against him was getting stronger in the army, and Oliver himself was beginning to fear that he was intriguing not for a settlement, but for a new war. He had refused to renew the parole that he had given, was believed to be negotiating with the Scots; therefore his guards had been strengthened. So when the Army Council met on November 1st, there was a strong demand that the negative voice of the King and House of Lords be taken away, indeed there were those who said that the time had come when liberty must be recovered by the sword.

All this was very disquieting. As for the King, Cromwell could only say that there had been faults on both sides, could only say as Christ did, "Let him that is without sin among you cast the first stone." If any of them could say that they were without transgression, he might say that it was just to cut off transgressors, "but considering that we are in our own actions failing in many particulars, I think there is much necessity of pardoning transgressors."

And then he came back to his main point, the point which, hoping against hope, he had been struggling to maintain through all those weary months, the authority of Parliament. England must not fall under military rule. "That which you have by force, I look upon as nothing." Again he preached the doctrine that he had preached at Saffron Walden. For much as he might object to any particular political position taken by any portion of the army, his main objection was to the fact that the army was claiming to be a political power at all. If there were to be changes in the Constitution, Parliament, not the army, must make them. There was much need, he said, for the army to conform to things that were within their sphere. "For the actions that must be done, and those that must do them, I think that it is their proper place to conform to the Parliament that first gave them their being, and I think it is considerable whether they do continue to suppress that power or no. Either they are a Parliament, or they are no Parliament. If they are no Parliament, they are nothing, and we are nothing likewise."

It had come to that. Everything else was gone. Parliament, imperfect as it was, unrepresentative of the people as it was, was the only vestige of the old constitution, the only legal authority that was left. And to that it was necessary to cling as to dear life. "For," he cried in his despair, "if anything have but the face of authority, if it be but a hare swimming over the Thames, I would take hold of it rather than let it go."

But again he, the man of the hour, must attend to the question of the hour. He knew that if he was to ward off anarchy in the state, the first step must be to put a stop to anarchy in the army itself. That was the immediate danger, that was the anarchy that would lead to the other anarchy. For the army had not only failed to acknowledge the authority of Parliament, it had also defied that of its own officers. There had been "declarations in the army and disobligations of the General's orders, by calling rendezvous and otherwise." He must call attention to that. "It is not," he said, "in the power of any particular man in the army to call a rendezvous of a troop or regiment, or in the least to disoblige the army from the commands of the General. This way is destructive to the army, and to every particular man in the army." He had been informed that some of the King's party had said that if they gave them rope enough they would hang themselves. They would certainly hang themselves if they did not conform to the laws of war.

He was in the greater haste to put an end to the insubordinations and divisions in the army, for he knew how much the King was counting upon them. So on November 8th a vote was passed for the suspension of the meetings of the Council of Officers, the agitators were sent back to their regiments.

On November 15th there was a grand review of the Army, divided into three parts to be held at three different places. In return for a pledge on the part of Fairfax to work for the redress of army grievances, and a better representation in Parliament, the soldiers were required to pledge themselves to obey the orders of the General and the Council of War. One of these divisions met at Cockbush Field near Ware. Some of the Levelers attempted to turn it into a demonstration in favor of the Agreement of the People, perhaps even to seize Cromwell as a traitor. So two regiments that had been ordered elsewhere appeared with copies of the Agreement of the People, and the motto "England's Freedom! Soldiers' Rights!" in their hats. But when Cromwell rode up to them, "his carriage with his naked sword daunted the soldiers with the paper in their hats, and made them pluck it out, and be subjected to command." That was true of one of the regiments, the other refused. So he ordered out eleven men by name, tried them by court-martial, condemned three to death, then ordered them to throw dice for their lives, he who threw lowest was shot. Thus at the cost of but one life the mutiny was suppressed. But even that troubled Oliver. His severity, he told Ludlow, was "absolutely necessary to keep things from falling into confusion."

He reported the affair to Parliament, and received the thanks of the House. Divisions in the army had been put down, and for the moment there was even peace between the Army and Parliament, the King's flight had united them. For on the 11th of November Charles had escaped from Hampton Court, and found refuge in Carisbrooke Castle on the Isle of Wight.

CHAPTER XI

The Second Civil War

AFTER the King's escape to the Isle of Wight Cromwell and the army washed their hands of him, ceased altogether to treat with him. Parliament however made another attempt, sent commissioners to him with fresh propositions. They reached him on the 24th of December, 1647. But next day, Christmas Day, Scottish commissioners arrived, and delivered "in the name of the Kingdom of Scotland," a protest against the English propositions. On the 28th, the King returned an unfavorable answer to the English Commissioners, giving the Scotch protest as his reason.

The truth was Charles had been in communication with the Scotch commissioners a long time, and had gone to Carisbrooke largely because it would be easier to treat with them there. When they came to him, they brought with them not only a protest against the English propositions but also a Secret Treaty or Engagement, which he signed December 28th, two days before the English Commissioners were dismissed. In this he bound himself to maintain the Covenant for those who had taken it or might take it, without forcing it on the unwilling, also to establish Presbyterian church government and the Westminster Directory of Worship in England for three years, with reservation of the Liturgy for himself and his household, and to suppress the Independents and all other sects and heresies. In return for this, the Scots were to send an army into England, for the purpose of restoring him to his full power in the three kingdoms. As it was not safe to bring this treaty out of the island with them, the Commissioners had it wrapped in lead, and buried in the garden of Carisbrooke Castle, whence they could recover it afterwards.

While Cromwell could not know the exact nature of the Engagement, he did know that the propositions of the Commons had been rejected, because the King was having dealings with the Scots, of whom he was more than suspicious. And it was the death blow to whatever faith he might still have had in him. When on January 3rd, 1648, the House voted that it would make no further addresses or applications to the King, he spoke so vigorously in favor of the resolution that a Royalist historian tells us "the glow worm glistened in his beak, and he began to spit fire." Only three months before he had "spoken much in the King's behalf" in order to defeat such a resolution in Parliament, only six weeks before he had made a three-hour speech in favor of monarchy. But at that time he had seen in the King's restoration England's best chance to return to a normal life, he had hoped against hope that he could trust him. Now he was thoroughly disillusioned, was determined no longer "to expect safety and government from an obstinate man whose heart God had hardened." He was always a man of strong passions. And he was not well, in February he was very ill.

Moreover, there was a family matter that he must attend to. He was negotiating for the marriage of his son Richard and Dorothy Mayor, daughter of Richard Mayor, Esq., of Horsley. His eldest son Robert had, as we have seen, died at Felsted School. Oliver, the second son, a cornet in the Parliamentary army, had died of smallpox shortly before Marston Moor. Richard was therefore the eldest surviving son. And he was a little worried about Richard, he was inclined to be indolent and extravagant. Perhaps marriage would sober him.

Mr. Mayor, Dorothy's father, seems to have been a Presbyterian. Some things of common fame, such as Mr. Cornwall's favoring the sectaries, and his rather tortuous doings the last few months "stuck with him a little." Cromwell heard his doubts and seems to have satisfied him. He "exceedingly liked Mr. Mayor's plainness and free dealings" with him. There were some delays about the marriage settlement, Cromwell wished to have the matter hastened. He wrote on April 3rd, "I think I may be at leisure for a week, to attend to the business from which perhaps I may be shut out afterward by employment." The Second Civil War was pending, that was the employment that would soon shut him out from everything else. Early in May he left London to take command against the insurgents in Wales. He was more or less distrusted by all parties, but he was needed now.

The Second Civil War was the direct result of that Engagement with the Scotch, accepted by the King, and buried in the garden of Carisbrooke Castle. When the substance of that Engagement was made known to the Committee of Estates at Edinburgh, there was considerable opposition to it. For much as they disliked the English sectaries, the Kirk party, headed by Argyle, did not care to make war upon them in company with Prelatists, and perhaps Papists. However, two-thirds of the Parliament adhered to it, and it was understood that an army of forty thousand Scots was being raised to invade

England in the King's behalf. It was hoped that as it approached there would be royalist risings in all parts of England and Wales.

And Cromwell knew that this hope was not without foundation, a fact which must have added greatly to his anxiety during the past few weeks, and perhaps increased his fear that the submission of the Agreement of the People to popular vote would only tend to further confusion and anarchy. The people as a whole had never been keen for the war, and now the long delay in settling matters was exasperating them. There was a disposition to pity the King, and to wonder whether his restoration, on almost any terms, would not be better than the present state of affairs. So everywhere disorderly mobs were shouting "For God and King Charles!"

As for the Presbyterian majority in the English Parliament, it wanted just what the Scotch invaders wanted, the restoration of the King, the establishment of Presbytery, and the suppression of the sects. But it was one thing to make terms with a defeated King, a King whom their own armies had defeated, another thing to make terms with a victorious King, victorious with the aid of a foreign army. That would be, as Cromwell put it, to "vassalize them to a foreign nation." So Parliament prepared to resist, and the Common Council of the City of London declared its willingness "to live and die with the Parliament."

The first loyalist uprising was in Wales, under Colonel Poyer, governor of Pontefract Castle. It was to quell this that Cromwell was sent to Wales. Whatever his final aim might be, for that job he could be trusted.

It was the most dangerous mission that he ever undertook. For although he believed that he was fighting in the cause of the Most High, and therefore would prosper, he had himself said, "We are too apt to call that faith which is but carnal imagining." If it should prove so in this case, it meant ruin to both himself and his cause, failure would mean for England a relapse into Royalism, for himself a traitor's death. A majority in Parliament, a powerful minority in the army already distrusted him, the King and a Scotch army hating sectaries would have no mercy on the great Independent. No doubt he wrestled long with his God in prayer before he went forth to victory.

For it was to victory that he went forth. The boastful Colonel Poyer, who had hoped that he would be the first man to charge Ironsides, and who had said that "if Cromwell had a back of steel and a breast of iron, he durst and would encounter him," was defeated by Colonel Horton before Cromwell reached Wales. His job was to besiege Pembroke Castle. He had no heavy artillery, the sustenance of his soldiers was for the most part but bread and water, he regarded it as a mercy that he was able to keep his men together in the midst of such necessities. But the garrison was still worse supplied, so after a siege of six weeks the castle surrendered to the mercy of the Parliament.

Meanwhile the Scotch army under Hamilton had entered England, not forty thousand strong but ten, though within a month additional troops from Scotland and English Royalists increased their number to twenty-three or four thousand. When Fairfax sent Cromwell to Wales, he had hoped to meet the Scotch army himself, but he had become engaged in putting down Royalist risings in Kent and Essex, and in the siege of Colchester. So as soon as Pembroke surrendered, Cromwell hastened to the North, where Major-General Lambert had been successful against the English Royalists, but had not a sufficient force to meet the Scotch.

Though their pay was in arrears, food insufficient and plunder forbidden, and many of them had to march barefoot from Wales to Yorkshire, his men did not hesitate. With only nine thousand dirty, ragged, hungry men he threw himself upon Hamilton's twenty-four thousand, and defeated them in the three days' battle of Preston.

And now the divisions in Scotland came to his assistance. As we have seen the Kirk Party, led by Argyle, known in Western Scotland as the Whiggamores, had opposed the Engagement from the first. They had almost made preparations to resist it. Indeed when Cromwell first fell upon Hamilton's forces at Pembroke, a Scotch chronicler tells us that the English Royalists "imagined that it was one, Colonel Ashton, who had got together about three thousand men to oppose us, because we came out of Scotland without the General Assembly's permission," and that "as soon as the news of our defeat came to Scotland, Argyle and the Kirk party rose in arms, every mother's son, and this was called the Whiggamore Raid." The followers of Hamilton were swept from power, the party of Argyle took possession of the Government.

Cromwell took advantage of this. To show the power of the English army, and to make it clear that it was on the side of the new Government, he decided to advance into Scotland. On the eighteenth of September, he addressed a letter to the Earl of Loudon, the new Chancellor of the Kingdom of Scotland. "We understand the posture you are in to oppose the enemies of the peace and welfare of both the kingdoms, for which we bless God for His goodness to you, and rejoice to see the power of the Kingdom of Scotland in a hopeful way, in the hands of those who, we trust, are taught of God to seek His honour, and the comfort of His people. We have thought fit to the end we may be in a posture more ready to give you assistance to advance into Scotland with the army. And we trust by the blessing of God, the common enemy will thereby the sooner be brought to a submission to you." He promised that, as soon as this was accomplished, the English army would depart out of the kingdom; in the meantime they would be "even more tender to the Kingdom of Scotland, than if we were in our own kingdom."

On October 4th Cromwell entered Edinburgh. He demanded that no Scotchman who had supported the Engagement be allowed to retain office under the new Government. That of course fell in with Argyle's views. As for religion, that was for the new rulers to settle. It would doubtless be Presbyterian without toleration. But that was Scotland's affair, not his or England's. Moreover, there were practically no Independents in Scotland to be either tolerated or persecuted. And he would not put her in the position of a conquered country, his aim was to establish peace and friendship between the two nations, by making her new rulers think of England as their protector, not their conqueror. To Hammond he wrote, "I profess to thee I have desired from my heart, I have prayed for it, I have waited for the day to see wiser and right understanding between the godly people, Scots, English, Jews, Gentiles, Presbyterians, Independents, Anabaptists and all. Our brethren of Scotland (really Presbyterians) were our greatest enemies. God hath justified us in their sight, caused us to requite good for evil."

But all through his life everything that he did was misunderstood by somebody, everything that he did increased the number of those who distrusted him. This time it was his friend Vane, and other Independents in England, who were alarmed to hear that the Apostle of Toleration had consented to such an arrangement. There were even rumors that Cromwell himself was turning Presbyterian. He was getting used to being misunderstood, he felt that he could be "passive and let it go, knowing that innocence and integrity lose nothing by a patient waiting upon the Lord." He had had to be passive and let a great many things go! But this was an attack from a new quarter, from friends who ought to have understood.

But what about Toleration in England? Would the English Parliament be softened by his victories to grant toleration to the army that had again saved them, whose successes had again proved that God was

on their side? On May 1st, the very day that he had been ordered
to Wales, an "Ordinance for Suppressing Blasphemies and Heresies,"
major heresies to be punishable by death, minor ones by imprisonment, had passed the Commons without a division. The next day it
had passed the Lords. To this he had paid no attention at the time,
he had something else to do just then, it was sufficient if Parliament
supported him in that.

But on June 28th, while still engaged in the siege of Pembroke, he
returned to the subject dearest to his heart and wrote to Fairfax, "I
beseech God teach this nation and those that are over us, and your
excellency and all us that are under you, what the mind of God may
be in all this, and what our duty is. Surely it is not that the poor
godly people of this kingdom should still be made the object of wrath
and anger, nor that our God would have our necks under a yoke of
bondage." Perhaps he did not have a general toleration in mind,
but at least the "poor godly people" who, under his leadership, had
won the first war, and were now winning the second, should be permitted to worship the God of their fathers in the way that their
conscience demanded.

Immediately after Preston had made final victory certain, he wrote
to the Speaker of the House, "Surely Sir, this is nothing but the hand
of God.—It is not fit for me to give you advice, nor to say what use
you shall make of this, (the victory that he had won for them), more
than to pray you and all to acknowledge God, and not hate His
people, (the poor godly people who had again saved them by winning
this victory), that are as the apple of His eye, and for whom even
kings are to be reproved; and that you would take courage to do
the work of the Lord, in fulfilling the end of your magistracy, in
seeking the peace and welfare of the people of this land; that all that
will live quietly and peaceably may have countenance from you."
But the Presbyterian majority hardened their hearts.

And now that the danger was over, the first question was, What
was to be done with the King?

CHAPTER XII

The Execution of the King

"If I would have given way to have all things changed, according to the Power of the sword, I need not to have come here."—CHARLES I.

"Be not offended at the manner, perhaps there was no other left."

—OLIVER CROMWELL.

"That which you have by force, I look upon it as nothing."

HERE are the bare facts connected with the execution of Charles I. On January 17th, 1648, the Houses had voted that no further addresses be made to him, yet the disposition of the majority in Parliament, army and country was to restore him in some way. In April, despite this vote, both Houses were discussing further negotiations, petitions from the city demanded them. Even on May 19th, when the Common Council of the City of London expressed their willingness "to live and die with the Parliament," they requested that fresh negotiations be opened with the King.

On September 18th, while the Second Civil War was waging, even before Cromwell entered Scotland, Parliamentary commissioners met the King on the Isle of Wight, and began negotiations known as the Treaty of Newport. The truth was Parliament was in a hurry to restore him before either the Scotch or the English army did so. They had no mind, as a conquered nation, to accept a king from the conquerors. Nor had they much more of a mind to accept him from their own army. That would mean toleration, perhaps military despotism. Moreover the fear was growing that the twice victorious army of sectaries was no longer seeking to restore him at all, and that they might make it impossible for others to do so.

The King rejected the terms offered him, the establishment of Presbyterianism without toleration, but after some bargaining consented to admit that Parliament had been justified in taking up arms, to agree to establish Presbyterianism for three years, to be followed by a limited Episcopacy, to allow Parliament to settle the affairs of Ireland, and to control the militia for twenty years. These proposals might have been worth considering, had not his tendency to slip out of all promises been clearly recognized by that time.

On the twentieth of November, the army in the South, not Cromwell's army, sent Parliament a Remonstrance. It was penned by Ireton. It set forth the danger and folly of treating with the King, whose concessions certainly sprang from neither remorse nor conviction, demanded the rupture of negotiations with him, and that he be brought to trial and punished, as the "grand Author of all our troubles." But Parliament insisted upon postponing the demands of a "council of sectaries in arms," and in fact never considered them.

Fairfax had objected to the first draft of the Remonstrance, had proposed that a plan be submitted to the King, by which the functions of the Crown would be reduced to something like the influence of the present day. He carried the officers with him. The plan was submitted to Charles, and rejected by him. He had signed his own death warrant. From that time there was no talk in the army of restoring him.

On December 1st he was, by order of Fairfax, removed from Carisbrooke to Hurst Castle in Hampshire. The next day Fairfax and his army entered London. On December 4th the Houses protested against removing the King without their knowledge and consent. On December 5th they voted that his answers on the Isle of Wight were "a ground for the House to proceed upon for the settlement of the peace of the Kingdom."

The army decided that they could delay action no longer. That evening there was a conference between the army commanders and the leaders of the minority in Parliament. Cromwell was not present, he had not yet come from the North. As a result the next day Colonel Pride, with an army behind him, arrested forty-five Presbyterian members of Parliament, and excluded ninety-six others. Thus the army got complete control of the House, no one was allowed to sit there, except as the army wished it. That evening Cromwell arrived in London, and the next day took his seat among the fifty or sixty members who continued to sit. He had been absent from Westminster more than six months.

On December 23rd the King was brought from Hurst to Windsor, delighted "to exchange his worst castle for his best." That day the purged Commons appointed a committee "to consider how to proceed in the way of justice against the King." Five days later the Commons passed an ordinance creating a tribunal to try him, it was to consist of three judges and a hundred and fifty commissioners. On the second of January 1649 this ordinance was sent to the Lords, with the resolution that "by the fundamental laws of the Kingdom, it is treason in the King of England to levy war against the Parliament and people of England." The Lords rejected it unanimously, the judges refused to act.

The Commons then passed a resolution, That the people are the original of power, That the Commons in Parliament assembled have the supreme power, That what they enact has the force of law without the consent of King or Lords. They then created a new court, omitting the three judges, and decreasing the number of commissioners to one hundred and thirty-five. This Act set forth that Charles Stuart "had wickedly designed totally to subvert the ancient fundamental laws of the nation, to introduce arbitrary and tyrannical government, had levied and maintained civil war against Parliament and the nation," and that "new commotions (presumably the Second Civil War) had arisen from the remissness of Parliament to prosecute him." Therefore in order that in the future "no chief officer or magistrate whatsoever may presume to imagine or contrive the enslaving or destroying the English nation, or to expect impunity for trying or doing the same," the persons whose names followed were appointed to try him.

Nearly half the commissioners declined to take part in the trial. The King refused to accept the body that tried him as a court of justice, he had before maintained that "a King cannot be tried by any superior jurisdiction on Earth." He kept his hat on his head, in no way showed any respect to the court, looked "very stern, with a countenance not at all moved, until the words "Charles Stuart to be a tyrant, traitor etc.," were read, when he laughed in the face of the court. Because he did not admit the jurisdiction of the Court, he refused to plead. "It is not my case alone," he said, "it is the freedom and liberty of the people of England; and do you pretend what you will, I stand more for your liberties. For if power without law may make laws, may alter the fundamental laws of the kingdom, (he too could talk about fundamental laws), I do not know what subject he is in England that can be sure of his life, or of anything that he calls his own." There was a point in this, it was military force, not law, that was trying him. And if so, might not military force control everything?

It was resolved to treat him as contumacious, and on Thursday, January 25th, it was voted to proceed to censure Charles Stuart to death. In order to give him another chance to plead, he was brought before the court to hear his sentence. He again refused to plead, but asked that before sentence was pronounced, he might speak to the Lords and Commons in the Painted Chamber. This was refused, the sentence was read, the King removed while still struggling to speak. As he went from Westminster to Whitehall "shop stalls and windows were full of people, many of whom shed tears, and some of them, with audible voices, prayed for the King." It was Saturday, the twenty-seventh of January, 1649.

On the thirtieth of January the sentence was carried out in front of Whitehall. The King had asked his servant Hubert to let him have "a shirt more than ordinary, by reason the season is so sharp as probably may make me shake, which some will imagine proceeds from fear." He did not shake.

What was Cromwell's part in all this? Upon examination we shall find him running true to form. Except on the battle field he was always a man of long hesitations. And he never originated anything, his function was to listen and pass judgment upon the plans of others. He waited also upon the course of events, for in these Dr. Beard's pupil saw the hand and heard the voice of God. It was his habit to turn the thing over on all sides, not to act until action could no longer be delayed. Then he would throw himself with all his might on the side on which the balance seemed to lie at the time, and when he had once done that, it was impossible to shake him. Perhaps this was not so much because he was sure that he was right, as because he was not sure, he may have been trying to drown the voice within him that said "Perhaps I am making a mistake." There could be no voice from Heaven to decide the matter, and he could not be eternally re-opening the question. That simply meant paralysis. And when his decision was once made, he seldom had any regrets.

"An executive," Woodrow Wilson is reported to have said to Lincoln Steffens, "is a man of action. An intellectual is inexecutive. In an executive job we are dangerous, unless we are aware of our limitations, and take measures to stop our everlasting disposition to think, to listen, to not act. I made up my mind long ago when I got into my first executive job, to open my mind for awhile, hear everybody who came to me with advice, information, or what you will, then some day, the day my mind felt like deciding, to shut it up and act. My decision might be right, it might be wrong. No matter, I would take a chance, and do something."

Cromwell was not an intellectual in Wilson's sense, but in this matter he was like him, and never more so than on this occasion. Of those who were responsible for the King's death, he was the last to come to the conclusion that it was necessary, but when he had once decided upon it, he was the one who knew no faltering. Indeed it can almost be said that Charles died because Cromwell willed it.

Let us try to trace the workings of his mind. The King made his escape from Hampton Court just three weeks after Cromwell had made his three hours' speech in the House in favor of monarchy. During those three weeks Cromwell seems to have completely lost faith in him. The long-spun-out negotiations had convinced him that Charles was simply trying to sow dissensions, to play off one factor against the other.

And there may be some truth in the famous story of the Blue Boar Inn and the man with the saddle, to wit, that Cromwell and Ireton, disguised as common troopers, went to the Inn, found the man, ripped open the saddle, and discovered in it a letter from the King to Henrietta Maria, in which he spoke of them as two army ruffians whom he had to cajole, but who should have their deserts at last, told her that he was courted by both the Scotch and the army, that whoever bid fairest for him should have him, but that he inclined toward the Scots, and added that she need not concern herself about any concessions that he might make, as he should not look upon himself as obliged to keep any promises made so much on compulsion, whenever he had power to break them.

At any rate it is clear that by November 1647 he was fully convinced of Charles' untrustworthiness. He, who in October had pleaded so hard for his restoration, had no word to say in his behalf at the meetings of the Army Council the next month. Yet he could not agree that God had laid upon him or upon the army the necessity of destroying him. When Harrison took the position that the King was a man of blood, and ought to be prosecuted, Cromwell did not deny that he was a man of blood, but thought that there might be prudential reasons for sparing him. David had spared Joab because he would not hazard the spilling of more blood, and because the sons of Zerniah were too strong for him. At any rate they must not do such a thing when it was disputable, and the work of others to do it, but only if it became an absolute and indisputable duty for them to do it. In any case it was the function of Parliament, not of the Army, to decide the matter.

Moreover it was necessary to wait until they could more clearly know the mind of God, revealed, as he believed, in the course of events. It might be possible that God had a purpose to destroy both King and House of Lords, but God could do it, without necessitating them to do a thing that was scandalous. They must wait upon God for such a way when the thing could be done without sin, and without scandal. Poor Cromwell! He was in a very hard place, in very great perplexity. King, Parliament and army had failed him, he would fall back upon God. He was ready to say with Hamlet,

"The times are out of joint. Oh, cursed spite
That ever I was born to set them right!"

His hope was that he was not born to set them right, that God would do it without him.

When Captain Bishop said that the attempt to preserve the King was the cause that the kingdom was in a dying condition, he made no answer. But he was turning it over in his mind, and beginning to think so himself. He believed in the voice of God speaking within him as much as Goffe did, but Dr. Beard's pupil also believed that God spoke through the course of events. In this way he gradually came to think God had told him that he had been wrong in trying to treat with the King. Not long afterward he said that "the glories of this world had so blinded his eyes that he could not discern clearly the great works the Lord was doing, that he was resolved to humble himself, and desired the prayers of the Saints that God would be pleased to forgive his self-seeking."

It is of course possible to argue from this that, in his efforts to restore the King, Cromwell really had been self-seeking, that when he said, "He who thinks we seek our own in this matter, much good may it do him with his thoughts," he was hypocritical. But the natural thing, the best thing for the kingdom, would certainly have been a restoration, if it could have been brought about in such a way as to secure parliamentary government, and religious toleration. History would have blamed him if he had not tried to effect this. And if Charles had accepted the very liberal terms offered him by the army in the Heads of Proposals, England would have been spared the military despotism of the next ten years, and the unbridled license of the Restoration period.

The probabilities are that Cromwell had been too busy to think much about what position would accrue to himself from the Restoration. Now he had time to examine himself. Whenever he had time for that there was always a little tendency to morbidness. Dr. Beard's pupil could not get it out of his head that when God approved of an action it succeeded, and that when it did not succeed, it was because God did not approve of it, because it was wrong. So he sought for wrong motives in himself, wondered whether there might not have been in his sub-conscious self, (only he did not say sub-conscious), a desire for his own aggrandizement.

After the King's escape to the Isle of Wight, Cromwell seems still to have felt that the monarchy should be restored, but not this monarch. He had completely lost faith in him. He felt around to see whether it would be possible to put the Prince of Wales or the Duke of York upon the throne. But none of the family of Charles I would consider such an arrangement.

When he gave a dinner to the leaders of the various parties, Edmund Ludlow, who was a Republican or Commonwealth man, was among the guests. He reports that Cromwell and Ireton "kept themselves in the clouds and would not declare their judgment, either for a monarchical, aristocratical or democratical government, maintaining that any of them might be good in themselves, or for us, according as Providence should direct us."

That was characteristic, Cromwell was "not wedded or glued to any form of government," he always waited for Providence, as manifested in the course of events, to direct.

The discussion on this occasion became too hot. Some of the guests, Ludlow among them, insisted not only that Charles should not be restored, but that he should be called to account for the blood that had been shed in England, Cromwell saw that nothing was to be gained by prolonging the debate, that his guests would "not draw together at all," so he ended it by throwing a cushion at Ludlow's head, and running downstairs. Ludlow threw the cushion back, and "made him hasten down faster than he desired."

The clouds in which Cromwell kept himself were owing to the fact that he too was trying to peer through a cloud not of his making. But they did not tend to decrease the distrust in him. The Republican Hazelrigg was perplexed, he saw what he wanted, and he did not perceive that the trouble was that Cromwell did not see what he wanted, or what it was possible to attain. "If you prove not an honest man," he said to him, "I will never again trust a fellow with a great nose." Lilburn had lost all faith in him. On the nineteenth of January 1648 he accused him at the bar of the Lords of high treason.

The Second Civil War made the army officers see red. And they attributed it solely to the King. For the first, evil counselors might share the blame, but now after God had declared Himself on the side of the Parliament, the King himself, by his agreement with the Scotch, was again plunging the nation into bloodshed.

So they met together at Windsor Castle "about the beginning of

Forty-Eight." There they spent a day in prayer. When they met again next morning "Lieutenant General Cromwell, as then was, did press very earnestly on all those present, to a thorough consideration of our actions as an army, and of our ways particularly as private Christians; to see if any iniquity could be found in them, and what it was, that if possible we might find it out, and so remove the cause of such sad rebukes as were upon us, by reason of our iniquities, as we judged at that time." On the morrow they met again, "having been led by the gracious hand of the Lord to find out the very steps, (as we were all then jointly concerned), by which we had departed from the Lord, and provoked Him to depart from us. Which we found to be those cursed carnal conferences on our own concerted wisdom, our fear and our want of faith had prompted us the year before, to entertain with the King and his party. And in this path the Lord led us not only to see our sin, but also our duty, and this so unanimously set with weight upon each heart, that none was able hardly to speak a word to each other without bitter weeping—And yet we were also helped with fear and trembling to rejoice in the Lord, who did direct our steps, and presently we were led and helped to a clear agreement among ourselves, not any dissenting; That it was the duty of our day, with the forces that we had, to go out to fight against those potent enemies, which that year in all places appeared against us, with an humble confidence, in the name of the Lord only, that we should destroy them. And we also were enabled then, after serious seeking His face, to come to a very clear and just resolution, on many grounds at large there debated amongst us, That it was our duty if ever the Lord brought us back again in peace, to call Charles Stuart, that man of blood, to account for the blood he hath shed, and mischief he hath done to the utmost against the Lord's cause and people, in this poor Nation."

So when, after the Second Civil War, it seemed as though the King might be restored, for the majority in Parliament and the majority in the country wished it, the army, that at the close of the First War had been inclined to be more lenient than Parliament, was now more determined upon vengeance, or at least upon taking such measures as would prevent its happening again.

For there was great danger that it would happen again. The Treaty of Newport, if completed and observed, would certainly mean persecution of the army that had twice saved the Parliament, perhaps it would mean a third civil war. And Cromwell knew that there was no hope that if completed, it would be observed. He of course did not know that, while the negotiations were going on, Charles was writing to a friend, "To deal frankly with you, the great concessions I made this day, the Church, militia and Ireland, were made merely in order to my escape. . . . My only hope is that now they believe that I dare deny them nothing, and will be less careful of their guards." Nor could he know that, while the King had sent a public letter to Ormond bidding him to go on in Ireland, he had also sent a private letter, telling him not to heed any open commands that he might receive from him, until he knew that he was free from constraint.

But while Cromwell did not know about these letters, he did know that the King was not to be trusted, so it did not make much difference upon what terms he was restored, he would not keep them. "All our security," he wrote, "would have been but a little bit of paper."

But he seems to have had nothing to do with the Remonstrance of the southern army on November 20th, he followed rather than led, as was his custom. On the twenty-fifth he wrote to Hammond, in charge of the King at Carisbrooke, "We in the Northern Army were in a waiting posture, desiring to see what the Lord would lead us to. And a Declaration is put out at which many are shaken; although we perhaps could have wished the stay of it until after the Treaty, yet seeing it is come out, we trust to rejoice in the will of the Lord, waiting His further pleasure."

And yet he also must have been somewhat shaken by this Declaration. For it meant that the army, in its zeal for toleration had put itself in the position of dictating to Parliament, that a minority, because they were armed, were drifting toward the control of all things. And only a short time before he had said that there was much need for the army to conform to the things that were within its sphere, that it was its proper place to conform to the Parliament that gave it its being, and he thought it considerable whether it continued to suppress the power of that power or no. And now Hammond was writing to him, "God hath appointed authorities among the nations, to which active and passive obedience must be yielded. This authority in England resides in the Parliament. Therefore active or passive obedience is to be yielded to them."

That was the doctrine that he had preached himself, but now under changed circumstances he was thinking it over again. For he made no God of Consistency. He wrote to Hammond that authorities and powers were the ordinance of God, but this or that species was of human institution, limited according to a particular constitution. He did not think that any authority could do anything it liked, and obedience still be due, all agreed that there were cases in which it was lawful to resist. (The agreement had been that there were cases in which it was lawful to resist a king, but if a king, why not a Parliament?) The query then simply was whether this was such a case. Then he asks three questions, the answers to which would determine the matter.

First, whether Salus Populi be not a sound position? Second, whether by the Parliamentary treaty this was provided for, or whether by it the whole point of the war was not likely to be frustrated, and all most like to turn out what it was before, and even worse? Finally, whether the Army be not a lawful power, called by God to oppose and fight against the King upon some stated grounds? And being in power to such ends, might it not oppose one name of authority for those ends as well as another, (Parliament as well as king)? Not by their power making the quarrel lawful, but it being so in itself. He wanted so much to conceal even from himself that it was because they were armed, that they could and were doing what they were doing! Yet this particular end was lawful or right in itself. But he had traveled a long way since he had said "If Parliament be nothing, we are nothing."

But after all "these kinds of reasonings may be but fleshly, though it's good to try what truth there is in them." Dr. Beard's pupil turns from them to the providences. Surely the victory of the army is an evidence of God's will in the matter, the fact that the hearts of so many of God's people, especially in the army, where the officers are almost unanimous, are disposed that way, is an internal evidence.

He was weighing and balancing the matter, looking on both sides, he had "not hitherto found clear direction." "Providence often decrees that men should walk in the dark," and he had had much experience of that. And yet a time was coming when he must throw his influence on the side on which the balance seemed to lie, too much weighing of the matter might lead to inaction when action was necessary. Tempting of God, he reasoned, might be of two kinds, either presumptuous action in carnal confidence, or inaction through unbelief and diffidence. He was beginning to fear that he might be guilty of the latter.

But in all this he was only defending the opposition of the army to Parliament. As to what should be done about the King, he had nothing to say. He would appear not to have thought the conclusion of the famous Windsor Castle prayer meeting final, and even if so, it had been rather vague. Charles Stuart was to be called to account for the blood that he had shed, but just how was not specified. And Oliver had not yet made up his mind about it, perhaps he hoped that he would not have to make up his mind.

There was a curious delay about his return to London. He was besieging Pontefract, the last stronghold in the hands of the Royalists, but why did he not leave Lambert in command there, and hasten to take his part in the great things that were going on in London? That was what he eventually did, why could he not have done it earlier? The truth seems to be that he did not know what part to take. He had said that if God had a purpose to destroy both King and House of Lords, God could do it without necessitating them to do it. Perhaps he hoped that God would somehow do it through the natural course of events, and he did not wish to forestall God's leading, not as yet very clear. He was not accustomed to take the lead in constitutional matters, he did not see what he could do if he went to London, he could besiege Pontefract.

He was not present at the meeting of the Council of Officers which decided to remove Charles from Carisbrooke to Hurst Castle. As for Pride's Purge, he declared that he had not been acquainted with the design, yet since it was done he was glad of it, and would endeavor to maintain it. He reached London that evening, and as it had only been decided upon the day before, he could not have known of it. In the preceding August, when he entered London at the head of an army, he had objected to any such action. He probably now agreed with Ireton and Harrison, who had said the previous evening, "We have neither law, warrant nor conscience to purge it, nor can anything justify us in doing it, but the height of necessity, to save the Kingdom from a new war, that they with the conjunction of the King, will presently vote and declare for." To save the kingdom from a new war! That was at the bottom of it all. Yet of course, so far as Parliament was concerned, there was little danger of a new war, if the army would yield on toleration, that is if the men who had won the war would remain passive, and allow their religion to be proscribed.

And now that "a lesser part of the Parliament had made the greater part of it a faction," what was to be done with the King? There was a difference of opinion among the officers. Ireton suggested that he be tried and sentenced, then left in prison until he consented "to abandon his negative voice, part from all Church lands, and abjure the Scots." Cromwell was not even willing to go that far, it was just to bring the King to trial, but it might not be expedient. At least there must be one more effort to induce him to make the concessions that the army demanded.

He carried the day, Lord Denbigh was dispatched to Windsor to lay new conditions before the King, and on Christmas Day Oliver urged the Council of Officers to spare his life if they were accepted. Exactly what they were we do not know, but if they were what Ireton had suggested, they would have put the Crown in very much the position that it is in at the present day, influence without power. Charles refused even to see Denbigh. For him it was a matter of conscience too. To him both monarchy and episcopacy were of Divine origin, he was prepared to die rather than to betray the ordinances of God. Within the limits of his conscience, and those limits were fairly wide, Cromwell was a man of compromise. He could not understand the man whose conscience allowed no compromise.

The King's action closed the last door of escape for him and also for Cromwell. He could no longer dodge the question, he must decide it now. And what should he decide? He took counsel with himself and with others, talked with Speaker Lenthall and others known to be cautious, legal, and conservative. He made an effort to postpone the King's trial, until after the trial of other important delinquents. During that month, December 1648, he "lay in one of the King's rich beds at Whitehall." He probably did not sleep much, no doubt he cried mightily upon his God. And then he made up his mind.

When the ordinance creating the High Court of Justice was being discussed, it is reported that he said, "If any man whatsoever hath carried on the design of deposing the King, and disinheriting his posterity; or if any man had such a design, he should be the greatest rebel and traitor in the world; but since the Providence of God and of Necessity hath cast this upon us, I shall pray God to bless our counsels, though I am not yet prepared to give you counsel."

"Not yet prepared to give you counsel!" Still hesitating! But it was to be his last hesitation. And when he had once made up his mind, it was, as it always was, impossible to divert him. He had thought about it long, had tried every other way, and now the time for action had come. He must no longer tempt God through cowardice or lack of faith. So it came to pass that the man who, up to the end of December, had fought almost alone in the Army Council to save Charles Stuart, was the man who at the end of January was chiefly responsible for his death. His friend Vane, whom he had called his brother, had disapproved even of Pride's Purge, he now refused to take any part in the trial, nor did he ever approve of the execution. "I cannot stop you," Algernon Sidney said, "but I will keep myself clean from having any hand in this business." Fairfax held himself aloof.

But Cromwell only grew more determined. He had put his hand to the plow, there must be no looking backward. When Sidney insisted that neither the King nor any other man could be lawfully tried by such a tribunal (had not the Petition of Right put an end to martial law?), he replied "I tell you we will cut off his head with the crown on it."

Nevertheless the question of their authority was one to which the Court would have to give an answer. And there is a story that on the 20th of January, the day on which the trial began, they had not yet found that answer. As they sat in the Painted Chamber, word came that the King was landing at the steps, which led up from the river. "At which Cromwell ran to the window, looking on the King as he came up the garden; he turned as white as the wall, then turning to the board, said thus: 'My masters, he is come, he is come, and now we are doing that great work that the whole nation will be full of. Therefore I desire you to let us resolve here what answer we shall give the King when he comes before us, for the first question he will ask us will be by what authority and commission we do try him?' " For a time no one answered. Then Henry Marten rose up and said "In the name of the Commons in Parliament assembled, and of the good people of England."

When Cromwell was dead and the King's judges were brought to trial, some of them attempted to prove that they had acted under coercion. And there can be little doubt but that Oliver used all the influence that he had to keep them to the resolution that had been formed. Colonel Ingoldsby went so far as to testify that he seized his hand, and guided his pen. But Mrs. Hutchinson, no friend to Cromwell, denies this, and the signature shows no sign of constraint. On the other hand the story that he inked Henry Marten's face, and was inked in return, is probably true. He was in a state of nervous excitement, the natural psychological reaction to his long hesitation. And at such times he sought relief in rustic buffoonery, as Lincoln did in story telling.

In Spence's Anecdotes there is a tale which Spence tells us that he got from the poet Pope, whose informant may have got it from Southampton himself. "The night after King Charles was beheaded," he tells us, "my Lord Southampton and a friend of his got leave to sit up by the body in the Banqueting House at Whitehall. As they were sitting very melancholy there, they heard the tread of somebody coming very slowly upstairs. By-and-by the door opened, and a man entered very much muffled up in his cloak, and his face quite hid by it. He approached the body, considered it very attentively for some time, and then shook his head, sighed out the words 'Cruel Necessity!' He then departed in the same slow and concealed manner as he had come. Lord Southampton used to say that he could not distinguish anything of his face, but that by his voice and gait he took him to be Oliver Cromwell."

And Dr. Gardiner thinks the story has much to recommend it. Cromwell had struggled against the deed for a long time, but had come to feel that "Necessity and Providence had thrust it upon him." "Be not offended at the manner," he wrote to Wharton, "perhaps there was no other way left." And it certainly agrees with the words of the Act that established the commission to try the King. This Act, after setting forth that Charles Stuart had wickedly designed to subvert the ancient laws and liberties of the Kingdom, and had shown himself impenitent in these courses, must stand his trial "for the prevention of the like and greater inconveniences, and to the end that no chief officer, or any magistrate whatsoever, may hereafter pursue tortuously or maliciously to imagine or contrive the enslaving or destroying of the English nation, and to expect impunity for so doing." Not so much because of what Charles Stuart had done, as because of what they feared that he and others would do. There can be little doubt but that Oliver had much to do with the wording of this.

Whether the execution was justifiable or not is a question upon which men will always disagree. It is certain that it was against the wishes of the people. When, in the course of the trial, Bradshaw used Henry Marten's formula, "In the name of the Commons in Parliament assembled, and of all the good people of England," a woman, perhaps Lady Fairfax, cried out that it was a lie, that not a half or a quarter of the people of England were with them. That was the truth, and the Commonwealth was hampered by that fact from the beginning.

And yet in a deeper sense the people of England were with them. For although they did not approve of the manner in which it was brought about, there certainly was a permanent national demand for the abolition of the old feudal monarchy, a demand which was to grow into the larger demand for the sovereignty of the people. And that was what the execution of the King effected. Mr. Belloc tells us that Charles I was the last real King of England. And Mr. Belloc regrets this fact, but the majority of his countrymen would hardly sympathize with his regret.

Whether the result could have been achieved in a less tragic way, it is impossible to say. It certainly could not have been while Charles was king. Even on the scaffold he maintained that liberty and freedom did not consist in the people "having a share in the government, that is nothing pertaining to them. A subject and a sovereign are clean different things."

But he also said "If I would have given way to have all things changed according to the power of the sword, I need not to have come here." And that was true.

CHAPTER XIII

The Commonwealth

IN 1653 Cromwell said to the Little Parliament "You remember well that at the change of government (the execution of the king) there was not an end to our troubles." Indeed it was only the beginning. He had torn down, now he must build up. Construction is always harder than destruction.

It must be borne in mind that technically he had as yet no position, other than that of a simple member of Parliament, and Lieutenant-General, that is second in command in the army, for although Fairfax had of late been keeping himself in the background, he was still first. But it was he who had won the war, he who had decided upon the execution of the King, so it was he, more than any other, who must decide upon the government that should succeed, and he shrank from it. No one ever desired such power more intensely than Oliver Cromwell shrank from it.

He had had no prejudice against a monarchy, or in favor of a republic. But the monarchy had gone, the republic had come. He must accept that, but he wished to make as little further change as possible. So when the resolution to abolish King and House of Lords was introduced into the Commons, he strove, though in vain, to retain the Lords as a consultative body.

And he wished to be as conciliatory as possible, to alienate no more than necessary from the new government. So when a Council of State, of which he was made President, was created to act as an executive body, and it was proposed that the Councilors take an engagement declaring approval of the High Court of Justice, the trial and execution of the King, abolition of the monarchy and the House of Lords, it was through his influence that the Commons agreed to a milder form of engagement, only binding those who took it to concur in the settling of the government for the future in the way of a Republic, without King or House of Lords, and to fulfill the duties imposed upon them by Parliament. Fairfax was allowed to take it in even a milder form.

But these were minor matters. The great problem before him, the problem that he was never to solve, was how to rid the country of military rule, establish a government that would command the affections of the people, yet secure the religious liberty for which he panted and yearned.

He knew that at present the government did not command the affections of the people. The new Great Seal was to bear the legend "In the first year of freedom, by God's blessing restored." But Cromwell knew, and the people knew, that it was not freedom, it was army rule. It was the army that had put the King to death. It was the army that had driven out all but ninety of the four hundred and ninety members of Parliament that the people had elected. It was a government by force and Cromwell himself had said "What you have by force, I look upon it as nothing."

The Council of Officers saw it just as he did. Step by step the army had risen to absolute control, each step had seemed unavoidable, they had hoped with him that each would be the last, and each had led to another. Now they wished nothing more than to abdicate in favor of the people. Provided however that religious liberty was secured.

Even before the execution of the King they had worked out a scheme, by which they hoped that that dreadful step at least should be the last, a new "Agreement of the People," which was presented to the House of Commons on the twentieth of January, 1649. In this it was provided that no Parliament was to have the power to take away the religious liberty for which the army had fought, though this liberty was not necessarily to extend to Popery and Prelacy. (Not that it was certainly not to extend that far, only not necessarily.) That matter being settled for all time, the army was ready to hand over the Government to a Parliament representing the people as no Parliament had ever represented them before. The existing Parliament, (none knew better than the army that it was no Parliament), was to be dissolved on or before the last day of April, 1649. Henceforth there were to be biennial Parliaments, elected by all those ordinarily assessed for the relief of the poor, except that those who had assisted the King were to be excluded for a term of years. The electoral districts were to be made more equal.

Parliament received the Agreement with thanks, but stated that, as it was long, it had not been read, but reserved for future consideration. No wonder, it was the first day of the King's trial, there was something else to think about. But it was never considered, and when the last day of April came, this Parliament, whose members sat, not because their constituents had elected them, but because the army had permitted them to sit, continued to sit. There was no sign of a dissolution. "It was better," Henry Marten said, "that the Commonwealth, an infant of weak growth, and very tender constitution, should be nursed for a time by the mother who had brought it forth. When Moses was found in the bulrushes, and brought to Pharaoh's daughter, she took care to find his own mother, and brought him to her to nurse."

And in this Cromwell agreed with him. Speaking in 1657 of the Long Parliament, which he had since forcibly dissolved, he commends them, that in 1649 "they were careful out of principles of Nature, (that do sometimes suggest best) and upon the utmost undeniable grounds, they did not think it was fit for them presently (immediately) to go and throw themselves and all the Cause into hands that perhaps had no heart or principle in common with them, to accomplish the end that they aimed at."

For he saw the new Republic so beset by enemies within and without, that the danger was not only that it would be overthrown, but that it would be overthrown by men so at variance among themselves that nothing but anarchy could follow.

He knew that outside of England it had no friends, that the Sovereigns of Europe, though not in a position to offer active resistance, were all more or less hostile, that war was threatening from both Ireland and Scotland, both of which had proclaimed other Governments.

And within England he saw an increasing Royalist reaction being fanned into a religious fervor by Dr. Gauden's "Eikon Basilike," which appeared only ten days after the execution of Charles I, and was generally believed to have been written by the martyred king's own hand. Royalist pamphlets were appearing in considerable number. Charles II was being prayed for in Presbyterian pulpits. The liberty loving Parliament, probably believing that it was acting in favor of ultimate liberty, was gagging both press and pulpit.

Cromwell, always endeavoring, within the limits of his conscience, to be all things to all men, if by any means he might gain some, was making an effort to conciliate the Presbyterians. He knew that the Scotch Presbyterians were negotiating with Charles II, he would try to win over the English Presbyterians. In April he offered to consent to the establishment of Presbyterianism with toleration for men of other creeds "who walked peaceably." He even went so far as to propose the readmission to Parliament of those excluded by Pride's Purge, if they would promise fidelity to the Republic. But the gulf between the Republic and the Presbyterians was too wide, it could not be bridged over.

Poor Cromwell! he had ample reason that March and April to try to reduce the number of foes without the Republican ranks, for he knew to his sorrow that the most formidable foes were not without but within, were those of his own household. Less than three months before he had written to Hammond of "this fear of the Levelers, of whom there is no (cause to) fear." But there was cause to fear them, he was realizing it now.

Of the Levelers there were two factions. There was the little band of True Levelers or Diggers led by Everard, who began to dig on St. George's Hill in Surrey, to sow parsnips, carrots and beans, and preached that the time was at hand when God would restore freedom to all to enjoy the fruits of the earth. To their prophet Winstanley the revelation had come that the earth should be the common property of all men. Man following his sensuality, had become an encloser, so that now all the land was held by a few while the many were practically their slaves. All landlords were breaking the commandment "Thou shalt not steal," and had reduced the plain hearted poor to work for them for small wages, while they themselves had made great fortunes. But the victory over the King had been won largely by the blood of the poor, and now, by virtue of the conquest, they claimed their share in the common land. When the earth became the common treasure, wars and enmities would cease. For at bottom all wars were economic in their origin.

In some ways these poor Diggers were anticipating Henry George, but they seem to have gone further, to have looked forward to a socialistic republic, in which there should not only be no private property in land, but no buying or selling, neither rich nor poor, communism rather than the Single Tax. But for the present they asked only for the right to cultivate the common or waste lands.

Alas! the common lands were rapidly disappearing, the system of enclosures against which these True Levelers were lifting up their voices, was well under way, and they were powerless to stop it. They were but few, mean and lowly, and the main body of Levelers did not sympathize with them.

As for Cromwell, he probably did not think much about them. Other things were occupying him. There were more formidable enemies of the Republic, he must conciliate some, he must destroy others. No one sympathized with the poor more than he did, no one denounced more vehemently "those who make many poor, to make a

few rich." Three times he had made enemies by opposing particular
enclosures, but he probably had no general theory on the subject. He
had never been given to theorizing, and he had no time for it now.

Later Winstanley published a book "The Law of Freedom," in
which, like many a twentieth-century thinker, he traced war, crime,
and the "inward bandages of the mind" to economic conditions. He
dedicated it to Cromwell. "Wee know," he told the Lord General
and the Council of War, "that England cannot bee a free Commonwealth, unless all the poore commoners have a free use and benefitt
of the land." He had struck at the root of the matter. Political rights
would avail little unless they were used to change economic conditions. But it was just after Worcester, Cromwell had much to attend
to, it is not likely that he read the book.

But the main body of Levelers, the political Levelers, headed by
John Lilburn, he could not ignore. These men protested that they
had no desire "to level men's estates, destroy property, or make things
common." Their motives were political, not economic. They demanded annual Parliaments, manhood suffrage and complete religious
liberty.

But what made Lilburn formidable, what made him the Voice of
England as a whole, drawing to him many who had no sympathy with
his specific demands, was his hatred of military rule. The tragedy of
it was that Cromwell hated it too. And it made it no easier for him
that he knew that in this Lilburn was fundamentally right. For to
give it up now would be to deliver England over to anarchy, at a time
when wars with both Ireland and Scotland were pending.

And in the army itself, the army that wished to abolish military rule
as much as Cromwell did, and saw no more of the practical danger
than Lilburn did, Cromwell knew that Lilburn's doctrine of the
sovereignty of the people was spreading. This troubled him most of
all. "I must needs say," he told the Council of Officers, "I think there
is more cause of danger from disunion among ourselves, than from
anything by our enemies."

So when Lilburn, brought before the Council to answer for certain
seditious writings, was sent out of the room, he put his ear to the
door, and heard Cromwell say, "I tell you, Sir, you have no other way
to deal with these men but to break them, or they will break you; yea,
and bring all the guilt of the blood and treasure spent in this kingdom upon your heads and shoulders, and frustrate and make void all
that work, that with so many years of industry, toil and pain you have

done; and so render you to all rational men in the world as the most contemptible generation of silly low spirited men in the earth, to be broken and routed by such a contemptible generation of men as they are, and therefore Sir, I tell you again, you are necessitated to break them."

Once before Cromwell's voice had been "sharp and untuneable" in defending this John Lilburn. Now it was equally sharp and untuneable in condemning him. Then he had spoken as though the very existence of government depended upon releasing him. Now he was sure that its existence depended upon condemning him.

Six months before, Cromwell had said at a meeting of the Army Council, at which Levelers were present, that however much they might differ in opinion, he was sure that they had all come together with the same integrity to the people. Even now he may not have doubted Lilburn's integrity, though Lilburn certainly did doubt his. But he was very angry that Lilburn did not see that even though his ideals might be right, (some of them he knew were right), to attempt to realize them now would be to "frustrate and make void all that work that with so many years of industry, toil and pain they had done." And he was afraid that he might succeed.

He had good reason to be afraid. He knew that Lilburn had many admirers in the city, (the citizens sent in three great petitions in his favor), and in the army his doctrines continued to spread. In April there was a riot among the soldiers in London. He went with Fairfax to put it down. This was accomplished quickly, and fifteen of the mutineers were tried by court martial. Five were found guilty, condemned to death, and four pardoned, but it was considered necessary to make an example of one. So Trooper Lockyer, twenty-three years old "of excellent parts, much beloved," who moreover had served seven years in the wars, was shot in St. Paul's Churchyard "many beholding and weeping." Here is Whitelocke's account of the funeral.

"About one hundred went before the corpse, five or six in a file; the corpse was then brought, with six trumpets sounding a soldier's knell. Then the Trooper's Horse came clothed all over in mourning, and led by a footman. The corpse was adorned with bundles of rosemary, one half stained in black, and the Sword of the Deceased along with them. Some thousands followed in rank and file; all had sea-green and black ribbons tied on their hats, and to their breasts, and the women brought up the rear. At the new churchyard in Westminster some thousands more of the better sort met them who thought not fit to march through the City. Many looked upon this funeral as an affront to the Parliament and Army, but they took no notice of any other's sayings." '

It is doubtful whether the "many of the better sort" who joined that procession were in sympathy with the Levelers' specific proposals, but they honored them because of the stand that they had taken against military rule. For, as Carlyle puts it, these men were "strong after their sort for the liberties of England, resolute to their very death." Perhaps Cromwell appreciated that too, for him it was again "cruel necessity."

That was on the twenty-sixth of April. On the first of May Richard Cromwell and Dorothy Mayor were married in Hursley Church. Cromwell wrote to Dorothy's father that he had hoped to be with them a few days earlier, but his aged mother was in such a condition of illness that he could not with satisfaction leave her; he hoped to get to the wedding, though he could stay but a single night, his occasions were causing these family affairs "to go in such a hurry, unbefitting the weight of them."

We will hope that he got there, but he certainly could not tarry long. There was a regiment at Salisbury that was refusing obedience to its officers, and roaming about the country seeking to enlist the sympathy of men of other regiments. Fairfax and Cromwell set out in pursuit of them, and in the night of May 14th Cromwell overtook them at Burford. Again there was a court martial, and three were shot. The rest having been addressed by Oliver in Burford Church, rebuked and forgiven, went to Ireland.

But still Lilburn and his like were making trouble. There was a pamphlet, "An Outcry of the Young Men and Apprentices of London," in which the army was called upon to disown Fairfax and Cromwell, to treat Parliament and the Council of State as tyrants and usurpers, and to reëstablish the army agitators. As a result there were further mutinies. There was also evidence that the Levelers were negotiating with emissaries of Charles II. Lilburn had hinted that a "regulated Kingship" might be satisfactory.

So he was again arrested, and in October brought to trial under a new Act passed by Parliament, which made it treason to write that the Government was a tyranny and usurpation. He had certainly written this, but he held that it lay with the jury to determine, not whether he had broken the law, as he certainly had, but whether the law was right in making his action treason. And the jury, in full sympathy with his position that the sword had no right to dictate law, acquitted him. Whereupon there arose "such a loud and unanimous shout as is believed was never heard in Guildhall, which made the Judges turn pale, and hang down their heads."

Cromwell was not there to hear it, he was in Ireland.

CHAPTER XIV

Ireland and Scotland

THE justification of Cromwell's severity with the Levelers lay in the fact that they were creating distractions in England and, most dangerous of all, in the army, at a time when the enemy was at the door. Whatever germs of truth there might be in their doctrines, this was not the time to consider them. England and especially the army, must be united to meet the foe.

For the present, he need not trouble himself about the continent of Europe. All governments there were more or less hostile to the new Republic, but none was in a position to make its hostility active. The immediate danger was from Scotland and Ireland.

While the new Government of Scotland owed its existence to Cromwell's overthrow of Hamilton and the nobility, he had noticed almost from the beginning, so he told the Council, "a very angry hateful spirit in Scotland against your army, as an army of sectaries. Although God hath used you as instruments for their good, yet hitherto they are not sensible of it, but they are angry that God brought them His mercy at such a hand."

Whatever semblance of friendship there had been between the two peoples had been destroyed by the execution of the King. The commissioners of the Scotch Parliament had made a public protest against it, had argued with Cromwell that the Covenant obliged both nations to preserve the King's person, and that to proceed to extremities was to break the league between England and Scotland. Cromwell had answered that the end of the Covenant was the defense of true religion, if the King was the greatest obstacle to the establishment of true religion, they were bound not to preserve him. Moreover it pledged them to bring to condign punishment all incendiaries and enemies to the cause, and "were small offenders to be punished and the greatest to go free?"

When the execution was actually accomplished, the Scotch government wished to make sure that England did not dispose of Scotland. It proceeded therefore to dispose of England. On February 6th, 1649, it proclaimed Charles II not only as King of Scotland, but as King of Great Britain, France and Ireland. It went further, and added that it would support Charles only as he engaged to rule according to the Solemn League and Covenant, thus advancing the monstrous claim not only to establish the government, but even to control the religion of England.

However Scotland was not immediately pressing, the Scotch had to complete their arrangements with the King. Ireland must first be attended to. There Ormond, the King's Lord Lieutenant, had succeeded in making a most unnatural alliance of Confederate Catholics and Anglo-Irish Royalists, the perpetrators of the Ulster massacre and the victims of it, and was preparing to attack Dublin, almost the only place in Ireland still holding out for the new government of England.

Cromwell regarded both the war with Scotland and the war with Ireland as defensive wars. His bitterest complaint against Charles I had been that he had tried to vassalize England to a foreign nation; now he said, "If we do not endeavour to make good our interest there (Ireland) we shall not only have our interest rooted out there, but they will in a very short time be able to land forces in England, and put us to trouble here. I confess I have had these thoughts with myself, that may perhaps be carnal and foolish. I had rather be overrun with a Cavalierish interest than with a Scotch interest. I had rather be overrun with a Scotch interest than with an Irish interest— Truly it is come thus far, and the quarrel is brought to this state, but that we can hardly return to the tyranny that formerly we were under the yoke of, which through the mercy of God has been lately broken, but that we must at the same time be subject to the kingdom of Scotland or the kingdom of Ireland, for the bringing in of the King. Now that should awaken all Englishmen, who perhaps are willing enough he should come in upon an accommodation, but not that he must come from Ireland or Scotland." Even men who were willing to bring in the King, wanted to bring him in, would not be willing to be subject to Irish or Scotch domination.

On the tenth of July Oliver, having been appointed for three years Lord Lieutenant of Ireland, and commander-in-chief of the forces there, set out from London. But he had to wait a month in the west, and during that time his wife, and perhaps some other members of his family, were with him. There was so little time in which he could see them, he must avail himself of what opportunities he could. And his mind and heart were much with the newly married pair. He was glad to know that they had leisure to make a journey to eat cherries, "it's very excusable in my daughter." To Dorothy's father he wrote "I have committed my son to you, pray give him advice—I would have him mind and understand business, read a little history, study the mathematics, and cosmography; these are good, with subordination to the things of God. Better than idleness or mere outward worldly contents. These fit for public services, for which a man is born."

And the new daughter had written to him, so he replied: "I like to see anything from your hand, because indeed I stick not to say that I do entirely love you." And then he gives some fatherly advice. "I desire you both to make it above all things your business to seek the Lord; to be frequently calling upon Him, that He would manifest Himself to you in His Son, and be listening what returns He makes to you, for He will be speaking in your ear and to your heart, if you attend thereunto, I desire you to provoke your husband likewise thereunto. As for the pleasures of this life, and outward business, let that be upon the bye."

One likes to linger a little over these sweet domestic touches, they form such a contrast to the story that follows. For Cromwell was going out to grim work. His career in Ireland does not fall properly within the scope of this narrative, and indeed over it, especially over the slaughter of the garrisons of Drogheda and Wexford, one would like to draw a veil. Yet as these slaughters are the worst blot upon his memory, a word may be necessary.

For the slaughter at Wexford he does not seem to have been directly responsible, but for that at Drogheda he gave the order, being as he says "in the heat of action." He was very angry, resistance had been offered at a time when he thought no more bloodshed necessary. He was "persuaded that it would tend to prevent much effusion of blood for the future, which are the satisfactory grounds to such action, which otherwise cannot but work remorse and regret."

His action was covered by the law of war at the time and indeed long afterward, in accordance with which, a garrison refusing surrender, was entitled to no mercy. Indeed as late as 1820 we find Wellington writing to Canning, "I believe it has always been understood that the defenders of a fortress stormed have no claim to quarter, and the practice which has prevailed during the last century of surrendering a fortress when a breach was opened in the body of the place, and the counterscarp had been blown in, was founded on this understanding. Of late years the French have availed themselves of the humanity of modern warfare, and have made a new regulation, that a breach should stand one assault at least. The consequence of this regulation was to me, the loss of the flower of the army in the assaults of Ciudad Rodrigo and of Badajoz. I should certainly have thought myself justified in putting both garrisons to the sword; and if I had done so at the first it is probable that I should have saved five thousand men in the assault of the second. I mention this in order to show you that the practice of refusing quarter to a garrison, which stands an assault is not a useless effusion of blood."

It is to be noticed that Wellington complained that according to the new French regulation a breach should at least stand one assault, before it was justifiable to give no quarter to the garrison. But in Cromwell's day not even a single assault was necessary. Drogheda had stood three, and it looked as though a fourth was in preparation, when Cromwell gave that fatal command. When the garrison made its third rally, Ludlow tells us that the Lord-General "resolved to put all upon it, went down himself to the breach; and calling out a fresh reserve of Colonel Ewer's men, he put himself at their head, and with the word 'Our Lord God,' led them up again and with courage and resolution, though they met with a hot dispute. But although the enemy had been forced to quit his entrenchments, and the English army was pouring into the town, many of the garrison betook themselves to Millmount, a place very strong and difficult of access, whether simply to retreat or to plan another assault, is not clear. It was then that Cromwell, being in the heat of action, and probably in the heat of passion, ordered that all be put to the sword.

But the fact remains that while, so far as the then law of war went, Oliver was merciful rather than otherwise at Drogheda, except in the case of Basing House he had never enforced that law in England, and it is noticeable that the defenders of Basing House, like the defenders of Drogheda, were Papists. The man, brought up on memories of the Spanish Armada, the Marian persecution, and the Gunpowder Plot, had not outgrown his inherited antipathy to Papists. When he and other commissioners went to the Guildhall to ask for a loan for this campaign, they told the Common Council that this was not a struggle between Independent and Presbyterian, but between Papist and Protestant, and that Papacy and Popery were not to be endured in that kingdom.

Then too Cromwell had been brought up in an atmosphere of special hatred for Ireland, a hatred which practically all Englishmen shared. He knew nothing of Irish civilization and culture, believed that the Irish were a barbarous race, and as Milton put it "indocile and averse from all civility and amendment." And if he did not conquer this barbarous race, and conquer them quickly, England would be in a desperate position. In the days of Elizabeth Ireland had been the place where Spain could land troops for the deposition of the excommunicated Queen. It was to Ireland that Charles I had looked for assistance. And now if the rebellion were not stamped out before Charles II could land in Scotland, England would be between two fires. What he did, he must do quickly and thoroughly.

Added to all this, were the memories of the massacre of 1641, exaggerated as it had been in England. If Cromwell had taken time to read May's "History of the English Parliament" published in 1647, he would have learned that "the innocent Protestants were of a sudden deprived of their estates, and the persons of above one hundred thousand men, women and children murdered, many of them with exquisite tortures, within the space of a month." And this had happened at a time when "forty years of peace had compacted these two nations into one body, and cemented them together by all conjunctions of alliances, intermarriages and consanguinity, which was in outward appearance strengthened by frequent entertainment and all kinds of friendly neighbourhood." Whether he had read it or not, this was what he and all Englishmen believed. So in speaking of Drogheda, he wrote "I am persuaded that this is a righteous judgment of God upon these barbarous wretches who have imbued their hands in so much innocent blood." Yet it is not likely that any one at Drogheda had taken part in the Ulster massacre.

But he found another justification for it, the justification that would have appealed to Wellington. (It is noticeable that he seems to have felt that it needed justification, perhaps he was the only Englishman who would have felt so.) He believed that it would "tend to prevent the effusion of blood for the future, which are the satisfactory grounds for such action, which otherwise cannot but work remorse and regret."

And indeed it did accomplish its immediate purpose, probably did prevent effusion of blood for the time being. The evening after Ormond wrote, "It is not to be imagined how great the terror is that these successes and the power of the rebels have struck into the people. They are so stupefied that it is with great difficulty that I can persuade them to act any thing like men for their own preservation." And yet later at Clonmel Cromwell met the strongest resistance he had ever encountered, and the lasting effect was to strengthen the hatred of the Irish for the English, which endures to this day.

It must however be said for Cromwell that he was more careful than other English commanders had been to protect non-combatants from plunder and violence. He was "resolved by the grace of God diligently and strictly to restrain such wickedness." "Give me an instance," he challenged the Catholic clergy, "of one man since our coming into Ireland, not in arms, massacred, destroyed or banished, concerning the massacre or destruction of whom justice has not been done, or endeavoured to be done." To which the clergy might have answered that both at Drogheda and at Wexford, priests at least had been put to death without mercy. But perhaps Cromwell regarded them as combatants, since it was believed that they had stirred up the whole trouble.

In ten months Oliver had conquered Eastern Ireland, others could deal with the West. So in May 1650 he was recalled to take care of Scotland. For the Scotch had come to terms with Charles II, or rather Charles II had come to terms with the Scotch. On June 11th he signed the Treaty forced upon him, on June 23rd he took the Covenant. Scotland was ready to strike.

The war with Scotland brought about a change in Cromwell's position. Hitherto he had been simply Lieutenant General under Fairfax, he went to Scotland as Lord General, Commander-in-Chief of the whole army.

For ever since the trial of the King, Fairfax had been more or less uneasy about the way that things were going. Each step might seem justifiable, but each had led to another. One must draw the line somewhere. He would draw it about leading an army into Scotland. So long as the English troops would act obviously in the defensive, he was willing to command them. If the Scots invaded England, he said, he was ready to lay down his life in opposing them, but he would not seek to prevent such an invasion, by invading Scotland.

Against this Cromwell protested. Mrs. Hutchinson tells us that "he laboured with him almost all the night with the most earnest endeavours." "I think," he argued, "we have a most just cause to begin, or rather requite their hostility first begun upon us, and thereby to free our country, if God should be pleased to assist us, (and I doubt not but that He will), from the great misery and calamity of having an army of Scots within our own country.—Your Excellency will soon determine whether it is better to have the war within the bowels of another country or of our own, and that it will be in one of these, I think it without scruple."

But his labors were of no avail. Fairfax resigned, giving as his official grounds, "debilities both in body and mind, occasioned by former actions and businesses." Cromwell took his place. "I have not sought these things," he wrote to a friend. But of course there were those who believed that he had. Ludlow was to become one of these, though at the time he said that in his pleadings with Fairfax he "acted the part so to the life that I really thought him in earnest."

Oliver was in earnest. His relations with Fairfax had always been exemplary and it is certainly to his credit that he had served as so faithful and courteous a subordinate, under a man with less than his military ability, and thirteen years his junior. And now his aim was to unite the Presbyterians and Independents of England, and ultimately to conciliate the Scots. So it was much better that Fairfax, suspected of being a Presbyterian, should command the expedition than that he, the great Independent, should do so.

Of Cromwell's campaigns in Scotland, of Dunbar and Worcester, it is not my purpose to speak. Of Worcester he wrote to Speaker Lenthall, "The dimensions of this mercy are above my thoughts. It is for aught I know a crowning mercy." It was indeed a crowning mercy, the last time that he was to appear in arms.

It is noticeable however that his attitude toward Scotland was entirely different from his attitude toward Ireland. He had never particularly loved the Scotch. "The way they now go on, pressing for their discipline," he had said, "I could as soon turn my sword against them as against any one." And now he was disappointed in them. "I had thought," he wrote, "that I should find in Scotland a conscientious people, and a barren country; about Edinburgh it is as fertile for corn as any part of England, but the people generally given to the most impudent lying, and frequent swearing, as is incredible to be believed." Yet he still counted them amongst the godly. He went against them reluctantly. To John Cotton in New England he wrote that "the greatest difficulty in our engagement in Scotland was by reasons we have had to do with some who were, I verily think, godly; but through weakness and the subtleties of Satan were involved in interest against the Lord and His people." The day after Dunbar he wrote to Lenthall: "Since we came into Scotland it hath been our desire and longing to have avoided blood in this business, by reason that God hath here a people fearing His Name, though deceived; and to that end have we offered much love unto such in the bowels of Christ."

So he lost no opportunity to plead with, to try to convince the godly in Scotland. To the General Assembly of the Kirk, he wrote on August 3rd, exactly a month before Dunbar, "Bring not upon yourselves the blood of innocent men.—I beseech you in the bowels of Christ, think it possible that you may be mistaken." From the camp at Pentland Hills, he wrote to the Honorable David Lesley, Lieutenant General of the Scots army, once his comrade in arms, that he speaks "to the honest people in Scotland, as to our own souls, it being no part of our business to hinder any of them from worshipping God in that way they are satisfied in their consciences by the Word of God they ought, (though differing from us), but shall therein be ready to perform what obligation lies upon us by the Covenant."

But he protests that "under pretence of the Covenant, and wrested from the most native intent and equity thereof, *a King should be taken in by you to be imposed upon us, and this called the cause of God and the Kingdom!*" If the Reformation was so perfect and spiritual, indeed the Kingdom of the Lord Jesus, did it need "such carnal policies, such insincere acting, such fleshly mixtures, as to pretend to cry down all malignants, and yet to receive and set up the Head of them?" They in their consciences must know that all Charles' promises and his declaration against his father's sins were made with regret, because of importunities and threats, and that to this very day he was against them.

Oliver's faith in a Providence manifesting itself in the course of events, was greatly strengthened by his campaigns in Scotland, for he regarded his victories there as the most signal proof that had yet been given him that God was on his side. "My weak faith hath been upheld," he wrote to his wife after Dunbar. "I have been in my inward mind marvellously supported." For this was a case in which the truly godly on both sides had invoked the God of Battles, and that God had given the victory to the English. "Did not you solemnly appeal and pray?" he asked the Scotch. "Did not we do so too? And ought not you and we to think with fear and trembling of the hand of the great God in this mighty and strange appearance of His?" And when they replied that they had not so learned Christ as to hang the equity of their cause upon events, he attributed it to the fact that "the things did not work forth their platform, and the great God did not come down to their minds and thoughts." He and they "ought to think with fear and trembling of the hand of the Great God in this mighty and strange appearance of His, instead of lightly calling it an event!"

For the next few years, Scotland and Ireland were incorporated into England. But they were treated very differently. In Scotland there was no wholesale confiscation of land as there was in Ireland. In Scotland too the national church was not proscribed, although it was deprived of all power in the civil government, the General Assembly being dissolved, but local presbyteries and synods continued to sit. In Ireland the old laws against the papists were rigidly enforced. They were not compelled to attend the Protestant churches, but they had no liberty of worship of their own. "I meddle not with any man's conscience," Cromwell wrote to the Governor of Ross, "but if by liberty of conscience you mean a liberty to exercise the mass, I judge it best to exercise plain dealing, and to let you know, that where the Parliament of England have power, that will not be allowed of—As for the people, what thoughts they may have in matters of religion in their own breasts, I cannot reach, but shall think it my duty if they walk honestly and peaceably, not to cause them in the least to suffer for the same." But in all this he was only an Englishman of his time, rather ahead of most of them.

There was some reform in the administration of the law, some improvement in trade, above all no attempt to prevent Irish manufactures from competing with those of England, perfect commercial equality between the two countries.

But so far as Ireland was concerned, the evil that Cromwell did lived after him, the good was interred with his bones. For with the Restoration all that was good in his policy was reversed, the evil remained.

CHAPTER XV

End of the Long Parliament

"I have sought the Lord day and night that He would rather
slay me than put it upon me to do this thing."
—OLIVER CROMWELL.

"That which you have by force, I look upon it as nothing."
—OLIVER CROMWELL.

AS Oliver journeyed slowly from Scotland to London, he seems to
have experienced a recrudescence of youth. He had had illnesses both in Ireland and Scotland, and they had taken his vitality.
"I grow an old man," he wrote to his wife after Dunbar, "I feel the
infirmities of age marvellously stealing upon me." But he was well
and young again now, for he felt that "God had ended all his troubles
by the marvellous salvation wrought at Worcester." He had done his
work, could return to his old pursuits and pleasures. When he reached
Aylesbury, Mr. Winwood, a member of the parliamentary commission
sent to offer congratulations, brought him his falcons, and as in by-
gone days, he "went out of his way a-hawking."

When, on the 12th of September, 1651, he entered London, he was
received as though he were a king returned from the wars, and there
were even some who said that he would make himself king, doubtless
there were some who wished that he would. Indeed if he had wished
to do it at all, he would probably have encountered less opposition
then than at any other time. But that was far from his thoughts.
When a friend commented on the great crowds that had turned out
to greet him, he jestingly replied that perhaps there would have been
still larger numbers to see him hanged. He was happy and humble,
"carried himself with great affability, and in his discourse about
Worcester, would seldom mention any thing of himself, but gave, as
was due, the glory of the action to God."

And now what should he do next? He held no civil position, was
only Lord General, Commander-in-Chief of the army. So it seemed
for a moment as though with Worcester he might consider that his
public work was really done, might really "go play." And he longed

to return to private life, to the wife that was "dearer to him than any creature," to Richard and Dorothy and their "little brat," born while he was in Scotland. Doll had written to him sometimes "very cunningly and complimentally," but on the whole neither Dick nor Doll had written often enough, if he had had the leisure that they had he would have written oftener. And Dick was still inclined to be idle and extravagant, and must be looked after a little. He had written him from Ireland to "take heed of an unactive vain spirit," and to recreate himself with Sir Walter Raleigh's History. Then there was Bettie and her husband "dear to him, very dear" but a little "cozened with worldly vanities and worldly company." And the dear little ones, Mary and Frances, who had sent him childish epistles during his absence. Moreover there would be hunting and hawking again, and all the old local interests, especially there were the Fens to be drained.

So he begged to be dismissed of his charge, begged it again and again, he says. But he could not obtain what he desired, what his soul longed for. "And the plain truth of the matter was, I did afterward apprehend, some were of the opinion (such the difference of their judgment from mine) that it could not well be."

And indeed it could not well be. Wherever he turned the country was in a most distressing condition. As wars go, these civil wars had been very humane, but they had brought about great economic dislocations. Estates had changed hands, and the new landlords were often less merciful than the old. Trade was bad, the overseas commerce had largely been destroyed, there was much unemployment, and many prisoners for debt. The taxation, necessary for the maintenance of the army, had added to the general misery. The law was severe, men could still be hung for stealing six and sixpence, the lawyers were reaping a harvest. The affairs of the Church were in a chaotic condition, and needed settling.

All these things had been troubling Oliver while he was in Scotland, and he had tried to stir up Parliament to remedy them. He had written to Speaker Lenthall that if Worcester were not, as he hoped, a crowning mercy, "such a one we shall have if this provoke those that are concerned in it to thankfulness, and the Parliament to do the will of Him, Who hath done His will for it and the nation," and he prayed that "justice and righteousness might flow from them, as a thankful return to our gracious God." After Dunbar he had been more specific; "Disown yourselves, but own your authority, and improve it to curb the proud and insolent, such as would disturb the tranquillity of

England, or if there be any one that makes many poor to make a few rich, that suits not a Commonwealth." He reminded the House, that it was that they might have liberty and opportunity to do these things, and not be hindered, that the army had been, and would be, willing to venture their lives.

But the Rump showed no disposition to use its liberty and opportunity in this way. The old leaders were gone, the old religious spirit was largely gone, many of the members cared about nothing except to feather their own nests. So it was not long before he came to feel that he was a chosen instrument of God "to use all the fair and lawful means that he could, to have the nation reap the fruit of all the blood and treasure that had been spent in the Cause." Who was to do this, if he did not? Had he not been called of God for this purpose, as was Abraham, or perhaps more exactly as was Joshua? In his failure to obtain the dismissal from his charge that his soul longed for, he to whom God always spoke through his providences, that is, through the course of events, found a confirmation of the call.

Others reasoned in the same way. "Great things God hath done by you in war, and good things men expect from you in peace," one wrote to him. And he had "many desires and thirstings in spirit, to find out ways and means whereby he might be in any way instrumental" to establish the things that his sword had made possible.

Yet, though assured of his call, it was with great reluctance and humility that he addressed himself to the work. "Indeed my dear friend," he wrote to John Cotton, "between you and me, you know not me, my weakness, my inordinate passions, my unskilfulness, and every way unfitness to the work." The weakness he had never had, the inordinate passions, if by them he meant the hot temper, he was learning to subdue. As for the skillfulness and fitness for the work, constructive work such as he had not done before, only time could show whether he possessed them or not, whether he who had done great things in war would be able to do good things in peace.

The first thing that he wanted to do was to divest the sword of all civil authority. No one, not even John Lilburn, had been more conscious than he, that since the close of the First Civil War, the government had been on a purely military foundation. Thus far it had seemed necessary, but he had not overthrown the royal despotism to establish a military despotism. He had never regarded the present government as anything but a necessary evil, to be tolerated, but only for a short time, because of the dangers within and without. But now the wars with Ireland and Scotland were over, European nations were beginning to be friendly, it was time to devise something permanent.

But he knew that very little could be done in this direction while this Parliament was sitting, this Parliament that was unpopular with the nation, and sat merely by grace of the army. For again he would have agreed with John Lilburn who wrote him that it was but "a picked party of your forcible selecting, and such as even your own officers, our lords and riders, have often and frequently styled no better than a mock Parliament, a shadow of a Parliament." Yet by an Act of May 1641, it could not be adjourned, prorogued or dissolved except by its own consent. That it had not been willing to dissolve itself while war was threatening from Scotland and Ireland was excusable, he himself had admitted that. But now he felt that his first task was to get rid of it. Until that was accomplished there was no hope of settling the nation.

So from the time that he resumed his seat in the House, he "pressed the Parliament, as a member, to period themselves." "I told them, for I knew it better than any one man in Parliament could know it, because of my manner of life, which led me everywhere up and down the nation, thereby giving me to see and know the temper of all men, and of the best of men, that the nation loathed their sitting." At last by a majority of only two votes, they were induced to fix November 3rd, 1654, as the date of their dissolution. That was three years ahead, therefore somewhat discouraging.

But at least a date had been fixed, this government would come to an end sometime, and it was well to consider what should succeed it. Therefore on the tenth of December, 1651, Cromwell called a meeting of divers members of Parliament, mostly lawyers, and some of the chief officers of the army, at Speaker Lenthall's house. It was with a heavy heart that he attended that meeting, for word had come only two days before that his son-in-law Ireton, the man on whose counsel he relied most, had died at Limerick on November 26th. However no time could be lost in grief. He told the assembly that "since the King was dead, and his son defeated, he held it necessary to come to a settlement of the nation; and in order thereunto, he had requested this meeting that they together might consider and advise, what was fit to be done, and to be presented to Parliament."

The real question, as they all saw it, was whether an absolute Republic or a mixed monarchical government would be better. No one thought of any other alternative. On the whole the officers were for a Republic, the lawyers for some form of monarchy. The Lord General sided with the lawyers. He was still not wedded or glued to any form of government, but he had never really wished to give up the monarchy, and he knew that the people wanted it back, that this desire was increasing in strength. To gain the affections of the people, that was what was necessary, before any government could be stable. Moreover, as Whitelocke had said, the laws of England were so inter-woven with the power and practice of monarchy that to settle a govern-ment without something of monarchy in it, would make so great an alteration in the proceedings of the law that it was not possible to see what inconveniences would arise thereby.

But when the question came up as to who the monarch should be, and Whitelocke even went so far as to suggest that a time might come when it would be feasible to think of the King's eldest son, or the Duke of York, Cromwell replied that that might be a business of more than ordinary difficulty. Perhaps his mind was running back upon all those interviews which he had had with the late King at Hampton Court, upon the time when he had thought him "the best and up-rightest man in the three kingdoms." As for his eldest son, who had taken the Covenant, and had put forth a "hypocritical and formal" Declaration against his father's sins, he had never been taken in by him. Whether at this time he had any one in mind who could supply the "somewhat of monarchical power which would be very effectual," can only be left to conjecture. Two months before he had thought much of the little Duke of Gloucester.

Nothing came of the conference. Cromwell was merely feeling for opinions that he might turn over in his mind. The time for action was not yet, he must await the Providence of God, that is the course of events. Meanwhile he must put up with this Parliament for a time—three years they had decided—do the best that he could do with it, at least get it to do something.

First something must be done to heal the wounds of war, it was desirable to have a nation as united as possible. So an amnesty must be granted to the conquered Royalists. It was necessary to be just to Royalists as well as to Puritans, to unbelievers as well as to be-lievers, he once said that it was even more necessary. In February 1652 he did succeed in getting Parliament to pass an Act of Amnesty for treasons committed before Worcester, but there were too many restrictions and exceptions to please him. And this, like everything else that he did, aroused suspicion. Ludlow and other doctrinaire Republicans thought that he did it "that so he might fortify himself with the addition of new friends to carry on his designs."

Next there must be a reform of the law, the law that in that

disorganized state of society, was serving "only to maintain the lawyers, and to encourage the rich to oppress the poor." Of course, in
his efforts in this direction, Oliver had to encounter the opposition
of the lawyers, but he succeeded in getting a little relief for poor
prisoners—not much—and in getting a committee of twenty-one members of Parliament appointed, with Matthew Hale as chairman, "to
consider the inconveniences of the law, and the speediest way to
remedy the same."

This committee drafted many good Bills, Parliament discussed
them, but failed to act upon them. "I will not say," Cromwell said
afterward, "that they were come to an utter inability of working
reformation, though I might say so in regard to one thing, the reform
of the law, so much groaned under in the posture that it is now. That
was a thing we had many good words spoken for, but we know now
three months together were not enough for the settling of one word
'Incumbrances.' "

Then there was the Church, what should be done about that? At
present it was in a state of chaos. True the Presbyterian discipline
had been established by law in 1648, but as Baxter tells us "though
Presbytery generally took in Scotland, it was but a stranger here."
Most congregations had failed to elect elders and deacons, and as
for the ministers "men made themselves ministers as they chose, got
themselves livings as they could." There were many lay preachers,
preaching as they chose and could. In 1652 the London Provincial
Assembly in Sion College expressed fear of "the utter dissolution of
the Presbyterial Government." A few years later a French Protestant
wrote home, "I extremely wondered to find those whom they called
Presbyterians, and who would imitate us of the religion in France
and Geneva, to have their discipline so confused and different.—You
may well imagine by the manner of the people, and their prodigious
opinions, that there is no catechism or sacraments duly administered."

And there were many, John Milton among them, who would have
liked to have the Church stay as it was, "men making themselves
ministers as they chose, getting themselves livings as they could."
But Cromwell could not see things that way, perhaps he did not
have faith enough, he felt that it was the duty of the Christian State
to maintain religious institutions and provide a regular educated ministry. There should be room for a considerable variety of opinion
among those within the State Church, there should be toleration for
those without, lay preaching should be permitted, he was not envious
that Eldad and Medad should prophesy. But as he had written to the

Governor of Edinburgh Castle, though "approbation was not a necessity to give faculty to preach the Gospel, yet it was an act of conveniency, in respect of order."

But in this, as in everything else, he had nothing constructive to offer. He listened to, and judged of the plans of others. And in this case it was the plan of a Rev. John Owen that appealed to him. Owen had preached before Parliament the day after the execution of the King. He wisely made no reference to the event that was uppermost in everybody's mind, but he upheld the supremacy of Parliament. The sermon was published with an appendix on the subject of religious toleration. In this Owen took the position that it was the duty of the government to maintain places of public worship, but that while the civil magistrate might punish those who in the name of religion, disturbed the public peace, he must not interfere in religious disputes.

This was quite in accordance with Cromwell's mind, he decided that Owen was "the person he must be acquainted with." So when he went to Ireland he took him with him as his chaplain, and later used his influence to have him made Dean of Christ Church.

In February 1652 a plan for an ecclesiastical settlement, doubtless suggested by Owen, and approved by Cromwell, was introduced into Parliament. There was to be a very broad National Church, controlled by two sets of commissioners, a commission of Triers to determine the moral and intellectual fitness of candidates for the ministry, and a commission of ejectors to go from place to place, ejecting unfit ministers and schoolmasters. Outside this established church, Dissenters might meet for worship "if they have constant meetings, in places publicly known, and give notice to some magistrate of this, their place of ordinary worship." The possible proscription of Popery and Prelacy was not even mentioned. But the opponents of those principles of the Christian religion, "without the acknowledgment whereof the Scriptures clearly affirm that salvation is not to be obtained" were "not to be suffered to preach or promulgate anything in opposition with such principles."

Cromwell heartily approved this general plan, on the face of it very liberal for the time. But he saw that its real liberality or illiberality depended upon how this last statement was defined. He was determined to make it as liberal as possible. So when in a committee appointed to discuss it, of which he was a member, Owen and his supporters were asked what principles they considered fundamental to Christianity, and they produced a list of fifteen such principles, he thought them too many. He demanded a more liberal interpretation of Christianity. "I shall need no revelation," he said, "to discover to me the man who endeavours to impose (his opinions) on his brethren." That was to Cromwell the supreme heresy.

And it was in the course of this debate that he made his famous statement. "I had rather that Mahometanism was permitted among us, than that one of God's children should suffer persecution." This in answer to one who, accusing him of being a lukewarm Laodicean, said, "I would rather be a persecuting Saul than an indifferent Gallia."

Outside the committee Milton was "humbly begging the Father of Spirits that He would either graciously please to stir up the hearts of these worthy men to put in some Christian retraction, or else the hearts of some of His faithful witnesses against such graven images, to present some faithful and truly Christian observations." And when the Lord General's position was known, he appears to have thought that he had made such "truly Christian observations," for it was then he addressed his sonnet to "Cromwell, our chief of men," and begged him to

"Help us to save free conscience from the paw
Of hireling wolves, whose Gospel is their maw."

But Parliament made no more progress in the reform of the Church than it did in the reform of the law. It discussed the plan but it did nothing. In fact it would do nothing about anything. Nothing could be carried, Cromwell said, without making parties unworthy of a Parliament. Vane even went so far as to complain that they would not even suffer things to be done that were so plain that they ought to do themselves.

There was some excuse for Parliament, it had other and more immediately pressing things to attend to than either the proposals of the Law Committee, or those of the Committee for the Propagation of the Gospel. A commercial war with Holland was threatening, largely the result of the Navigation Act passed in October 1651, which struck at the Dutch monopoly of the carrying trade, by enacting that all goods entering England or English territory must be brought in English ships or in ships of the country to which the goods belonged. And this war finally broke out, when the Dutch admiral Tromp failed to lower his flag to the English admiral Blake on the narrow seas off Dover.

It was very distasteful to Cromwell, it was war between the two great Protestant countries, it increased the economic and financial difficulties of England, and above all it delayed the reforms on which his heart was set, and made it still more difficult for him to deal with Parliament. He was sent to investigate, decided that England was in the right, but he did not like the war. "I do not like the war," he said, "and I will do everything that I can to bring about peace." And in every attempt to come to terms with the Dutch, he was to be found with the peace party.

Moreover, the war led to another difference between him and Parliament. For to meet the expenses caused by it, Parliament confiscated the estates of about six hundred and fifty Royalists, most of whom had done nothing to justify such action. And Oliver, whose heart was set upon "healing and settling" was indignant. "Poor men," he said, "were driven like flocks of sheep by forty of a morning, to confiscations of goods and estates, without any man being able to give a reason why two of them should forfeit a shilling."

And yet he stood by Parliament, because it was the only constitutional authority, the only link with the past that was left, though he knew full well that its constitutional authority was more of a semblance than a reality. There had been some by-elections since 1649, its membership had been increased to about a hundred and twenty-five, but in no sense could it be said to represent the people, whole districts were unrepresented. And yet it was assuming to itself "all the authority of the three estates that were before," executive, legislative, and judicial. "It so assumed them," he said later, "that if any man had come and asked, 'What rules do you judge by?' it would have answered, 'Why we have none. We are supreme in legislature and in judicature.'" And it sat all the year round, never taking more than three or four days' holiday. So, as he put it, "the country was governed by a perpetual Parliament, always sitting."

However, perhaps the constitutional question did not trouble him so much, as the difficulty about getting things done; he would have been patient with any Parliament that he saw really healing and settling the nation. But in fundamental matters this Parliament would do nothing. He knew that many were getting positions for sons and nephews, taking bribes to let off Royalists easily who had to compound for their estates, while they were often too severe to those who did not offer such bribes. And, perhaps most serious of all, some of them were buying up estates, largely those of Royalists, and then depriving the tenantry of their ancient rights. So he was sure that this Parliament must be dissolved, both because it did not represent the people, and because it was unworthy, yet he was also sure that it ought to dissolve itself. It was at least a semblance of authority though it was "but a hare swimming over the Thames." And there was no one else to dissolve it, except the army, and the army must not do it, it had been forced to take too many steps already, it must not take this one. The mere thinking of dissolving it by "an act of violence was to him worse than any engagement that ever he was in."

And the Council of Officers agreed with him, so that "for a long time they were very tender even to so much as petition." But toward the end of July 1652, they did consider a petition "that a new representative be forthwith elected." Cromwell could not even go so far as that. So owing to his influence the petition was changed to a request that Parliament would consider the qualifications which would secure "the election of such as are pious and faithful to the Commonwealth to sit and serve as members of the said Parliament," and the demand for a dissolution was changed into a demand for particular elections to fill vacancies. This was what Vane had been advocating since 1650. But even with this change Cromwell would not sign the petition. After all it was the duty of Parliament to decide upon its own dissolution, the filling of vacancies, and the manner of election. If only Parliament would see its duty, and do it! But it was the duty of Parliament, not of the army.

Well, if they would not dissolve themselves, they must at least do something, if only they would do something, they might stay, so in August the Council of Officers "seeing that nothing would be done— did a little to remind them by petition." This petition asked that speedy and effectual means be taken to carry out a long list of reforms. But the Army "had no return at all for our satisfaction, a few words given to us; the things presented by us were, we were told, under consideration, to those not presented by us there was little or no consideration at all."

And so Cromwell's dilemma was the Parliament, the only constituted authority, was not ruling, and the army must not rule. And yet some one must rule. Evidently in England at least there must be a government with "somewhat monarchical" about it. In September he seems again to have been thinking of the Duke of Gloucester. How about making him King, and himself Protector? But that hardly seemed practical.

So the weeks went on, and there was no solution, the situation was becoming almost unbearable. Cromwell knew that in every corner of the nation the people were dissatisfied, that every man was complaining of the "non-performance of those things that had been promised, and were of duty to be performed," and that "the blame was being laid at the Army's door." And the officers came to the conclusion that, whatever the constitutional position might be, they must do something about it. They alone had the power, and the country expected it.

So in October there began to be meetings of the Army Council to which they invited "divers members of Parliament." There were ten or twelve such meetings. The officers "most humbly begged and besought the members of Parliament that by their own means they would bring forth those good things that had been promised and expected; that so it might appear that they did not do them from any suggestion from the army, but from their own ingenuity, so tender were we to preserve them in the reputation of the people, yet how little we prevailed we very well know."

And Cromwell's dissatisfaction increased. Was it because there was no king in Israel that every man was doing that which was right in his own eyes? In November he had a conversation with Whitelocke. He spoke of the distraction in Parliament, in the army and in the nation, of the danger of being fooled out of the mercies of God "by our particular posings and animosities, one against another." Whitelocke sympathized, but thought that the root of the trouble lay in the ambitions of the officers, and the mutinous spirit of the soldiers. Cromwell replied that that did not trouble him, that he was able to control any difficulties that might arise in that way, but that the army did begin to have a strange distaste against members of Parliament, and he wished that there were not too much cause for it. He spoke of their self-seeking, their delay of business, and design to perpetuate themselves, the scandalous lives of some of them. "These things, my lord, do give much ground for people to open their mouths against them, and to dislike them, nor can they be kept within the bounds of justice or law or reason, they themselves being the supreme power of the nation liable to no account to any, nor to be controlled or regulated by any other power; there being none superior or coördinate with them." There must be some authority or power so full and so high as to restrain and keep things in better order.

Whitelocke could only hope that a time would come when the majority of the members would be better advised. And Oliver, who had been hoping against hope, now declared that there was "no hope for these men, some course must be thought of to curb or restrain them, or we shall be ruined by them." And when Whitelocke continued to argue the point he, following the tenor of his own thoughts, rather than the arguments that were being presented to him, burst out, probably nervously and impetuously, with what perhaps seemed to him at the moment the only possible solution, "What if a man should take it upon himself to be king?"

Eleven months before he had said that a government with "somewhat monarchical" in it, would be very effectual, yet it is not at all certain that he was thinking of himself as the monarch. But when he confronted Whitelocke with this sudden question, there can be no doubt but that he was turning such a possibility over in his mind. The Voice of God, speaking through the course of events had called upon him to do so many unexpected things, what if that Voice were now calling upon him to undertake this duty too? But he put it from him, the call was not clear enough; more vigorously than before he set himself to work to bring about an understanding with Parliament.

In both army and Parliament the question had arisen, if this Parliament is dissolved, how should its successor be chosen? It must be borne in mind that there never had been a Parliament that technically represented the people, though probably this Parliament, in its early days, had represented them in spirit. But now no one dared to trust a Parliament freely elected, the times were too troubled for that. There was just a ferment of thought, naturally every thing and every one at cross purposes. So it is now in almost every land in this period succeeding the Great War. So it always will be when we overturn, overturn, overturn. People go on in accustomed grooves, without thinking or feeling much, then all begin to think and feel, and all in different ways. To get any action at all a dictator seems to be necessary, or at least inevitable.

Among the officers two parties had developed, led respectively by Lambert and Harrison. Lambert stood for an immediate dissolution, by force if necessary, after that keep as close to the old idea of Parliamentary government as seemed safe at the time. Harrison, drifting towards Fifth Monarchy ideas, demanded a government of moral and religious men, not to be elected by the people, but to be chosen by those whose judgment could be trusted to pick them out. Cromwell thus described the two parties, both of which were urging him "to do things which made his hair stand on end." "One of these is headed by Major General Lambert, who will be content with nothing less than a dissolution. Of the other Major General Harrison is the chief, who is an honest man and aiming at good things, yet from the impatience of his spirit, will not await the Lord's leisure, but urges me on to that which he and all honest men will have cause to repent."

That January 1653, the month in which Cromwell wrote the above, the officers began to hold daily prayer-meetings. That meant that they were fortifying themselves to do something. Oliver was anxious when at All Hallows some soldiers prayed for a new representative, he was apparently in sympathy with the Government that silenced them. On January 28th the officers addressed a circular letter to the regiments in England, Scotland and Ireland, asking for the support of soldiers as well as officers, in demanding from Parliament first the establishment of successive Parliaments, consisting of "men faithful to the interests of the Commonwealth, men of truth fearing God and hating covetousness," second, the reform of the law, third, liberty of conscience, without encouragement to such as are popish, or profane in the exercise of their superstitious forms and licentious practices," fourth, "due countenance and encouragement to those who faithfully dispensed the Gospel."

Cromwell could not have found much fault with these demands, they were about what he wanted himself. Only he still hoped that Parliament would grant them voluntarily, rather than they should be forced upon it by the army. He was disturbed because soldiers were preaching in favor of the violent expulsion of Parliament. Indeed on March 11th the Council of Officers at St. James had resolved to turn them out, "had not the General (Cromwell) and Colonel Desborough interceded, asking them 'if they destroyed that Parliament what they should call themselves, a State they could not be.'" And when they answered that they would call a new Parliament, "Then," said the General, "the Parliament is not the supreme power, but that is the supreme power that calls it." It was not for the army to make itself the supreme power in that way, or in any way. He would still keep hold of the hare swimming over the Thames.

So, on into April, the very month that he turned them out, indeed in a sense up to the day that he turned them out, Cromwell was fighting for Parliament. "Our soldiers," says a newsletter of April 1st, "decide speedily to have a new representative, and the Parliament resolve to the contrary; the General sticks close to the House." As he had not gone to the House for three or four weeks this can only mean that he was upholding it. And because he was upholding it, he was "daily railed upon by the preaching party, who say they must have both a new Parliament and a new General before the work is done, and that these are not the people that are appointed for the perfecting of that great work of God, which they have begun." But a week later there was less talk of a new representative, "the heat of the soldiers being somewhat abated by the General's sticking close to the House, and sending some of the maddest of them into Scotland."

And Parliament had at last been roused to action, had itself taken up a Bill for a new representative. But it was only what Vane had been advocating for three years, there were to be elections to fill vacancies, but the present members were to keep their seats. The franchise was to be fairly broad, neutrals and men who had deserted the cause were to be allowed to vote, but this was counteracted by the fact that the present members were to be judges both of the eligibility of new members, and of the validity of the votes cast. And these rules were to apply not only to the next, but to all succeeding Parliaments. That is they, and the men chosen by them, were to rule England.

This bill was not one which Cromwell could contemplate with pleasure. "We should have had fine work then," he said, "a Parliament of four hundred men, executing arbitrary government without intermission, except some change of a part of them; one Parliament stepping into the seat of another just left warm for them; the same day that one left another was to leap in." He thought that was a "pitiful remedy."

So he who had been fighting for Parliament against the Council of Officers, was once more at one with the Council. However they might differ on other things, they would unite to defeat this Bill. For it would deprive the Army of what they had fought for, it would give the people no rights. "We came to the conclusion among ourselves," Cromwell afterward said, "that if we had been fought out of our liberties and rights, necessity would have taught us patience, but to deliver them up would render us the basest persons in the world, and worthy to be accounted haters of God and of His People." Yet still "the thinking of an act of violence was to us worse than any engagement that ever we were in." For they were still "willing, even tender and desirous if possible, that these men should quit their places with honour."

So, on the fifteenth of April, having been absent from the House about a month, he again took his place, and endeavored to persuade it. The Bill had already passed its second reading. So strong was his opposition, that it led some of the members to say, "It is high time to choose a new General." Whereupon Cromwell offered his resignation, he was always glad to give up power, but as no one could be found to take his place, that idea was soon dropped.

And he still clung to the Parliament. On the evening of the nineteenth of April there was a conference of officers and members of Parliament. "It is necessary," said one of the officers, "that the thing be done (the Bill be defeated) one way or the other, and the members of Parliament not suffered to prolong their power." Cromwell rebuked him, and proposed as a compromise that Parliament dissolve itself at once, but themselves appoint a provisional government, that the members devolve their trust to some well-affected men, such as had an interest in the nation, and were known to be of good affection to the Commonwealth. To this the officers were well inclined, and undertook to demonstrate by historical precedents that "this was no new thing when the nation was under such hurly burlies." With the exception of St. John, the members of Parliament were not so favorable to it, Sir Arthur Haselrigg opposed it violently, Sir Henry Vane was critical. The discussion lasted far into the night, got nowhere, broke up from sheer weariness, but Vane and other members promised to suspend proceedings on the Bill in the House next morning, and to meet with the soldiers again in the afternoon.

So when the fateful twentieth of April came Oliver, relying upon that promise, decided not to go to the House. He had grown more careful about his dress of late, but this morning he put on "a plain black suit, and grey worsted stockings," that would do to stay at home. Some of those who had been present at the discussion the night before dropped in to talk with him, but when it was announced that Parliament was sitting, they went off to take their places in the House, Cromwell was left alone.

Then came a message from Harrison, that in spite of the promise of the previous evening, the House was proceeding with the Bill. Probably Vane had intended to keep his word, but the House had called for it, for they hoped to get it through before Oliver could be informed, then adjourn until November, thus making it impossible to either repeal or amend it. Sir Arthur Haselrigg was leading them. Perhaps Vane could not have stopped them, but it is not on record that he tried. After all it was his Bill.

Cromwell could not believe what he had heard. Had his friend Vane, whom he called Brother Heron, and who had been closer to him than a brother, been false to him? He waited. A second, a third messenger came. Then he called an officer, and bade him summon a guard of soldiers. Taking them with him he stationed them at all the approaches of the House. After that had been attended to, he himself entered the House.

He had come to dissolve that House by force. He had come to do that, "the mere thinking of which had been worse to him than any engagement he ever yet was in." How far was he acting upon his own best judgment, or to what extent was he influenced by the feeling that, having withstood the pressure of the army officers so long, it would be impossible for him, in view of this latest development, to withstand it any longer? We cannot know. But in 1637 he told some of the officers that it was they who had made him dissolve the Long Parliament.

He "sat down, as he was wont to do in an ordinary place." For a short time he watched and listened in silence. Then he beckoned Harrison to him, and whispered in his ear that he thought this Parliament ripe for a dissolution. As usual, when he had once made up his mind he went further than even those who had urged him on, could go with him. "Sir," said Harrison, "the work is very great and dangerous, therefore I desire you seriously to consider of it, before you engage yourself."

Oliver sat still fifteen minutes longer. Then the Speaker put the final question, "That this Bill do pass." No, this Bill must not pass! "This," he said to Harrison, "is the time that I must do it." So he stood up, as if about to speak to the question, talked of the great things that this Parliament had done in its earlier and better days, of its "pains and care of the public good."

Was he planning simply to urge them, to shame them into being true to their traditions? If so, his mood changed. He began to speak rapidly and angrily of their delays of justice, self-interest and personal faults. "Charging them not to have a heart to do anything for the public good, that they had espoused the corrupt interests of Presbytery, and of lawyers who were the supporters of tyranny and oppression, and finally they had resolved to perpetuate themselves in power."

He had removed his hat when he began to speak. Now he clapped it on again, this Parliament was not worthy of that mark of respect, in fact it was not a Parliament at all. "It is not fit," he shouted, "that you should sit as a Parliament any longer. You have sat long enough, unless you had done more good."

Sir Peter Wentworth rose to complain of such unparliamentary language, the more horrid, as it came from their servant whom they had so highly trusted and obliged. Perhaps Cromwell thought that the obligation was not all on one side, at any rate he was only the more incensed. "Come, come!" he cried. "I will put an end to your prating! You are no Parliament, I say that you are no Parliament!" Then to Harrison, "Call them in, call them in!" and as the door opened thirty or forty musketeers tramped into the House. "This," exclaimed Vane, "is not honest, yea, it is against morality, and common honesty!" And Cromwell, who thought that it was his old friend who had not had common honesty, cried out in the bitterness of his soul, "O Sir Henry Vane! Sir Henry Vane! The Lord deliver me from Sir Henry Vane!"

The members, there were only about fifty present that morning, began to file out. The Speaker, Lenthall, he who eleven years before had told Charles I that he had neither eyes to see, nor tongue to speak in that place, but as the House was pleased to direct him, said that he would not come down until forced. "Sir," said Harrison, "I will give you a hand." Upon which he came down. Then Cromwell, fixing his eyes upon the mace, said, "What shall we do with this bauble? Take it away, take it away!" and a musketeer did so.

And Oliver called out after the departing members: "It's you that have forced me to do this! I have sought the Lord day and night that He would rather slay me than put it upon me to do this thing!" There can be no doubt but that he had.

In his dealings with the Long Parliament, he had acted exactly as he had in the matter of the execution of the King. Up to Christmas Day 1648, he had tried to save Charles I. On the twentieth of January 1649 the High Court of Justice met which was to condemn him to death, and Cromwell was its animating spirit. Up to the nineteenth of April 1653, he had resisted the illegal dissolution of Parliament, opposed every one who advised it, on the twentieth he dissolved it on his own sole responsibility, forcibly and in anger. In both cases he had kept his mind open for a long time, listened to everybody, tried not to act. Then a day came when he closed his mind, listened to no one, acted.

This time he had the approval of the nation. "Not a dog barked at their going." Under cover of night a wit scribbled on the door of Parliament, "This House to let unfurnished."

And there was no link left to bind England to the past, not a vestige of authority, not even a hare swimming over the Thames.

Only Oliver Cromwell, Lord General, and Commander of the Forces in England, Scotland, and Ireland.

He was not to find it any easier. Two years later he told the First Parliament of the Protectorate that even the Long Parliament would have done better than they were doing.

Was it a mistake? Would it have been, as Mr. Buchan says, better for him and for England, to let Parliament blunder and bluster, and to guide it firmly toward self-dissolution? Could he or any man have done that? The old schoolmen used to debate the question, "Does God know what would have happened, if some antecedent thing had happened, which did not happen?" To which the only answer can be, God may know, but we do not.

CHAPTER XVI

Barebone's Parliament

"Truly I will now come and tell you a story of my own weakness and folly. And yet it was done in my simplicity. I dare avow it was. It was thought that men of our own judgment, who had fought in the wars, and were all of a piece upon that account, it was thought, 'Why surely these men will hit it and these men will do it to the purpose, whatsoever can be desired!' And truly we did think, and I did think so, the more blame to me! And such a company of men were chosen, and did proceed into action. And truly this was the naked truth, that the issue was not answerable to the honesty of design."

—OLIVER CROMWELL.

IF Cromwell had been inclined to have any misgivings as to the wisdom of his hasty action in dissolving the Long Parliament, they would have soon been laid at rest, for it made him popular in a sense that he had never been before and was never to be again. The French Ambassador told his Government that "the nobility and populace universally rejoiced at General Cromwell's deed." Hyde, hearing in exile of the expulsion of the Parliament of which he had been a member, called it a "most popular and obliging act." At home the ballad-mongers were singing:

> "Brave Oliver came to the house like a Sprite:
> His fiery face struck the Speaker dumb;
> 'Begone,' said he, 'you that have sat long enough,
> Do you mean to sit here till Doomsday come?'"

There was another popular street song, in which each verse ended with, "Twelve Parliament men shall sell for a penny."

And now that the work of destruction was fully accomplished, and Oliver was the only authority that was left, how would he build up? That was what every one was asking, that was what he was asking himself.

And naturally there were many who thought that he would make himself King, many who would have been glad to have him do so.

Indeed the army officers proposed it, petitions were coming in from all parts of the country asking him to assume the crown, there were even royalists who said that they would rather have him as sovereign than "any other in the three nations." As his son Henry, home from Ireland to be married, strolled about Spring Gardens, there were shouts of "Room for the Prince!" Some one hung a picture of Cromwell with three crowns in the Exchange, beneath it were the words

"Ascend three thrones, great Captain and Divine
By the will of God, O Lion, for they are thine.
.   .   .   .   .
Then shout, O merchants, cits and gentry sing,
Let all men bare head cry, God save the King!"

But when the Lord Mayor took the picture down and asked Oliver what he should do with it, he only laughed, and said such trifles were not to be considered in so serious a time.

For while he had maintained that "a government with somewhat monarchical about it would be very effectual," and while when only a few months before he had asked, "What if a man should take it upon himself to be King?" he was undoubtedly thinking of himself, he had no idea of making himself King at this juncture. For the Lord General to do that, would seem like the permanent establishment of the rule of the army. And he was convinced that now at last the army had really "done its do," and ought to abdicate. It wanted to abdicate, and he wanted to lay down his dictatorship.

But there were some things that he could do in this period of popularity and temporary power. He could for instance pardon poor prisoners, thus anticipating the reform of the law that he so longed for. "To hang a man for six and eight pence, and I know not what," he said, "to hang for a trifle, and acquit for murder, to see men lose their lives for petty offences, this is a thing that God will reckon for." He wished that it were so that "none should hereafter suffer death for theft, because we read not of any such law in the Holy Scriptures." If he could not get the law of England changed, he could at least, in this brief period of absolutism, pardon some who had broken it, and he pardoned many on their way to Tyburn.

And he could try to do something to unite the discordant nation, produce a feeling of general good will. So we find him sending a guard to protect a Presbyterian minister turned out of his pulpit by an Independent, interfering to save Royalists and even Catholics from persecution, so that a newsletter of May 6th reported that he was "very kind to the old malignant party, and some have found much more favour since the late dissolution, than in seven years' solicitation before." Indeed the hopes of the Royalists were so aroused, that some of them even thought that he was planning to restore Charles II. There was a story that Mazarin had proposed to him that Charles marry his daughter, so that his seed might inherit the throne.

But Oliver was not planning to restore the Stuarts, he was trying to devise a plan by which he could lay down his own dictatorship. For he clearly recognized that it was a dictatorship, and worse, a military dictatorship that he, the Lord General of the forces of England, Scotland, and Ireland was absolutely the only authority left in the land. And "in that unlimited condition he did not wish to live a day."

So, soon after the dissolution, he sent for Major Salwey and Mr. John Carew "to whom he complained of the great weight of affairs, that by the undertaking was fallen upon him." The consequences thereof, he said, made him tremble, he desired them to free him of the temptation that might be before him. To that end he asked them to go immediately to Chief Justice St. John, Mr. Selden and some others, and endeavor to persuade them to draw up some instrument of government that would take the power out of his hands. To which Major Salwey replied, "The way, Sir, for you to free yourself of this temptation, is for you not to look upon yourself to be under it, but to rest persuaded that the power of the nation is in the good people of England, as formerly it was."

And that was exactly what Cromwell would have liked to do. But it would have meant a general election. And neither he, nor the Army Council, just as anxious as he was to prove that the Long Parliament had not been turned out to make room for themselves, could see their way clear at that time to a general election. So long as there was no constitution, while everything had to be decided upon, that could only breed confusion worse confounded.

Oliver himself had no plan, and in the Army Council, there were still the two factions, led by Lambert and Harrison. In fact in the reaction in favor of monarchy, each had been talked about as a possible king.

Now Lambert was proposing that there should be first a small

Council, perhaps only ten or twelve, that should draw up a written constitution, more or less on the lines of the Agreement of the People. When that was accomplished, a regular Parliament could be elected.

But Harrison had become an out and out Fifth Monarchy man. The Fourth Monarchy of Daniel, the Roman Empire, was tottering to its fall, now was the time for the saints to take the kingdom and possess it, to set up the laws of God instead of the laws of man. The vacancy of the English throne, the dismissal of the Long Parliament, had clearly prepared the way for King Jesus. So Harrison wanted a nominated Assembly of Saints, perhaps seventy persons, like the Jewish Sanhedrin.

And Cromwell hesitated, seems at first to have inclined toward Lambert's plan. Godly men might make the best rulers, but Parliamentary government would be more acceptable to the people of England. And he knew that no government could be permanent that did not command the affections of the people.

But why not try Harrison's plan, or a modification of Harrison's plan, for a short time, call together a number of godly men, who would "put the nation in some way of certain settlement," and then when they had done their job, hand the government over to a regular Parliament?

So on the twenty-ninth of April, nine days after he had expelled the Parliament, he drew up a proclamation, that to provide for the present government, there was a decemvirate already sitting, seven military men and three civilians, and to this would be added "certain persons of approved fidelity," to be called from various parts of the kingdom.

But he did not publish it for eight days. For he was still hesitating. He really wanted something a little different from what Harrison had in mind, an assembly of real Puritan notabilities. Godliness was not enough, there must be definite achievement, such as would command the respect of the nation. And he hoped to include some who, while they might disapprove of the execution of the King and the expulsion of Parliament, would yet be willing to coöperate in devising some form of government. With this end in view, he offered a seat in the Council to Fairfax. But when Fairfax declined, he felt that others of like mind would do the same. There was nothing then to do but to try Harrison's plan. So on May 6th he issued his proclamation. And as was his wont, when he had once decided to do the thing, he became enthusiastic about it.

Therefore letters were dispatched, in the name of the General and the Council of the Army, to Puritan churches in each county, asking them to send in the names of men fit to be members of the new representative, which the Venetian ambassador said was "to be and not to be a Parliament." When the list was completed, the Army Council might both strike out and add names. Cromwell afterward said that there was not a man of the rank of a captain but named more members than he himself had done.

By the end of June the roll was made up. There were to be a hundred and twenty-nine members for England, five for Scotland, and six for Ireland. It was a larger and more representative assembly than Harrison had proposed. And it consisted, as the writs sent out by Cromwell stipulated, "of men fearing God, and of approved fidelity and honesty." There were some well-known names among them, but not so many as Cromwell wished. Fairfax hesitated, as late as the twentieth of June his name was on the printed list, but then he declined. There was an effort to secure Vane, but he replied that though the reign of the saints was about to begin, he preferred to take his share of it in Heaven.

This strange assembly came together at Whitehall on the fourth of July, 1653. Standing by the window, opposite the middle of the table, the Lord General addressed them. And he certainly spoke the mind of himself and his officers when he told them that they had been called together because of the necessity of divesting the sword of all power and authority in the civil administration. To transform the military state into the civilian state, to lay down the burden which he and his council had found too heavy to bear, and which ought not to be in military hands, "no, not for a day" that was his object. And here was his opportunity.

And yet it was plain that the army was the source of the authority with which this assembly was to be invested. There were as many officers present as the room could well contain, some on his right hand, some on his left.

Then he went off into an ecstatic fervor, showing how thoroughly the scheme at which he had at first hesitated had taken hold of him. For the time being, he might himself have been a Fifth Monarchy man. This was the age of miracles. Why should not God work a miracle through this body of men, as he had through the army? Had not that been "a poor and contemptible company of men, neither versed in military affairs, nor having much natural propensity to them?" Yet God had owned them, blessed them, and furthered all their undertakings. This Parliament was a company of men, perhaps as little versed in political affairs as the army had been in military affairs, perhaps it had no more natural propensity to them. But God could work "in the civil powers and authorities," as He had in the army. This might be the door to usher in the things that God had promised, which had been prophesied of, and which He had set the hearts of His people to wait for and expect. It has been noticed that apocalyptic visions have generally come to men in times of despair. Perhaps the height of Cromwell's apocalypse only measures the depth of his despair.

But just as he thought that the army had been given power by God, but only temporarily, and having performed their mission were now handing it over to this assembly, so he believed that these army nominees were but an intermediate step to handing it over to the people. "Who can tell how soon God may fit the people for such a thing?"

And it was given to them to work together with God to fit them, by showing the people that they loved them, that they laid themselves out, their time and spirits for them, by convincing them that as men fearing God had fought them out of their thralldom and bondage, so men fearing God were now ruling them in the fear of God, and taking care to administer good unto them. They must be just to all, "as just towards an unbeliever, as towards a believer. I confess I have said sometimes, foolishly it may be, that I had rather miscarry to a believer than to an unbeliever. This may seem a paradox, but let's take heed of doing that which is evil to either."

And then, the toleration that was so dear to his heart, that desire for toleration which really lay at the bottom of all his difficulties. They were "to be very much touched with the infirmities of the saints, to have a respect unto all, to be patient and tender towards all, though of different judgments. And if I did seem to speak something that reflected on those of the Presbyterial judgment, truly I think if we have not an interest of love for them too, we shall hardly answer this of being faithful to the saints."

Finally "I beseech you, but I think I need not, have a care of the whole flock. Love the sheep, love the lambs. And if the poorest Christian, the most mistaken Christian, shall desire to live peaceably and quietly under you, I say if any shall desire but to live a life in godliness and honesty, let him be protected."

He ended with the sixty-eighth Psalm, "Let God arise, let His enemies be scattered, let them also that hate Him flee before Him—But let the righteous be glad, let them rejoice before God, yea, let them exceedingly rejoice." "The triumph of that Psalm," he said, "is exceeding high."

And "when the Lord General Cromwell had ended this very grave, Christian and seasonable speech, his Excellency produced an instrument under his own hand and seal," whereby he devolved on them the supreme authority until November 3rd, 1654, and directed them to choose, three months before their dissolution, another assembly to succeed them, the second assembly to sit a twelvemonth, and in that time to make provision for a further succession in government.

That was on the fourth of July. On the twenty-second of August we find Oliver writing to Fleetwood in Ireland: "Truly I never more needed help from my Christian friends than now.—Alas! I am in my temptation ready to say, 'Oh, would I had wings like a dove, then I would fly away and be at rest,' but this, I fear is my haste."

What had so changed his mood? It was only seven weeks since, his heart swelling with enthusiasm, he had made that triumphant, prophetic speech. But in that time there had been much, both without and within Parliament, to disturb him. There had been considerable squabbling between Presbyterians, Independents and Baptists. He had arranged conferences between the ministers of the various sects, and had sought to persuade them to live peacefully together, but in vain. The only result was to make them more or less hostile to himself, "Being of different judgments," he wrote, "and each sort most seeking to propagate its own, that spirit of kindness that is to them all (his spirit) is hardly accepted of any.—It would fall out as when the two Hebrews were rebuked, you know upon whom they turned their displeasure." And then the root of the whole matter, that for which he was always striving, "If every one, instead of contending, would justify his form of judgment by love and meekness, Wisdom would be justified of her children."

Among the Presbyterians there had been a strong recrudescence of Royalist feeling. Presbyterian ministers were openly telling their congregations that England would never be happy without a king, and the Episcopalians were also asserting themselves. Before the end of July it was noticed that there was a great increase in the number of conventicles for common prayer, at which the prospects of a Restoration were freely discussed.

But the greatest, or at least the most turbulent opposition, came from the Fifth Monarchy men, whose preachers were describing the parochial clergy as "hirelings," and "priests of Baal," and the Church as the "outworks of Babylon, part of the Kingdom of the Beast," and declaring that Christ would destroy all such anti-Christian forms as churches and clergy all over the world. In private they were caballing to make Harrison Lord General instead of Cromwell.

And worst of all Lilburn was back in England, making trouble. For a libel against Haselrigg the Long Parliament had, in January 1652, banished him from England, on pain of death if he returned. Whether Cromwell had any part in this or not, does not appear. On the Continent he had made friends with Royalist exiles, there had previously been a little leaning toward Royalists on the part of the Levelers. Now he was reported to have said that with ten thousand pounds he could set Charles Stuart on the throne. Learning of the dissolution of the Long Parliament, he petitioned Cromwell to allow him to return to England. To this Cromwell made no reply, but in June 1653 he returned. The Council of State ordered the Attorney General to prosecute him. Sympathetic crowds flocked to the trial. He argued that if Cromwell had turned out the Long Parliament justly, its unjust action in banishing him ought not to be maintained, if unjustly Cromwell ought to be punished. He was acquitted, London rejoiced, and even the soldiers who guarded the Court joined in the general acclamation. That was on August 20th, two days before Cromwell wrote his despairing letter to Fleetwood, perhaps it had something to do with his mood.

That did not end the trouble made by Lilburn. On the night of September 14th his followers scattered in the streets printed broadsides, accusing Oliver Cromwell of high treason "to their lords, the people of England." The breaking up of the Long Parliament, it was argued, was probably justifiable, but the omission after that dissolution, to entreat "the lords, the people of England" to elect representatives according to their indubitable right, that was high treason. The people of England were invited to convene on the sixteenth day of October, in their several counties, to elect "a true Parliament, by manhood suffrage." This manifesto ended with an appeal to the soldiers. No doubt some of them had imbibed Lilburnian principles, that was very dangerous.

And within the godly Assembly that he had called together, there was not much to comfort Cromwell. On July 6th, it voted to assume the name of Parliament. Then it proceeded to the reform of the law, which Cromwell had so long urged. After a very short debate, it was voted to abolish the Court of Chancery, and a committee appointed to reform the law talked of reducing the great volumes "into the bigness of a pocket book as is proportionable in New England and elsewhere." Certainly something should have been done about the Court of Chancery, its delays and costliness were causing great scandal, at this time there were twenty-three thousand cases of from five to ten years' standing undetermined. It would be well also to simplify the law. But in the body that undertook this stupendous task so glibly, there was not a single practicing lawyer. No wonder that Cromwell was aghast. "I am more troubled now," he said to a friend, "with the fool than with the knave."

And when they took hold of the Church, it was with the same idea that old things had passed away, that all things had become new. The Fifth Monarchy men, not content with denouncing the parochial clergy as "hirelings," were teaching that the Church itself was an "outwork of Babylon" and part of the "Kingdom of the Beast." It was the duty of the Saints to destroy Babylon. There should be no organized Church, nothing but lay preachers.

There was a strong party in Parliament that sympathized with them, and hoped that Cromwell would do so too. But he was beginning to feel like many a modern today, who has fought against Victorian conventionalities and hypocrisies, yet now could almost wish to see them back again. He had always defended lay preachers, but he was alarmed at this tendency to go to the other extreme. "The former extremity that we suffered under," he said to the first Parliament of the Protectorate, "was that no man, though he had never so good a testimony, might preach, unless ordained. So now I think we are at the other extremity, when many affirm that he who is ordained, hath a nullity, or an Anti-christianism, stamped thereby upon his calling, so he ought not to preach or ought not to be heard."

On the second of December the Committee on Tithes presented a scheme for reorganizing the Church. They recommended that itinerant commissioners be appointed to eject unfit ministers, and to fill vacant livings, that the present provision for maintanance of approved ministers be guaranteed by Parliament, that for the present tithes be continued, but suggested a plan for their commutation in cases of conscientious objectors. On this plan, very similar to Oliver's, there were prolonged debates. On Saturday, December 10th, the vote was taken. The first clause of the report was rejected, fifty-six votes against it, fifty-four for it. This was regarded as tantamount to the rejection of the whole scheme, indeed to the rejection of an established Church altogether.

That alarmed Cromwell, and in fact alarmed the majority of the

Parliament. For the truth was that, even in this Parliament of the Saints, the moderates were in a majority, there were eighty-four of them against sixty extremists. But moderates are moderates, even in advocating moderation, while extremists are always extreme in advocating extremes. So the extremists were always in their places, while the moderates, wearied by long and foolish debate, were often not there when matters came to a vote.

But this vote alarmed the moderate party. The next day, Sunday, they held consultations with various army officers, apparently not with Cromwell. Monday morning they were up betimes, and before many members of the opposing party, which now called itself the Godly Party, got there, they voted their own dissolution. It was moved and carried "that the sitting of this Parliament any longer, as now constituted, will not be for the good of the Commonwealth; and that therefore it is requisite to deliver up unto the Lord General Cromwell the power which we received from him." The debate was very short. When there was an attempt to spin it out until there was a fuller House, old Rouse, the Speaker, whose version of the Psalms is so familiar to Presbyterians, rose from the chair without stopping to put the question and, preceded by the mace, accompanied by the clerk of the House and fifty or sixty members, marched off to Whitehall. There they proceeded to sign a paper (eventually about eighty signed), returning their powers to Cromwell. Twenty-seven stayed behind in the House, and proceeded to draw up a protest. Two Colonels entered, and ordered them out. They at first refused to go unless there was a command from the Lord General that they should. The Colonels had no such order from Cromwell, but when they fetched in two files of musketeers, the members dispersed. Thus ended this strange assembly, to be known afterwards as "Barebone's" Parliament, because a certain Praise-God Barebone happened to sit in it. Unfortunately this has given the false impression that such names were common among the Puritans. They were not.

Cromwell had had nothing to do with these proceedings. "I can say it," he afterward said, "in the presence of divers persons here, who know whether I lie or not, that I did not know one tittle of the resignation, till they all came and brought it, and delivered it into my hands." But doubtless he was relieved by it.

He had said a few months before that Major-General Harrison was "urging him on to that which he and all honest men will have cause to repent." But he had finally adopted Harrison's plan with modifications. Whether Harrison repented of it or not, Cromwell did. Later he spoke of it as "a story of his own weakness and folly." "And yet," he said, "it was done in my simplicity. It was thought that men of our own judgment, who had fought in the wars, and were all of a piece on that account, why surely these men will hit it, and these men will do it to the purpose, whatever can be desired. And such a company of men were chosen, and did proceed to action. And this was the naked truth, that the issue was not answerable to the simplicity and honesty of the design."

As he said, he had had his disappointment, and would not again repeat the experiment. But it "had had much teaching in it, and he hoped that it might make them all wiser for the future." It had taught him once for all, how difficult it was to find the saints, and perhaps that the saints, when found, would not necessarily be the best rulers.

But he was again in the position which he wished to avoid, and from which again he must find some way of escape. "My own power," he said, "was again by this resignation as boundless and unlimited as before, all things being subjected to arbitrariness, and myself the only constituted authority that was left, a person having power over the three nations, without bounds or limits set." And Vavasour Powell was advising his congregation to go home and pray and say, "Lord, wilt Thou have Oliver Cromwell or Jesus Christ to rule over us?" At Blackfriars he was being called "the Old Dragoon" and "the Man of Sin."

And again it was the army officers who offered the solution. For if the army was not to rule, it alone was in a position to decide who should. For some time the officers had been alarmed, not only by the political and religious situation, but also by the fact that Parliament was not acting honorably with respect to the capitulations made with royalist commanders, and was also opposing the renewal of monthly assessments for the maintenance of the army. So they had already evolved a plan, which they had been pressing upon Oliver for some time.

And this time it was Lambert and his party who were getting the upper hand. They had reverted to the idea of a written constitution. Under that, they would at least know where they stood. Such a constitution had been in preparation during October and November. It differed from the Instrument of Government, afterward adopted, chiefly in the fact that the chief executive was to be King, rather than Protector. In 1648, when the Agreement of the People was prepared, the main idea had been to check the executive. But conditions had changed, now it was Parliament that must be checked.

Toward the end of November this Instrument was submitted to Cromwell. "They told me then," he said, "that except I would undertake the Government, they thought things would hardly come to a settlement, but blood and confusion would follow." He refused. Much as he was in favor of a government with something monarchical about it, he felt that he himself could not accept the title of King, and especially when it was offered him by the army; that would seem like a continuation of the military rule that must come to an end. Moreover, he had empowered the Little Parliament to sit until the end of 1654. One Parliament was enough to expel by force of arms. His answer was given December 1st.

But eleven days later the Little Parliament dissolved itself. Then there seemed to be nothing for him to do but to accept the accomplished fact, and undertake the task offered to him. Some one must undertake it, and there was no one else. He accepted it, but his title was to be Protector, not King.

CHAPTER XVII

The Protectorate

"One thing now this government hath done, it hath been instrumental to call a Free Parliament, which, blessed be God, we see here this day.—It's that which I have desired above my life.—And if this day this meeting, prove not healing, what shall we do?"—OLIVER CROMWELL.

ON the sixteenth of December 1653 Oliver Cromwell was installed as Lord Protector of England, Scotland and Ireland. Henceforth he was to sign himself not Oliver Cromwell, but Oliver P. For he was no longer His Excellency, the Lord General, but His Highness, the Lord Protector. And again his buoyant optimism asserted itself, it was a new beginning. He always threw himself so eagerly into new beginnings! And this time the goal seemed in sight, the goal that he had been aiming at through six troubled years! Now at last he could divest the sword of all civil authority! Military rule would soon be over, the rule that he was beginning to find as irksome to him as it was to the nation. He and the nation would soon be free together! So he took the oath of office, clad not in scarlet as a general, but in black as a civilian.

And he was to have a free Parliament, not a close oligarchy, but a Parliament that would represent the nation as no English Parliament had represented it before. For there was to be a redistribution of seats, according to the general plan of the Agreement of the People. In the counties the franchise was to be extended to all who possessed personal property to the value of two hundred pounds. And while in the boroughs the various franchises of the pre-war period were to be continued, inasmuch as the number of the county members had greatly increased, the borough members were not as large a proportion of the whole as they had been. No one who had assisted the King in the war could vote in the next Parliamentary election, or sit in any of the next four Parliaments, but that was a temporary arrangement. Roman Catholics and those who had aided in the Irish Rebellion were permanently disqualified.

There was to be but one House, it was to meet at least once in three years, and to remain in session at least five months. On its legislation the Protector had no veto, he could only ask it to reconsider. All Bills were to be presented to him for signature, but if after twenty days he had not given his consent, or persuaded Parliament to withdraw the Bill, it became law, unless it were contrary to the Instrument of Government.

There was to be a Council, upon whose advice the Protector was supposed to act, the members of the first Council named in the Instrument, vacancies to be filled by a rather complicated joint action of Protector, Council and Parliament. When Parliament was not in session, the Protector and Council might pass ordinances, to be regarded as law until Parliament confirmed or rejected them.

The country, with the exception of the Levelers and Lilburnians, accepted the new constitution not enthusiastically, but as necessary for the times, the only protection against anarchy on the one hand, and military rule on the other. And Oliver accepted it in the same way. He had not much faith in written constitutions, but when nations break entirely with their past, they are necessary. Moreover, anything to get away from military rule! And to him the crowning merit of the Instrument was that it assured religious toleration for so long a time as the Government established by it should stand.

For inasmuch as none knew better than the army officers that the people did not really want toleration, and that no Parliament that they were likely to elect would want it, they had arranged to make it impossible for either an intolerant Parliament, or an intolerant people to disturb it. The Christian religion as contained in the Scriptures was to be "held forth and recommended as the public profession of the nation." There were to be "able and painful teachers for the instructing of the people, and for discovery and confutation of errors, heresy, and whatever is contrary to sound doctrine," and until some better arrangement could be made, they were to be maintained by tithes, as heretofore. But no one should be compelled, either by penalties or otherwise, to the public profession held forth. On the contrary, all who professed faith in God through Jesus Christ, "though differing in judgment from the doctrine, worship or discipline publicly set forth," were only not to be restrained from, but were even to be protected in the profession of their faith and exercise of their religion, "so they abuse not this liberty to the civil liberty of others, or to the actual disturbance of the public peace." For political reasons, however, this liberty was not to be extended to Popery and Prelacy (in this the Instrument was narrower than some of the preceding plans had been) ; and for the maintenance of morality, it was not to be extended to "such as, under the profession of Christ, hold forth and practice licentiousness."

According to the Instrument, the first Parliament of the Protectorate was not to meet until September 1654. That gave Oliver nine months in which, with the advice of the Council, he might issue ordinances, which had the force of laws "until order shall be taken in Parliament concerning them." He was very diligent about it, between December 1653 and September 1654, he issued eighty-two such Ordinances. Most of these were confirmed by the second Parliament of the Protectorate, but all were annulled at the Restoration, many of them to be reënacted in the nineteenth century.

There was an ordinance establishing the union of Scotland with England, and another for the distribution of seats in Ireland. There was an ordinance against dueling, another which forbade cock-fighting because it led to the disturbance of the peace, and was frequently accompanied by gaming and drunkenness. Another suppressed horse-racing for six months, because the Cavaliers made use of race meetings to carry out their designs. But at the very time that Oliver was suppressing cock-fighting, as being a practice that led to "sundry evils dishonouring to God and ruinous to men," he himself attended a hurling and wrestling match. He no longer had the time for these things that he used to have, but he availed himself of such opportunities as came to him, for he had no objection to sport as sport. He said later that he had discovered that there was "a great deal of grudging, because we cannot again have our horse races." He did not "think that these were lawful, except to make them recreations. But it was folly not to be able to endure it when they were for necessary ends (preventing Royalist plots) abridged of them." And when in 1656 Lord Exeter asked Major-General Whalley whether he would allow the Lady Grantham cup to be run for at Lincoln, "I assured him," Whalley reported to the Protector, "that it was not your Highness' intention in the suppressing of horse races, to abridge gentlemen of that sport, but to prevent the great confluence of irreconcileable enemies." Lord Exeter got his horse race.

But now as always, it was the religious question that interested Oliver most. The Instrument of Government had provided for an Established Church with toleration. Now was the time to put Oliver's scheme into effect. For the doings of the last few weeks had convinced him, if he had needed convincing, that there should be a Church endowed and supervised by the State. He hoped to be able to make this church so broad that there would be very few outside to tolerate. But these must be tolerated.

So in March an ordinance was issued, appointing a Committee of Triers to examine into the qualifications of all candidates for livings. No doctrinal tests were to be imposed. But no one could be admitted to a benefice except as the Committee found him to be "a person for the grace of God in him, his holy and unblameable conversation, as also for his knowledge and utterance, able and fit to preach the Gospel." Outside this ministry there might, of course, be preachers, but they were not to receive the public maintenance and stipend.

In August there was another ordinance, appointing Commissioners of Ejectors, for ejection of "scandalous and inefficient ministers and schoolmasters," no matter at what date they had been appointed. It will be noticed that Oliver had his eye upon education as well as upon religion, perhaps largely because he regarded it as the hand-maid, or even foster mother, of religion. Not only did he make pro-vision for competent masters in the lower schools, he appointed com-missioners to visit the public schools and universities. While in Scotland, he was made Chancellor of the University of Oxford, and Clarendon testifies that Oxford under him "yielded a harvest of extraordinary good and sound knowledge in all parts of learning." He defended her endowments, presented manuscripts to the Bodleian, was interested in her individual scholars. "If there was a man in England," says Neal, "who excelled in any faculty or science, the Protector would find him out, and reward him according to his merit." To Dr. Cudworth of Cambridge he gave orders to "mark among the ingenious youths of that University such as he deemed fit for public employment, and make him aware of them." And he was planning a new University at Durham.

While the Commissioners of Triers moved from place to place to examine candidates, the Commissioners of Ejectors were local com-mittees, fifteen to thirty gentlemen in each county, with ten or twelve divines. Most of the well-known English gentlemen and clergy of the day were included in their membership, some of them not ad-herents of Cromwell, among others Richard Baxter.

And Baxter has a very good word to say for these Commissioners. "To give them their due," he tells us, "they did abundance of good to the Church. They saved many a congregation from ignorant, un-godly, drunken teachers—from all those that used the ministry but as a common trade to live by. While they may have been a little partial to Independents, Separatists, Fifth Monarchy men and Anabaptists, yet so great was the benefit above the harm to the Church, that many thousands of souls blessed God for the faithful ministers that they let in." He also found Cromwell himself an exemplary patron. For "having near one half the livings in England in his own immediate disposal, he seldom bestoweth one of them upon any man, whom himself doth not first examine, and make trial of in person, save only at such times as his great affairs happen to be more urgent than ordinary, he useth to appoint some others to do it in his behalf; which is so rare an example of piety that the like is not to be found in the stories of princes."

Baxter did not like Oliver, he was convinced that he had worked all along for his own aggrandizement, that he had even "caused and permitted distractions to hang over us to necessitate the Nation, whether they would or not, to take him for their Governor." Yet he was constrained to admit that he "soon saw that it was his design to do good in the main, except in those particulars that his own interest was against, and to promote the Gospel and the interest of godliness, more than any one had done before."

Outside the national Church, the Instrument had guaranteed liberty of worship to "all such as do profess faith in God by Jesus Christ," except that Popery and Prelacy, regarded as idolatrous and politically dangerous, were excepted by name. But though the Liturgy had been prohibited since 1645, many Anglican clergy retained their livings, sometimes using portions of the Prayer Book from memory, in other cases confining themselves to preaching and the Sacraments. And many Episcopal congregations met in private houses, and were not molested.

Next to the reform of the Church, the Protector was most interested in the reform of the law, especially in cutting down the number of capital offenses. He wanted to make the English law "conformable to the just and righteous laws of God." But unlike the Saints of Barebone's Parliament, he realized his ignorance on that subject. "If any one should say to me, 'How would you have it done?' " he said, "I confess that I do not know." So he appealed to the lawyers to help him, "being resolved to give the learned of the robe the honour of reforming their own profession," and "hoping that God would stir them up to do it." Again there was a commission of lawyers with Matthew Hale at the head, to "consider how the laws might be made plain and short, and less chargeable to the people." And they prepared several Bills.

So Oliver was very busy, apparently successful, and probably fairly happy, during those first nine months of the Protectorate. There was, of course, some trouble with Republicans and Levelers. Christopher Peak and Vavasour Powell were denouncing him from the pulpit as the "dissemblingest perjured villain in the world," and bidding any one present to repeat it to him, and tell him that his reign would be short. And there was a Royalist plot against his life. But on the whole those early days of the Protectorate were a period of comparative ease and calm. It was when he had to meet his first Parliament that his troubles began again in earnest.

In that first Parliament the majority were either Presbyterians or moderate Independents. The experience with the Little Parliament had made the country conservative. But it had made Oliver conservative too, so he had no fault to find. He was pleased to hear that "the Presbyterians were fully reconciled to the Government, walk hand to hand with the true-hearted Independents as to civil matters." And he "favoured them greatly," for he hoped that they might become "a great strength to the Settlement."

Indeed such was his confidence in his position, that when a proposition was made in the Council to ask the members to accept personally the engagement already taken for them by their constituents, that they would do nothing to alter the Government as settled in a Single Person and a Parliament, he rejected it on the ground that it would only lead to irritation, and the Instrument had not empowered the Council to make such a demand. He was to change his mind later.

The third of September, the day of Dunbar and Worcester, was considered Oliver's fortunate day. So it had been chosen for the opening of this first Parliament of the Protectorate. But as it happened that year to fall on a Sunday, there was only a brief meeting with him in the Painted Chamber after a service in the Abbey. The next day he addressed them. He was full of relief and hopefulness. Now the army might indeed give up. The Constitution, it was true, had been drawn up by the officers, but the constituencies had accepted it, and there was at least a Parliament elected by the people, in some respects more representative of the people than any Parliament had been before.

So, after reporting upon what had been accomplished thus far, especially for the Church and for the Law, he announced as the crowning achievement, "One thing more this Government hath done, it hath been instrumental to call a Free Parliament, which, blessed be God, we see here this day. And that it may continue so, I hope is in the heart and spirit of every good man in England. . . . It's that which

I have desired above my life, so I shall desire to keep it so above my life."

That morning the Rev. Thomas Goodwin had preached a sermon in the Abbey, in which he had found much that he liked. He had spoken on "Israel's bringing out of the Wilderness into a Place of Rest." Egypt was the old Prelacy, and the Stuart rule; the Wilderness, all that the English people had been through since then; the Protectorate, or what it might lead to, the Place of Rest. And Cromwell's heart beat high, he too felt that they were reaching a Place of Rest. And that Goodwin especially reprobated the latter part of that wilderness way, the cry for leveling in the State, and voluntarism in the Church, was not displeasing to him.

For he himself had little that was good to say of the Levelers, and he made no distinction between the followers of Lilburn, and the followers of Winstanley. A typical Englishman, he stood for Order, and the kind of order that Englishmen knew. And these men were trying to upset all that, all those things "whereby England hath been known for hundreds of years. A nobleman, a gentleman, a yeoman, the distinction of these, that is a good interest in the nation, and a great one! The natural magistracy of the nation, was it not almost trampled under foot, under despite and contempt, by men of levelling principles?"

And while he still believed in liberty of conscience and liberty of the subject, "two as glorious things to be contended for as any that God has given" he maintained that "both of these are often abused for the patronising of villainies." In this and in his defense of an established church, "to put a stop to that heady way of every man making himself a minister," he seemed to many to have gone back on some of his former utterances. But like Abraham Lincoln he had an aim, but no policy, when the tent blew too much over on one side, he put in a peg on the other.

As for the Fifth Monarchy men, he admitted that there were among them "many honest people, whose hearts are sincere, many belonging to Christ." But "for men to entitle themselves on this principle, that they are the only men to rule, truly they had need to give clear manifestation of God's presence with them, before wise men will receive, or submit to their conclusions." Such manifestation had not been given by the members of Barebone's Parliament. There had been nothing in their hearts and minds but "Overturn, overturn, overturn!"

But now the wilderness period was over, a door of hope had been opened, they were within sight of the Promised Land. And it was for this Parliament to put the topstone to the work, and make the

nation happy. "And therefore I wish you to go forward, and not backward." They had been called together in the hope that through them
the Ship of the Commonwealth might be brought into a safe harbor.
The end of their meeting was Healing and Settling. "And if this day,
this meeting, prove not healing, what shall we do?"

Alas! not yet was the Ship of State to be brought unto the desired
haven. That day's meeting was not to prove Healing and Settling.
Oliver had said that this was a Free Parliament, and that he had desired above his life to keep it so. But its members did not consider
themselves free, while acting under an Instrument drawn up by the
army officers, rather than by themselves. In January 1649 Parliament
had claimed to be the supreme power in the State, representing the
sovereign people. A body that had made that claim could not accept
a constitution drawn up by the army.

So on Thursday, September 7th, (Oliver had made his speech on
Monday), a resolution was carried to refer the Instrument to a Committee of the Whole House. As there was a strong Republican element
in the House, there was a motion to settle the government not in a
Single Person and Parliament, but in Parliament alone. It was argued
that power should not be put into the hands of one man, after so much
blood had been spilt to put it into the hands of the people. But as the
majority did not really wish to unseat the Protector, but only to assert
the paramount power of Parliament, this motion was changed so as
to read "in a Parliament and a Single Person qualified with such instructions as Parliament should see fit."

No doubt Oliver himself would have preferred to receive his power
from Parliament rather than from the army. Oxenstiern, the Swedish
ambassador, had told Whitelocke that but one thing remained for the
Protector to do, "to get him a back and breast of steel." When asked
what he meant, he had replied "I mean the confirmation of his being
Protector by your Parliament, which will be his best and greatest
strength." And probably the Protector agreed with him.

But it soon became evident that what this Parliament chiefly wanted
was the power to do away with the broad toleration so dear to him and
to the army officers, an Instrument of Government, in which the clause
decreeing toleration for all time, should be stricken out. That was the
price that they demanded for "the back and breast of steel."

And strangely enough, it was the Republican element, generally Independent, that at first pushed this demand even more energetically
than did the Presbyterian. It was Haselrigg, the man whom Lilburn
had libeled, and got banished from England therefor, the man who

perhaps more than any other, had been responsible for the action of the Long Parliament which had led Cromwell to expel it, who, even as early as Tuesday, two days before the motion to refer the Instrument to a Committee of the Whole, had demanded that religion be made their first care. Now Haselrigg was supposed to be an Independent, but he was primarily a Republican. Therefore he was willing even to cast aside Independency and Toleration, if only he could establish a Republic without a Protector. So, knowing that there were many Presbyterians in Parliament, he proposed that they establish "one good form," and suppress sects.

The next move was to declare that no questions should be reserved from Parliamentary legislation, that is, that Parliament and not the Instrument, should determine whether there was to be toleration or not. On Monday, September 11th, it was voted that an Assembly of Divines, nominated by Parliament, be summoned to advise on such matters as that body should lay before it. Evidently this was to do away with the toleration of the Instrument, and of the Protector's Ordinance, and to establish an intolerant Church.

And that was just the price that Oliver would not pay for his "back and breast of steel." He had longed for Parliamentary government, but only because it was the form of government to which the people were accustomed, therefore probably the only form under which England could have peace and quietness. So he had "desired a free Parliament above his life." But he desired religious toleration even more than he desired a free Parliament, because he believed that it was fundamentally right, right in the sight of God.

And herein lay the root of all his difficulties. He had once said that Major General Harrison "aimed at good things, yet from the impatience of his spirit, would not await the Lord's leisure." In this matter of toleration, it may be said that that was true of Oliver himself. He could not bring himself to allow a Parliament, freely elected by the people, to do wrong in this respect, in the hope that in time they and the people would learn by experience. He was bent upon forcing England several generations ahead of her time.

But consider his position. If he had been a modern King, he would have had no real responsibility in the matter. If he had been a modern Prime Minister, he would have resigned, and let the majority have its way, but the responsibility for the wrong action would not have been his. He was not a modern King, he did have a real responsibility. He was not a modern Prime Minister, he could not resign.

So, on Tuesday the 12th, only eight days after his first address to

the House, he again summoned its members to the Painted Chamber,
and fairly poured out his heart to them, in what is perhaps the most
notable speech that he ever made. First he told them the story of
his own life, how he was "by birth a gentleman, living neither in any
considerable height, nor yet in obscurity." How he had been called
to several employments in the nation, and had endeavored "to discharge the duties of an honest man in these services to God and His
people's interest, and to that of the Commonwealth" and of how, step
by step, steps which could not have been foreseen, he had been brought
to the Protectorate. "I have not called myself unto this place, I say
that I have not called myself unto this place!" he repeated it again
and again. It was only when all government had been dissolved, and
there was nothing to keep things in order but the sword, that he had
consented to take upon himself an office, which indeed had limited
rather than increased his power.

He had told them that they were a free Parliament, but he had
thought that they understood that he was Protector. And he insisted
if he was not Protector, then they were not a Parliament. For it was
only the Instrument of Government which had made him a Protector
that had made them a Parliament. And this Instrument had been read
at the various places of election, and the voters had agreed that the
Persons chosen by them "should not have power to alter the Government, as it was now settled in a Single Person and a Parliament."
And now for you to sit, and not own the authority by which you sit,—
doth as dangerously disappoint and decompose the nation, as any thing
that could be invented by the greatest enemy to our peace and welfare, or that could well have happened." They were decomposing the
nation just at the time when he was hoping that it was possible to
compose it. That was the agony of it. But in reality the pity of it
was that in their opposition to toleration, the nation was probably
more in sympathy with them than with him, the main difference of
opinion being as to who should be the persecutor, and who should be
the persecuted. That was the tragedy of it. "That," he said, "hath
been one of the vanities of our contest. Every sect saith Oh, give me
liberty! But give it to him, and in his power he will not yield it to
any one else."

Yet he was not averse to Parliament revising the Instrument of
Government, in fact he was rather pleased to have them do so, for
he too did not wish a constitution drawn up wholly by the army.
Provided four Fundamentals were retained, Government by a Single
Person and a Parliament, Provision against Parliaments making them-

selves perpetual, Liberty of Conscience, and a Joint Control of the Militia by Protector and Parliament. "These must be delivered over to posterity, as the fruit of our blood and travail," the army's blood and travail. Anything else they might change.

And it is evident to one who reads his speech that it was the third fundamental that was essential to him, the others were largely for the sake of that. For "that *ought* to be so. It is for us and for the generations to come."

He ended by telling them that now he must do "what at first upon a just confidence he had forborne to do." He must put a stop to their entrance into the Parliament House until they had signed a paper, pledging themselves to be faithful to the Commonwealth and Protector, and not to alter the Government, as settled in a Single Person and Parliament. This was after all no more than to give their personal assent to the terms on which they had been elected. Nevertheless, he said, and one can still feel the emotion in his voice, "I am sorry, I am sorry, and I could be sorry to the death that this is necessary!" But he could "sooner be willing to be rolled in his grave, and buried with infamy, than he could give his consent to the wilful throwing away of this Government, so owned by God, and approved by men."

About a hundred irreconcilables, mainly Republicans, refused to sign. Having got rid of them he got on fairly well for a time with those that were left. Indeed he seemed to get on better with them than with the horses in which he had always delighted. On October 14th we find a foreign Ambassador writing home, "The Protector might better have sat in his chair in the Painted Chamber to govern the Parliament, which is more pliable to his pleasure, than on the coach box to govern horses, which have more courage to put him off the box, than the three hundred members of Parliament have to put him out of his chair." For on September 24th, Oliver, accompanied by Thurloe, had "taken the air" in Hyde Park, in a coach drawn by six spirited horses, the gift of the Duke of Oldenburg. Moved by his habitual desire to manage horses, he had changed places with his coachman. But this time he did not know his horses. He used the whip too freely, was jerked forward, thrown first on the pole, then on the ground, his foot caught in the reins, and a pistol exploded in his pocket. There were some scratches, and a slight wound in the leg, so that it was some days before he could leave his room. But it might have been much more serious.

As for the House, there was no difficulty at all about the first two fundamentals. An article was passed giving supreme power to the Protector and Parliament, and a Triennial Bill provided against perpetual Parliaments. An effort was made to keep the Council, like a modern Cabinet, in constant harmony with Parliament, by enacting that the Councilors should be nominated by the Protector, and approved by Parliament, and that none of them was to retain office more than forty days after the election of a new Parliament, except as that Parliament should pass a vote of confidence in them. As Oliver's accident had made the necessity for providing for the succession to the Protectorate very conspicuous, that matter was taken up, and it was decided that the Council should elect, except when Parliament happened to be sitting, in which case the election should be as Parliament saw fit.

Thus far Oliver had no particular objections. But the last two fundamentals, the two that he cared most about, were not to go so well.

As for religious toleration, the proposal for an Assembly of Divines was dropped, instead there was a committee to consider ecclesiastical arrangements. There was no objection to an Established Church in which, according to the Instrument, "the true reformed religion, as it is contained in the Holy Scriptures, shall be asserted and maintained, as the public profession of religion." But who was to decide what that "true reformed religion, as contained in the Holy Scriptures" was? And what was to be done with those whose consciences forbade them to accept that decision?

One thing Oliver had thought that the Instrument of Government had settled. There were to be no Bills restraining tender consciences, unless they "abused their liberty to the prejudice of the civil liberty of others, or to the disturbance of the public peace." Parliament assumed that as a matter of course there would be such Bills, but it was willing to concede that the Protector's consent was necessary before they could become law. And there was a proviso to the effect that Parliament without the Protector might pass Bills for the restraint of "atheism, blasphemy, damnable heresies, popery, prelacy, licentiousness, and profaneness." That would always leave the question open as to what "damnable heresies" were, and on that subject not only might Protector and Parliament differ, but different Parliaments would vary in their judgments.

But the House was more interested in the fundamentals that should be required in the Established Church. And the Common Councilors of the City were preparing a petition to encourage Parliament in the settlement of Church government, evidently intolerantly. "When," sighed Oliver, "shall we have men of a universal spirit? Every one desires to have liberty, but none will grant it." It will be remembered that the Ordinance establishing the Triers required no theological examination of candidates for state stipends. And Cromwell wished that to remain so.

He had been worried about the matter for some time. As early as November 16th, a committee had come to him to ask his advice on matters relating to toleration. It found him in a hopeless, irritable mood, and he answered that "he was wholly dissatisfied with the thing, and had no propensity or inclination to it; that the Parliament had already taken the government abroad, and had altered or changed it in other matters, without his advice, and therefore it would not become him to give any advice at all, simply and apart as to this matter."

Indeed it was an ill time that they had chosen to come to him. At that moment he was troubled and saddened by another matter. On that day, his mother, in her ninetieth year, lay dying. That evening when her wearied and anxious son visited her for the last time, she gave him her final blessing in words which must have remained with him during the little time that he himself had yet to live. "The Lord cause His face to shine upon you, comfort you in all your adversities" (to her, so near to him, the Protectorate was not splendor, but adversity, for she knew that it was so to him), "and enable you to do things for the glory of the Most High God, and to be a relief unto His People. My dear son, I leave my heart with thee. A good night!" The next day she was gone. Except for the year at Cambridge, and the five years at St. Ives, he had always lived with her, or she with him.

But a public man has no time to indulge in private grief. The Committee on Ecclesiastical Affairs was at that time listening to certain divines who were urging acceptance of the fundamentals formulated in 1652 (when Oliver had said that he would rather see Mohammedans in England than that a single Christian should suffer persecution), as conditions of toleration. Owen still stood out for these, and was supported by all his colleagues, except Baxter and Viner. Baxter proposed that nothing be required except the Lord's Prayer, the Apostles' Creed, and the Decalogue. Even that was not broad enough for Oliver, but at least Baxter was worth arguing with. So he summoned him to an interview, but this time he was not in his usual mood of preferring to make others talk, rather than to talk himself. Baxter tells us that he smothered him with a torrent of words, to which he was not permitted to reply. Probably the loss of his mother, added to the terrific anxieties about the Cause nearest to his heart, had unnerved him.

But his conduct did not help a good man, rather bent on misunderstanding him, to understand him any better. Baxter was convinced that Cromwell was working for his own aggrandizement, and he had now come to the conclusion that it was with this end in view that he had encouraged the sects from the beginning. So on Christmas Eve when he preached in Westminster Abbey, "Cromwell and many honourable members of Parliament being the chief part of the audience," he chose as his text, "Now I beseech you, brethren, through the name of our Lord Jesus Christ, that there be no divisions among you," and he pointed out how mischievous a thing it was for politicians to maintain such divisions for their own ends, that they might keep the Church, through its divisions, in a state of weakness, lest it should be able to offend them. Such was his prejudiced interpretation of the man who was risking everything that he might keep the unity of the Spirit, in the bond of peace, rather than the impossible, and if possible, intellectually deadening unity of form and doctrine.

But Cromwell had got used to prejudiced interpretations. In January we find him writing to a friend, "If I mistake not, my exercise of that little faith and patience I have was never greater." For "such as fear the Lord" were "divided in opinion, and ready to fall foul upon one another—so that whoever labours to walk with an even foot between the several interests of the people of God—is sure to have reproaches and anger from some of all sorts."

The House continued its intolerant legislation. It was voted to exclude damnable heresies from toleration, even without the consent of the Protector. Only by a great effort did Oliver's friends succeed in carrying a Resolution that such heresies should at least be enumerated beforehand. And it was decided that Parliament was to have the sole right of legislating against atheism, blasphemy, Popery, Prelacy, licentiousness and profaneness, and those who openly attacked, by speech or in print, doctrines set forth as the public profession.

As an example of its views on blasphemy, on January 15th the House appointed a committee to prepare charges against John Biddle, to be known later as the Father of English Unitarianism. The Long Parliament had in 1648 passed an Ordinance punishing deniers of the Trinity and Incarnation with death. But during the period of Army and Independent ascendancy it would appear not to have been enforced, and Biddle had promulgated his doctrines without let or hindrance. But now he was summoned before Parliament, condemned to prison, while his book was to be publicly burnt. Now even Cromwell was inclined to draw the line at "men who denied the divinity of Our Saviour," and thus made other Christians idolaters. But he hated persecution more than he hated heresy. If Biddle remained in England, he might be put to death, so he sent him to the Scilly Islands, and subsequently released him. After the Restoration he was again arrested, and died in prison.

As for the fundamentals to be accepted by the Established Church, the divines who had been called in consultation presented a list of twenty. "Their propositions were printed for the Parliament, but the Parliament was dissolved, all came to nothing, that labour was lost."

And no doubt Oliver was relieved that it came "to nothing," but it was not directly in order that the labor expended upon it might be lost, that he dissolved the House. The final break was to come on the control of the army.

For during the weeks that Parliament had been discussing the third of the fundamentals, it had also been discussing the fourth. Oliver had insisted that the control of the army be divided between Protector and Parliament. But Parliament was determined to get rid of army rule. It was the army that had made it possible to put the King to death, it was because he had an army at his back that Cromwell had been able to dissolve the Long Parliament, it was the army that had imposed a written constitution on both Parliament and the nation, it was because the army must be maintained that the land was groaning under a weight of taxation almost four times as great as it had been in the king's day. And now it was the army that was insisting upon a toleration, distasteful to the majority both of Parliament and of the nation.

So although when a certain Thomas Tawney, who called himself Theauros John, lighted a bonfire, into which he threw a Bible, a saddle, and a sword, saying that these were the Gods of England, and proceeding to the door of Parliament, laid about him with a drawn sword, the House had him arrested, and committed to prison, it was just as determined as he was to get rid of or control the saddle and the sword, and to arrange that the Bible should not be interpreted by them.

And Oliver was as desirous as it was to get rid of the saddle and the sword. He had never wished to rule England through the army ("that which you have by force, I look upon it as nothing"), and now he was becoming more and more aware that it was not he that was ruling England through the army, but it was the army that was ruling

England through him, that to be the master of fifty thousand men, he must necessarily be their servant. But he was not willing to get rid of army rule in the way in which Parliament wished, in the only way in which it could really be done, he was not willing to hand over the entire control of the army to Parliament.

It was all, or almost all, this matter of toleration. "I had rather that Mahomedanism were permitted among us, than that one of God's children should suffer persecution." As things were now, in case Protector and Parliament should be at variance, with an armed force at his back, he could defy both Parliament and the nation.

And they were at variance, would probably always be at variance on the subject of religious toleration. That was the real reason that Oliver insisted upon the control of the army. One of his Parliamentary supporters put it in a nutshell when he said that "to exclude the Protector from the command of the standing forces would be to give up the Cause, that eminent and glorious Cause, which had been so much and so long contended for, for such Parliaments might hereafter be chosen as would betray the glorious liberty of the people of God."

And herein lies the whole difficulty of the Protectorate. Oliver was not willing to trust "the glorious liberty of the people of God" to any Parliament whatsoever. He knew that he could not. "Love the sheep, love the lambs," he had said to the Little Parliament, "and if the poorest Christian, the most mistaken Christian shall desire to live quietly and peaceably under you, I say if any shall desire but to live a life in godliness and honesty, let him be protected." But he knew now that that was more than could be expected of any Parliament. So in dissolving this Parliament he said, "If it (the control of the army) should not be equally placed between the Protector and the Parliament, it determines his power for hindering Parliament from imposing what religion they please upon the conscience of men." Yet he had no desire that the "people of God" should rule (the Little Parliament had cured him of that), but only that they should be safe. By army rule, much as he hated it, if it were possible in no other way. "That which you have by force I look upon it as nothing," he had said, but he had added, "I do not know that force is to be used, *except we cannot get what is for the good of the kingdom without it.*"

But Parliament was intent not only upon avoiding military government, but also upon cutting down the excessive taxation caused by the existence of a standing army. It wished to return to the militia system as soon as possible. The Instrument had provided for an army of thirty thousand, but it now numbered fifty-seven thousand. The House proposed that for the present it be reduced to its legal figure, and that during Oliver's life-time Parliament have a voice with him in fixing the number, and that after his death, it alone should determine the disposal of it. And it would vote money for it for only five years, at the end of which time it would be determined whether it would be disbanded or not.

This vote was taken on January 5th, 1655. According to the Instrument the Protector could not dissolve Parliament until it had been in session five months. But that day the newspapers under the influence of the Government began to talk about five lunar months. No doubt Oliver had been watching the calendar anxiously, and there is also evidence that the officers were forcing his hand. The four calendar months would not be up until February third. But five lunar months would be up on January twenty-second.

So on that day he summoned the members to the Painted Chamber, and made them a speech.

"There be some trees," he said, "that will not grow under the shadow of other trees. There be some that choose, a man may say so by way of allusion, to thrive under the shadow of other trees. I will tell you what have thriven, I will not say what you have cherished under your shadow. That would be too hard. Instead of peace and settlement, instead of mercy and truth being brought together, righteousness and peace kissing each other, weeds and nettles, briars and thorns, have grown under your shadow. Dissettlement and division, discontent and dissatisfaction, together with real dangers to the whole, have become more multiplied during the five months of your sitting than in some years before. Therefore I think myself bound, it is my duty to God, and to the people of these nations, to their safety and good in every respect. . . . I think it my duty to tell you, that it is not for the profit of these nations, nor fit for the common and public good, for you to continue here any longer. And therefore I do declare with you, That I do dissolve this Parliament."

And yet he looked upon them as "having among them persons that he could lay down his life individually for." And he still had "a hope fixed within him, that this Cause and this Business was of God." Had it not been for that, he "would many years ago have run away from it."

If he had been more of a statesman, less, as Mr. Belloc calls him "the soldier out of place," would he have managed better? Certainly if he had been willing to give up religious toleration, he might have managed better. But in that case he would have considered himself a traitor to the "hope fixed within him," that the Cause and the Business were of God.

But there were in the very nature of the case other reasons for his failure. In the first place after a violent revolution, the choice, at least for a term of years, seems to be only between anarchy and despotism. The present state of Europe is demonstrating this on a very large scale. Oliver dared not permit anarchy, he was loath to establish despotism.

And in the second place experience has shown that sovereignty cannot advantageously be divided between a Single Person and a Parliament. There will be constant conflict, and before things can go smoothly, one or the other must get not only the upper hand, but become the supreme power.

Something like this division of authority is being tried under exceptionally favorable circumstances in the United States of America, but the success is not so conspicuous as to tempt other nations to adopt it. In England the problem has been solved by making a Parliament representing the people supreme, the Executive and Legislative united in the Cabinet, the King a useful symbol, and at times a helpful adviser.

If Cromwell had read Hobbes' "Leviathan," published in London in 1651, he would have learned that men might give authority to one man to represent them, or they might give it to an assembly, but when they have chosen either, that must be the sovereign power, it cannot be shared with another. For "where there is already erected a Sovereign Power, there can be no other Representative of the same people. For that were to erect two Sovereigns, and every man to have his person represented by two Actors, that by opposing one another, must needs divide the Power which, if men will live in peace, is indivisible; and thereby reduce the multitude into the condition of Warre contrary to the end for which all Sovereignty is instituted."

CHAPTER XVIII

Absolute Power

"Truly I have, as before God, often thought that I could not tell what my business was, nor what was the place I stood in, save comparing myself to a good constable, set to keep the peace of the parish."—OLIVER CROMWELL.

"I have found a great deal of truth among professors, but not much mercy—But when we are brought in the right way, we shall be merciful as well as orthodox—God give us hearts and minds to keep things equal."—OLIVER CROMWELL.

FROM January 22nd, 1655 until September 17th, 1656, there was no Parliament. During that period Oliver and the Council, as he himself put it, "endeavored to walk as those that would not only give account to God of their actions, but withal had to give an account of them to men." That is, after dismissing the first Parliament of the Protectorate, he tried, so far as it was possible, to conform his government to their wishes. They had planned to reduce taxation by reducing the army, so during the summer and autumn of 1655, he disbanded ten or twelve thousand soldiers.

But he was beset on all sides by difficulties, not the least of which was that his health was failing. He was often ill, he was growing prematurely old, foreign ambassadors noticed that his hand shook when he greeted them. And this was not helped by the fact that he already realized, and soon came to realize more fully, that his government was threatened both by constitutional opposition, and by armed insurrection. The Instrument of Government had allowed him to levy, without consent of Parliament, sufficient taxes to meet ordinary expenses, but there were those who objected on the ground that the Instrument, not having been ratified by Parliament, was not binding. When a man named Cony refused to pay customs duties, his counsel questioned the validity of the ordinance imposing them, and Chief Justice Rolle resigned rather than pronounce judgment. Oliver heard a great deal of talk about Magna Carta. And the worst of it was, he knew that, theoretically and ideally, his opponents were right. He could

249

only plead that in times of revolution all laws are off, that necessity knows no law. He became nervous, excited, determined. "If nothing should ever be done," he said, "but what is according to law, the throat of the nation may be cut, while we send for some one to make a law." Yet Clarendon testifies that "in matters which did not concern the life of his jurisdiction, he seemed to have great reverence for the law, and rarely interfered between party and party."

And when the Republican Ludlow told him that he would not own the legality of his government, because it seemed to him "a re-establishment of that which we all engaged against, and had with a great expense of blood and treasure abolished," he was already painfully aware that there was some truth in the criticism. "What is it that you would have?" he asked. "That which we fought for," was the reply, "that the nation might be governed by its own consent." "I am as much for government by consent as any man," answered the harassed Protector, "but where shall we find the consent?" That was the trouble, there was no consent anywhere. When Oliver read Harrington's "Oceana," he said, "that he approved the Government of a Single Person as little as any of them, but that he was forced to take upon himself the office of High Constable, to preserve the peace among the several parties in the nation, since he saw that being left to themselves, they would never agree to any certain form of government, and would only spend their whole power in defeating the designs, or destroying the persons of one another." And now he knew that when Ludlow spoke of consent, he meant only Republican consent, and the Republicans were but a small minority in the nation.

For himself he was still not wedded or glued to any form of government, was ready to establish any form that would command the affections of the people, and insure religious toleration. But there was no clear majority for any form of government, and there was a clear majority against religious toleration. Even before he dissolved the last Parliament, Wildman was urging him to call a Parliament, freely elected by the people, in the hope that in this way religious freedom might be secured. Oliver knew that it was the last way to secure it.

And he knew that there was danger from armed insurrection. There were the fanatic Republicans led by Wildman and Sexby, there were Royalists watching their chance from the nearest continental shores. And these two forces, so unlike in their final aim, seemed ready to combine for the first step, the overthrow of the present government. Through Thurloe, who was at once Secretary of State, chief of police, and head of the secret service, Oliver knew all about these things. In

February, 1656 Wildman was arrested near Marlborough while dictating a "Declaration of the Free and Well-affected People of England, now in arms against the tyrant Oliver Cromwell." Early in March a Royalist outbreak in Yorkshire was suppressed. On the eleventh of that month two hundred Cavaliers under Penruddock and Wagstaff entered Salisbury during the assizes, seized the judges in bed, but disappointed in their efforts to rally the inhabitants, withdrew to South Molton in Devonshire, where they were defeated by government forces. As usual the Protector was not vindictive, only nine of the rebels suffered death, but a number were shipped to the plantations.

He had not found it difficult to put down these individual uprisings, the real trouble was that he knew that everywhere there was smoldering discontent, that everywhere there was danger of rebellion and anarchy. Some one told him that nine out of ten of the people were against him. And he knew that it was probably true, but he also knew that the nine out of ten could unite on nothing except being against him. If they could have united for anything, he would have been obliged to retire and let them have their way, and perhaps he would have been glad to do so. As it was, he replied, "Very well, and what if I disarm the nine, and put a sword into the tenth man's hand, would not that do the business?"

Who knows? He may have spoken in a moment of nervous exasperation, he may have spoken in a mood of stern determination, but in any case he looked upon it as a temporary expedient. "That which you have by force, I look upon it as nothing," but he was coming to feel that there were times when "the people would prefer their safety to their passions, and their real security to forms." And he very soon decided that such a time had come.

It was the country districts that were giving him most anxiety. There he felt that more than local control was needed. For in them the justices of the assizes exercised a general administrative oversight, and being country gentlemen of the class elected to the Long Parliament, they naturally were not favorable to the government, the sects had robbed them of the victory that should have been theirs. And Cromwell felt that the danger was so great that he entered upon the most doubtful of all his experiments, that of the Major Generals. He divided England into eleven districts, over each of which he set a Major General. They had under them the local militia, supplemented by special troops of horse. This experiment, like all the others that he tried, probably did not originate with him; it was Lambert who now had the upper hand in the Council, and it is almost certain that the scheme was invented by him. But Oliver made it his own, and as usual when he did that, entered upon it enthusiastically, and defended it emphatically. Yet there is evidence that it was troubling him.

Having sinned against his conscience in one way, it was easier for him to sin against it in another way, his plea in both cases necessity. The Major Generals were paid for by taxation levied upon Royalists only. He who would rather be "just to an unbeliever than to a believer," he who had tried so hard to conciliate the Royalists, he who had objected so strenuously to the taxes levied upon them to support the Dutch war, had come to that! For the recent Royalist uprising had roused him. It might seem unjust to punish all Royalists for the fault of a few, but he believed that "the whole party was involved in the business directly or indirectly." He called attention to the fact that they were keeping themselves "distinct and separate from the well-affected, marrying only among themselves, as if they would avoid the very beginning of union, breeding their children under the ejected clergy, as if they meant to entail their quarrel, and prevent the means to reconcile posterity." Had he not at first been lenient, he said, he could not with any comfort and satisfaction to himself take the course which he was now compelled to take. But he had been lenient, and they had abused his leniency.

It was all the desperate expedient of a desperate man. He did not pretend that it was within the law. And he was ill at ease with himself, impatient with his critics. "It was for ordinary governments," he said, "to live within the law, if a Government in extraordinary circumstances, go beyond the law, it should not be clamoured at or blottered at."

But it was clamored at and blottered at. So far as preserving the peace went, it seems to have worked well. But it was natural that such an extension of military rule should bring odium, and the more so, as it was the business of the major generals not only to preserve order, but to suppress vice. So their brief rule was a period of espionage, of arbitrary and capricious punishment, and the name of the Protector began to stink in men's nostrils. "What you have by force, I look upon it as nothing." This was worse than nothing. And it had all grown naturally and almost inevitably out of that June day in 1647 when, because there was nothing else for him to do, he had left London to throw in his lot with the army.

There were those who said, "If we have civil liberty, religious liberty will follow." He knew that that was not true, that the mind of the people was not for religious liberty. So it was in the interest of religious liberty that he had deprived them of whatever civil liberty they had. Of course he hoped that it would be only temporarily. For while he believed that the "civil liberty and Interest of the Nation ought to be subordinate to the more peculiar Interest of God," he could not believe that they were "inconsistent and two different things," or that they would clash very long. And it must be added that in the present clash of factions, political as well as religious, he saw that under no system could they have civil liberty, that it would only degenerate into anarchy.

But having sacrificed civil liberty, how much religious liberty was he able to secure? He announced as his general principle that "whatever pretension to religion would continue quiet and peaceable, they should enjoy conscience and liberty to themselves, but for whatever was contrary and not peaceable, tending to combination, interests and factions, let the pretence be never so specious," for such he was against all liberty of conscience. And since he had found "a great deal of Truth among professors, but not much Mercy," he was determined "not to suffer a man of one form to be trampling upon the heels of another form," for "when we are brought in the right way, we shall be merciful as well as orthodox—God give us hearts and minds to keep things equal!"

So he made it his chief task "to keep things equal," to "keep all the godly of separate judgments in peace"; he was "as a constable to part them, and keep them in peace." And on the whole, so far as the principal Puritan sects were concerned, Presbyterians, Independents and Baptists, he was "not unhappy in preventing any one Religion from trampling upon another." He was so pleased with the work done by his Commissioners of Triers that he thought the time had come to celebrate a little. So one day in April 1655 he invited them to dinner at Whitehall, "sat at table with them, was cheerful and familiar in their company." It was good to be able to relax a little, and "by such kinds of little caresses," says Whitelocke, "he gained much upon many persons."

But he knew that the Fifth Monarchy men were not so well pleased with these commissioners, that they were proclaiming that they were absolutely anti-Christian, that one could with as good conscience go to the Pope and his cardinals for approbation as to them. He knew that they were maintaining that earthly rule should be entirely in the hands of the saints, that the present Government was to be condemned, because "it had a Parliament in it, whereby power is derived from the

people, whereas all power belongs to Christ." He had heard that they
were saying that when the Little Parliament was dissolved, he had
"taken the crown off the head of Christ, and put it on his own," therefore "that Whitehall where he dwelt stank of the brimstone of Sodom,
and of the smoke of the bottomless pit; the flying roll of God's curses
would overtake the family of that great thief there, who had taken for
himself the benefit, purchased by those who shed their blood for the
cause of Jesus Christ, and the interest of His kingdom."

So far as this railing concerned himself alone, he was inclined to be
good-natured, even amused, but it was not a time when he could allow
his authority to be thus openly questioned. When a certain preacher
called John Rogers, who had been imprisoned for his fierce denunci-
ation of his government was admitted to his presence, he listened
patiently to what he had to say and responded, "I believe you speak
many good things, according to the Gospel, but what you suffered for
is railing and evil doing." There was always a germ of truth in what
these people had to say, Cromwell recognized this, and it interested
him. He sent for Simpson, another of these preachers and argued
with him for the better part of a day. Simpson was unconvinced, told
him that he was a traitor, and had incurred the penalty for high treason. To which Oliver replied, probably with a smile, "Well said,
Simpson, thou art plain indeed," but added firmly "The Government
I have taken, and I intend to maintain it." Nevertheless he allowed
him to remain at liberty.

Later he sent for four of the chief Fifth Monarchists, among whom
was Harrison, and asked them "whether they would engage to live
peaceably, and not disturb the peace of the nation." When they refused, they were told that "if they would return to their own counties,
and promise not to come forth without leave," they would suffer no
harm. But they refused even that, in fact they were preaching the
lawfulness of taking up arms against the government, "endeavouring to
seduce some great officers from their trust," and opposing the payment of taxes. So they were committed to prison. But Oliver was
very loath to deal thus with them, Harrison had been his friend, he
still believed that he was "a good man, who would not await the
Lord's leisure." "I know it is a trouble to my Lord Protector to have
any man, who is a saint in truth, to be grieved or unsatisfied with him,"
wrote Thurloe. But imprisonment had been inflicted upon these men
"in pity to them, and other people who are led by them, as well as for
the sake of the nation, that they may not put things into blood and
confusion, and be made use of by the Cavaliers, and the vile Levelling

party, to destroy and utterly root out all that are good and godly in the land."

About this time Oliver was beginning to hear a great deal about a new sect lately risen up, who called themselves the Society of Friends, but who were frequently spoken of as Quakers. He knew that because they refused to have the Scriptures called the Word of God, spoke of the churches as "steeplehouses," and railed at ministers as "hirelings, deceivers and false prophets," the justices of the peace frequently prosecuted them under the Blasphemy Act. He probably was not much incensed against them because of that, he knew how easy it was to call men blasphemers, and he had not taken time to inquire into their particular form of blasphemy. But it distressed him to hear that they would burst into churches, interrupt services, call out to the preachers, "Come down, thou deceiver, thou hireling, thou dog!" This did not seem to him "a pretension to religion that would live quiet and peaceable."

So on February 15th, 1655 he issued a proclamation, which Dr. Gardiner thinks may be justly called the charter of religious freedom under the Protectorate.

God, the Protector said, Who had wrought so many mercies and deliverances in late years had, as not the least token of His favor and good will, crowned the people of England, by granting them a free and uninterrupted passage of the Gospel amongst them, and liberty for all to hold faith, and profess with sobriety their light and knowledge, according as the Lord in His rich grace and wisdom, had dispensed it to every man. A mercy till of late years denied to this nation, and still denied to most of the nations round about it. And he, the Protector, reckoned it as a duty, and would take all possible care, to continue and preserve this freedom to all persons in the Commonwealth fearing God, though of different judgments. But on no pretense whatsoever should this freedom be extended beyond the bounds which the royal law of love and Christian moderation have set in our walking towards one another.

"And his Highness cannot but sadly lament the woful distemper that is fallen upon the spirit of many professing religion and the fear of God in these days, who so openly and avowedly, by rude and unchristian practices, disturb both the public and private meetings for preaching the word and other religious exercises, and vilify, oppose and interrupt the public preachers in their ministry. Whereby the liberty of the Gospel, the profession of religion and the name of God is much dishonoured and abused, and the spirit of all good men much grieved. His Highness therefore, having information from divers parts of the Commonwealth of such practices by divers men lately risen up under the name of Quakers, Ranters and others, who do daily both reproach and disturb the assemblies and congregations of Christians in their public and private meetings, and interrupt the preachers in dispensing the Word, and others in their worship, contrary to just liberty, and to the disturbance of the public peace, doth hold himself obliged by his trust, to declare his dislike of all such practices, as being contrary to the just freedom and liberties of the people,—and doth hereby strictly require that they forbear henceforth all such irregular and disorderly practices; and if in contempt hereof any person shall presume to offend as aforesaid, we shall esteem them disturbers of the civil peace, and shall expect and do require all officers and ministers of justice to proceed against them accordingly."

It is not likely that at the time that this Proclamation was issued, Oliver knew much about the Quakers. To him they were probably nothing but "divers men lately risen up, who do daily both reproach and disturb the assemblies and congregations of Christians." Moreover he, like many others, would seem to have had a tendency to confuse them with another sect called Ranters who, without their virtues, exaggerated their peculiarities. But eleven days later he was to learn more.

For, on February 26th George Fox, having been arrested and brought to London, was admitted into his presence, while he was dressing. He entered with the salutation "Peace be to this House," and then exhorted the Protector "to keep in the fear of God, that he might receive wisdom from Him, and that by it he might be directed to order all things under his hand to God's glory." To which Oliver could have had no objection, but as soon as he could get in a word, he questioned him about the one thing to which he did have an objection, the thing that had troubled him at the time that he penned the proclamation, why he quarreled with the ministers. Then he listened patiently, while Fox poured forth his arguments against those who preached for filthy lucre, arguments which he did not find very convincing, though he "carried himself with much moderation." But Fox also gave him glimpses of his deep spiritual insight, and with this he was in profound sympathy. As he spoke, he would sometimes interrupt him to say, "That is very good," and "That is true." Then "persons of quality, so-called" began to come in, and Fox "drew back, lingered, and then was for retiring." As he left him, the Protector caught his hand, and said, "Come again to my house; for if thou and I were but an hour a day together, we should be nearer one to the other. I wish no more harm to thee than to my own soul." He had found a kindred spirit.

And not only did Fox go out a free man, but he addressed meetings in London and elsewhere, though they had been closed by Government orders only a few days before. And "so great were the throngs of people, that I could hardly get to and from the meetings for the crowds of people, and the truth spread exceedingly." It was "a great commencement in London, and some in the Protector's house and family."

But of course Oliver could not be everywhere, and there were still local persecutious, warranted, it was not unnaturally thought, by his own proclamation. Many held that the Quakers were crypto-Catholics, so some local authorities tried to impose upon them the oath of abjuration, which they of course refused to take, since their principles forbade them to take any oath. "It was never intended for them," cried the Protector when he heard it, "I never so intended it." And when they were punished for refusing to pay tithes, he again objected. He intervened to save when he could, generally by using his right of pardon. When Fox himself was re-arrested and one of his followers, Humphrey Norton, came to Whitehall to intercede for him, offering to go to prison in his stead, "Which of you," asked Oliver of his Council, "would do as much for me?" To Norton he simply replied that it would be a breach of the law to accept his offer, but he sent orders to his brother-in-law Desborough, the Major-General of that district, to let Fox and the other imprisoned Quakers go free.

There were signs that English Puritanism was broadening. It must have been a satisfaction to Cromwell to know that Baxter had created a system of voluntary associations, soon to extend to fourteen counties, in which Presbyterians, Independents and Baptists took part amicably. Over in Cambridge the Vice-Chanceller Whichcote was developing a creed, founded on the text, "The spirit of man is the candle of the Lord." Not Fox's inner light, that was something supernatural, but the reason, given by God to enable man to discover Truth. "What," asked Whichcote, "doth God speak to but my reason? Should not that which is spoken to hear? Should it not judge, discern, conceive what God is meaning?" So Puritanism was leading in some quarters toward latitudinarianism and rationalism. And in Oxford Cromwell's brother-in-law Wilkins was presiding over a little group of scientific men. In London Hobbes was publishing his philosophical treatises unmolested, Davenant, protected by Cromwell, was reviving the drama, and a new word "opera" was being introduced into the language.

So much for the Protector's attitude toward the great and ever increasing number of Puritan sects. But what about those who were not called Puritans, those whom at one time at least he would hardly have reckoned among the godly, those to whom the Instrument had not promised protection?

As we have seen, although the Liturgy had been prohibited since 1645, there were Episcopal clergymen who retained their livings, and Episcopal congregations that met in private houses. But after Penruddock's rising, an edict was issued to the effect that no one was to keep in his house an ejected clergyman as chaplain or tutor, under pain of heavy fine, that no such clergyman was to teach school, preach or administer the sacraments, celebrate marriages or use the Book of Common Prayer on pain of three months' imprisonment for the first offense, six months for the second, and banishment for the third. However even before he finished writing this Declaration Oliver grew more merciful, for at the end it was stated that to those who had given a "real testimony of their godliness and good affection toward the present government, so much tenderness shall be used as shall be consistent with the safety and good of the Nation."

And in February 1656 he summoned some of the leading Episcopal clergymen to Whitehall, told them that he understood how they felt, and all he asked was a promise that if liberty were allowed, they would not use it to excite fresh disorder. They assured him that such a pledge would be forthcoming. So while the Declaration was not withdrawn, it was seldom if ever put in practice. No longer were services held in St. Gregory's as they had been openly all along, but in private houses in London, Oxford, and elsewhere the Prayer Book was used, the sacraments were administered. And when a deputation of London ministers waited upon the Protector, and complained that the Episcopal clergy had got away their congregations, "Have they?" he asked, making as though he would say something to the captain of the guard, then suddenly, "But hold, after what manner do they debauch your people?" "By preaching," was the answer. "Then preach back again," retorted the Protector, and so left them.

In March 1656 Archbishop Ussher died. He had advised Charles I not to consent to Strafford's execution, in 1648 had preached a sermon in Lincoln's Inn, denouncing the attitude of the Parliament to the King, and shortly afterwards preached to the King himself, urging the doctrine of Divine Right. Yet the Protector ordered him a public funeral in the Abbey, himself contributed £200 toward the expense, and the Anglican service was used at the grave. In January Ussher had presented a petition in behalf of the "poor ousted clergy." To this Oliver had given no definite answer, but it is probable that the leniency shown to them was in a measure the result of his pleading. However Cromwell's own heart and conscience would never allow him to be a persecutor. But again he could not be everywhere, there was a major-general who sent Jeremy Taylor arbitrarily to prison.

Dr. Gardiner thinks that it was easier to be lenient, because at that time there do not seem to have been many who were attracted by the Episcopal form of worship, that while Royalists were numerous, they were actuated by other motives than attachment to the Church. But there were times when Cromwell could show mercy even to Royalists. It was while he was Chancellor, and Owen was Vice-Chancellor of Oxford, that Dr. John Wilson was appointed Professor of Music in that university, and proceeded almost immediately to publish his "Psalterium Carolinum, The Devotions of His Sacred Majesty in his solitude and suffering rendered into verse for three Voices, and an Organ or Theorbo," in which twenty-seven of the Psalms were adapted to events in the late war, and the words of David were put into the mouth of Charles I. Cromwell may not have been consulted about the appointment, but he certainly knew about the Psalterium Carolinum. However it is probable that he could forgive anything in a real musician. Under his government there was a "Committee for the Advancement of Musicke."

As for the Catholics, the Protector had had a life-long prejudice against them, it was in the blood, and he never wholly got over it. But even toward them he was becoming more lenient. No doubt this was partly because the complicated duties of his office had led him to take a more mundane view of some things. He wished to keep on friendly terms with France, and he saw that he could not consistently ask Mazarin to tolerate the Huguenots of France, while he persecuted the Catholics of England. But persecution was not his role, experience had taught him that the Catholics were not the only persecutors, and he admired the sincerity of some of them.

According to the Instrument of Government fines were no longer to be collected from those who refused to attend church, but they might still be exacted from those who refused to take the Oath of Abjuration, in which the Papal authority and transubstantiation were renounced. However they had been very irregularly collected, Oliver hated to interfere with religion. But after the Royalist insurrection of 1655 there was a proclamation announcing that the law would be strictly enforced. This was no doubt actuated partly by alarm, but largely by a desire to increase the revenue. In October 1655 the Venetian ambassador described the Protector's policy as a resolution to deprive the Catholics of their possessions, but let them hear as many masses as they would.

And they were hearing masses. Bordeaux, the French ambassador, was writing to Mazarin that his Church was more frequented than that of any ambassador had been before. Every festival day there were three or four thousand in attendance, and no one was molested as they went out, not even the priests who served, "a thing that the Queen (Henrietta Maria) was never able to prevent." Sagresti, the Venetian, reported that the hall of his embassy would not hold those who came to attend mass, and that English priests were allowed to preach in their own language. And when the Council suggested that Sagresti be warned, the Protector replied that he had done no more than the ambassadors of other nations. He could not however prevent guards being placed around the Embassy next Sunday, and they arrested more than four hundred of the worshipers. But they probably all escaped with a warning not to repeat the offense. And probably many of them did repeat it, and were not again arrested.

But the outbreak of war with Spain roused greater hostility to them. Oliver himself contributed to this by representing it as a religious war, and declaring that "the Papists in England have been accounted Spaniolised ever since I was born." A bill enacting severer penalties against recusants was introduced into the Second Parliament of the Protectorate. Mazarin was alarmed, wrote to the Protector urging toleration. To which Cromwell replied that he had the matter "set home upon his spirit, but he might not, (shall I tell you that I cannot?") at this juncture, and as the face of his affairs then stood, answer the call for legal toleration. But he had of some, of very many, had compassion, "making a difference" had "plucked many out of the fire, the raging fire of persecution, that did tyrannize over their consciences, and encroached by an arbitrariness of power upon their estates." And it was his purpose, as soon as he could "remove impediments, and some weights that pressed him down, to do more in relation to that." Meanwhile he believed that under his government there was less reason to complain in behalf of the Catholics as to rigor upon men's consciences, than under the Parliament.

And although the objectionable bill passed, and Oliver signed it, there is no evidence that there was really any increased activity against the Papists. It is true that in December 1657 eight priests were arrested in Covent Garden, their crosses, jewels and vestments confiscated, and Pepys tells us that Cromwell made some of his gentlemen try on their copes, which "caused abundance of mirth," but the priests themselves were neither indicted nor punished.

As a further instance of liberality, it is commonly said that it was under Cromwell that the Jews, expelled from England by Edward I in 1290, were first allowed to return. Technically that is not quite true. For some years Spanish and Portuguese Jews, mostly men of wealth and commercial connections, had been stealing into London, trying to escape observation. But now the question came up, would not the Puritan reverence for the Old Testament, and Oliver's spirit of toleration permit larger and more open immigration? Manasseh Ben Israel, an Amsterdam rabbi and physician, arrived in London in October, 1655, published a Humble Address to the Protector in November, arguing for the admission of his race. War with Spain was threatening, Spanish Jews in London might give valuable assistance to England, there were also commercial advantages that might be gained through them. Oliver referred the matter to his council, which passed it on to a committee of its own members, a committee which met at Whitehall two or three times a week, the Protector himself being generally present. It is on record that on December 12th he spoke in favor of granting Manasseh's petition in such a way that one of his auditors said "I never heard a man speak so well." Nevertheless Manasseh was obliged to return to his own country, with a pension from the Protector, but no answer to his request.

However, in the course of the discussion, the two Judges, Glyn and Steele, had expressed the opinion that there was no law forbidding the Jews to return to England, nothing but the proclamation of Edward I. So, unless a successful action should be brought against one of them for residence there, it might be assumed that they had a right to come. They began to settle freely in the country, no such action was ever brought against them.

In July 1656 Oliver issued writs for the election of a new Parliament. The Instrument did not require him to do this for another year, but he had embarked on a war with Spain, and needed money.

In March 1654 the war with Holland had come to an end, the Dutch agreeing to submit to the supremacy of the British flag in the English seas, and to abandon all demand for the modification of the

Navigation Act. And immediately the Protector began to contemplate war with Spain. For although somewhat more liberal toward Catholics than of old, his liberality did not extend to Spanish Catholics. Spain was a natural enemy of England, "by reason of that enmity which is in her, which is against whatever is of God." He harked back to the days of "Queen Elizabeth of famous memory," when the Spaniard's design was "by all unworthy, unnatural means to destroy that Person, and to seek the ruin and destruction of these kingdoms." He read in Sir Walter Raleigh's "History of the World," that "the Turks and the Spaniards were the two nations to be regarded, the one seeking to join all Europe to Asia, the other the rest of all Europe to Spain." To him Spain was still "the head of the Papal interest." To persecute the individual misguided Papist might be wrong, to make war to uproot the whole Papal interest was preëminently right. And while he was not a persecutor, he was a warrior.

Moreover England had a great navy, and he wished to use it. And he himself had a great reputation abroad, the Queen of Swedes had said to Whitelocke, "Your General hath done the greatest things of any man in the world." Clarendon tells us that Oliver's reputation at home was but a shadow compared with his greatness abroad. His prestige was England's prestige, he must use it to increase her influence. Moreover he was a dictator, and it is the nature of a dictator to wish to advance his country's interest abroad. And with him this was also religion. For since, as Milton had said, and Cromwell believed, God had a way of revealing His will first to Englishmen, through them God's will must be revealed to other peoples. He had so often said that the English were the best people in the world. So the desire for national aggrandizement, which in so many statesmen is religion without God, was in Cromwell, as later to some extent in Bismarck, religion based upon God. "God has not brought us where we are," he said, "but to consider the work we may do abroad as well as at home." It is possible to enter into and understand his feeling, even although one condemns his judgment.

So, not realizing that the Peace of Westphalia had ended religious wars, he was dreaming of a great Protestant League headed by England. With this end in view, he made overtures to the various Protestant powers, but in vain. The truth was Europe and England were becoming more mundane, it was for commerce, not for religion, that they were now willing to fight. And no doubt Oliver, while still keeping his religious enthusiasm, was also to a certain extent catching the mundane spirit of the times, no doubt he had his eyes partly on the

Spanish colonies, and the commercial advantages that were to be gained by a Spanish war.

But Spain and France were at war, and each was bidding for the assistance of England. And there were those among his advisers who saw the position that France was gaining, and that eventually she would be the enemy. Better attack her rather than Spain, and that before she grew too strong. So he began to think it might be just as well not to ally himself with either side, to try to maintain friendly relations with both. But when he planned to renew treaties of commerce and friendship with Spain, demanding that English merchants should have free exercise of their religion in Spanish ports, and that English colonists and traders should be allowed to go to the West Indies without being treated as enemies, the Spanish ambassador answered that that would be to ask for his master's two eyes.

That settled the matter. He had a navy that was doing nothing, he calculated that it would cost no more to put it in action than to lay it up. So in August 1654 he sent out two fleets, one under Blake to go to the Mediterranean and get reparation from the pirates of Tunis and Algiers for wrongs done to English commerce, the other under Penn and Venables, to seize a Spanish island in the West Indies. Strangely enough, he seems to have thought that the latter could be done without bringing on a war with Spain in Europe. But that was the way these things were done in the days of "Queen Elizabeth of famous memory," and in all his dealings with Spain Cromwell was back in those days.

He was negotiating a commercial treaty with France when word came of the massacre of the Vandois by the troops of the Regent of Savoy. Milton called upon God to avenge His slaughtered saints, Cromwell set to work to do something about it. He appointed a day of humiliation, opened a collection for the relief of the sufferers, himself contributing £2000, summoned the Protestant powers to intervene, even thought of sending Blake's fleet to attack Nice and Villa Franca. But France, desirous of the friendship of England, put pressure to bear upon Savoy, the massacre stopped, the Vandois were reinstated in their valleys, Oliver's praises rang throughout Protestant Europe. Then a treaty was signed with France, on the face of it nothing but a commercial treaty, but there was a secret clause, providing for the expulsion of English Royalists from France, and a private promise from Mazarin to protect the Huguenots in their rights under the Edict of Nantes.

Meanwhile Blake had been very successful in the Mediterranean, but in August 1655 word reached England of the defeat of the expedition sent to the West Indies. And Spain, having decided that she would not stand such irregular proceedings, declared war. That made it necessary to summon Parliament.

CHAPTER XIX

The Second Parliament of the Protectorate

"I profess I had not the apprehension, when I took this Place, that I could do much good; but I did think I might prevent imminent evil.—But this I do say, that I do think from my very heart, you, in settling of the peace and liberties of this Nation, which cries as loud upon you as ever nation did for somewhat that may beget a consistence, ought to attend to that; otherwise the Nation will fall to pieces.—And therefore I am not contending for one name compared with another.—I am ready to serve, not as a King, but as a constable, if you like!"

—OLIVER CROMWELL.

WHEN Oliver decided to call a new Parliament, the Major-Generals had assured him that they could secure the return of members favorable to his government. That proved a false hope. Since they themselves were the most prominent cause for the opposition, it was probably a mistake that they acted as electioneers. At any rate, although they were all returned, so many hostile members were elected with them, that one of them, Kelsey, wrote to the Protector, "There is such a perverseness in those chosen, that without resolution in you and the Council to maintain the interest of God's people, which is to be preferred before a thousand Parliaments, we shall return to our Egyptian taskmasters."

Seeing the danger, the Council, falling more and more under the influence of Lambert, assumed the right to decide upon qualifications, and about a hundred disaffected members were excluded. Oliver seems to have stood back and given the Council a free hand.

To this Parliament Oliver made his opening speech on the seventeenth of September 1656. There was not the same enthusiasm and hopefulness that there had been in former speeches, he had been too often disappointed and the election itself had been ominous. But amid many digressions and repetitions there was an urgent call to action. He would speak, he said, "of Being and Well-Being, of Being first, because there was a question as to whether they could continue to be at all, there were enemies at home and abroad who were threatening the very existence of the nation." Yet this should not cause despondency, and he thought that it would not, "because we are Englishmen and much more than English. Because you all, I hope, are Christian men."

The war with Spain must be prosecuted with vigor, for in fighting Spain they were fighting for all the Protestant interests. To all the Spaniard's other iniquities must be added the fact that he had "espoused Charles Stuart with whom he is fully at agreement," (what else could Cromwell have expected!), and this had brought him in league with all the disaffected in England. The various plots against the government were recounted, the appointment of the Major-Generals justified, the Protector's views upon toleration, and the limits to which, under the circumstances, it must be subjected, were clearly stated.

Above all, he must rouse them to do something. "Now if I had the tongue of an angel, if I were so certainly inspired as the holy men of God have been, I could rejoice for your sakes, and for the sake of God and of the Cause we have engaged in, that I could move affections in you to that which, if you do it, will save this Nation! If not, you plunge it, in all human appearance, it and all the Interests, yea and all Protestants in the world, into irrecoverable ruin!—Therefore I beseech you, I beseech you, do not dispute of unnecessary and unprofitable things that may divert you from carrying on so profitable a work as this is."

And then, the most important thing of all, this Parliament and the Protector must not work at cross-purposes, they must be so united that the nation may say, "These two are knit together in one bond." If that should be apparent, there would be little danger either at home or abroad, for "that and nothing else can work off these disaffections from the minds of men, which are as great, if not greater, than all the other oppositions you can meet with."

"Therefore," he said in conclusion, "I beseech you, in the name of God, set your hearts to this work. And if you set your hearts to it, then you will sing Luther's Psalm, 'God is our Refuge and Strength, a very present help in time of trouble.'" He repeated it two or three times, "The Lord of Hosts is with us, the God of Jacob is our refuge."

And Parliament, stripped of its opposition members, did at first set its heart to the work, in a way that he found encouraging. On October 9th Thurloe wrote, "The Protector and Parliament do agree very well," on November 13th, "The Parliament do mostly intend the reformation of the law (Oliver had urged this strongly in his opening speech), and the raising of money for prosecuting the Spanish war. This, and the agreement which is between His Highness and them, is a great cause of the quiet which we have in all parts of the Kingdom."

But it was not long before a difference of opinion arose in the case of James Naylor, a saintly, but apparently at the time, a neurotic Quaker, in need of a sanatorium. He had been imprisoned at Exeter, and when released, he made a triumphant entry into Bristol, somewhat in the fashion in which Christ entered Jerusalem. He rode not on a donkey, but on a horse, while his admirers shouted "Hosanna!" and sang "Holy, Holy, Holy, Lord God of Sabaoth!" In this way he and his friends seem to have intended only to bring home forcibly the doctrine so emphasized by the Quakers, but not peculiar to them, that the living Christ dwells in the heart of every one of His followers. When he was arrested, and brought before the Bristol authorities, and asked, "Art thou the Son of God?" he replied, "I am the Son of God, but I have many brethren—The Lord hath made me a sign of His coming." The local magistrates were at a loss as to what to do with him, so they sent him to London, and Parliament appointed a committee of forty-five to consider the case.

Some of the members of this committee were more or less in sympathy with him. "That which sticks most with me," said one, "is the nearness of his opinion to that which is a glorious truth, that the Spirit is personally in us." Another said, "I wonder why any man should be so amazed at this. If you hang every man that says that Christ is in you, the Hope of Glory, you will hang a great many." And one, Colonel Holland, made a general plea for liberty of conscience. "Consider the state of this nation, what the price of our blood is, liberty of conscience, the Instrument of Government given to us. We remember how many Christians were formerly massacred under this notion of blasphemy, and who can define what it is? I am wholly against the question."

Nevertheless the majority decided that Naylor was guilty of horrid blasphemy, and he was sentenced to be set in the pillory in Palace Yard, Westminster, for two hours, whipped by the hangman through the streets to the Old Exchange, London, to stand in the pillory there for two hours, his tongue to be bored through with a hot iron, and his forehead branded with a B, then to be sent to Bristol, carried through the city on horseback face backward, to be whipped there on the market day following his arrival, then to be imprisoned in Bridewell without pen, paper or ink, until Parliament chose to release him. And the Speaker, after reading this sentence, told Naylor that the House had mingled mercy with justice! To which he replied, "God has given me a body, God will, I hope, give me a spirit to endure it."

The truth was that it had frequently been predicted by both the Roman and the Anglican church that the toleration of schism in the Body of Christ would lead to vulgar absurdities, blasphemies, and all manner of disorder. So even the advocates of toleration were zealous to show that their toleration did not extend to these things.

And Oliver was alarmed. It was not only that he was averse to religious persecution and savage punishment, but this Parliament, without consulting him, had arrogated to itself the judicial power of the former House of Lords, nay more, it had been both prosecutor and judge. It would have been possible, in its strictly legislative capacity, to have passed a Bill of Attainder. But that would have required the Protector's signature, and one member argued, "We may thus bring him into a snare, unless he heard the matter. His opinion may stick and demur as to the offence, for the Instrument says all shall be protected that profess faith in Jesus Christ, and that I suppose this man does." So it was argued that it was in their power to proceed judicially, for with the extinction of the House of Lords, its judicial power had devolved upon the Commons.

It was difficult to see whereunto this might lead. Chief Justice Glyn had argued against it that the Protector was under oath to protect the lives and liberties of the people. "If we proceed in this manner judicially against any man that we please," he said, "we divest him of that power, and take the sole power of judging men without law, or against law. It is true such things have been done by Parliament alone, but never without great regret." That was the way that it looked to Oliver. To the officers he said two months later, "The case of James Naylor might happen to be your case. By their judicial power they fall upon life and member, and doth the Instrument enable me to control it?—By the same law and reason that they punished James Naylor, they might punish an Independent or an Anabaptist."

So he wrote to the Speaker that although he detested and abhorred the giving the least countenance to persons of such opinions and practices as James Naylor, yet "we being entrusted in the present government on behalf of the people of these nations, and not knowing how far such proceedings, wholly without us, may extend in their consequences, do desire that the House may let us know the grounds and reasons whereon they stand."

But he could do nothing, the sentence was carried out. In the case of a man condemned by an ordinary court he had the prerogative of pardon, but this was an action of Parliament, and his power was limited by the Instrument. However, he could not get poor Naylor off his mind, during his imprisonment he endeavored to lighten his sufferings, and just a month before his own death, he sent to inquire after his health, for he heard that he was very ill.

As for the Major-Generals, the really crying grievance of the nation, this Parliament sat three months before the question came up. And then it came on the question of supply. On Christmas Day, 1656, Desborough asked for "leave to bring in a Bill of Assessment for the maintenance of the militia forces; the same to be levied upon such persons as have been in arms against the Parliament, or sequestered for their delinquency in the late war, with exceptions and proviso to be contained therein for some persons."

When the debate on the first reading of this Bill came on January 7th, 1657, there was a great surprise for the House. Oliver's son-in-law Claypole, who had never before taken a serious part in debate, rose and moved its rejection! Could it be possible that he was acting as the Protector's mouthpiece? Other members of the family took the same position. To Major-General Boteler who had argued that because some of the Cavaliers had done amiss, all deserved to be punished, Harry Cromwell, Oliver's cousin, replied, "By the same reasoning, because some of the Major-Generals have done amiss, which I offer to prove, all of them deserve to be punished." Then he went to Whitehall, repeated what he had said to the Protector, bringing papers with him to prove his statement. Oliver laughed, took the scarlet coat which he had worn when he opened Parliament from his back, his gloves from his hands, and threw them at him. The next day he strutted about the House in them, leaving the members to wonder whereunto this might tend.

Claypole had opposed the Bill on the ground that it was inconsistent with the Act of Oblivion, (no doubt Oliver's conscience was troubling him about that inconsistency), and the debate turned almost wholly on that Act. When it was urged that the tax was necessary to preserve internal peace, and therefore it was just to levy it upon those by whom the peace had been endangered, Broghill replied that to make no distinctions among the cavaliers, to treat them as though they were united against the government, was the very thing that would force them thus to unite. "Surely this will harden them. I wish this do not make them a corporation, and make men of estates and no estates desperate."

But there were speakers who struck at the root of the matter, condemned not only the method by which the Major-Generals were paid, but the institution itself. "That which makes me fear the passing of the Bill," said one, "is that thereby His Highness' government will be more founded on force, and more removed from that national foundation, which the people in Parliament are desirous to give him." Another declared that the new militia tended "to cauterize our nation, and prostitute our laws and civil peace to a power that was never set up in any nation without dangerous consequences."

When the Bill was finally rejected by a majority of thirty-six, some of the Major-Generals went to the Protector, and complained "how much thereby the House reflected on him, and discouraged the godly, and that their aim was to pass nothing which might tend to his accommodation, and that they would raise no money," Oliver only replied that he hoped better things of Parliament. He knew that, now that the means for their support had been taken away, the Major-Generals would soon disappear. And no doubt their disappearance was a relief to him. Their institution had been against his general principles; he was a man who always kept his ear to the ground, and in that way he had learned that they were a source of weakness rather than of strength to his government. And while, in his opening speech to Parliament, he had defended them, on the ground that it was for ordinary governments to live by law and order, but a government in extraordinary circumstances must sometimes go beyond the rules for self-preservation, Being must sometimes be considered before Well-Being, now that the English arms were being successful against Spain, (word had come that Staynes had captured the Spanish treasure ships), and Parliament, working in harmony with him, had the very day after the militia bill was rejected, voted £400,000 to carry on the war, perhaps his government could be what he had always wanted it to be, an ordinary government.

And Parliament was taking every means to make it so, working very hard to get back into the old and tried paths. As early as October a plan had been brought forward to make the Protectorate hereditary. There had been a similar movement in 1654, but Parliament had vetoed it. And Oliver had acquiesced. "Who knows," he had said, "but that a wise man may beget a fool?" But now the idea was gaining in favor, in fact it had become "the great towne talk." Just before the general election of 1656 an anonymous pamphlet had appeared, urging it upon the incoming Parliament. There was no historical precedent for election, and there was great danger attendant

upon it. "If there be so much danger of division and civil war dependent on elective principalities even because they are elective, what
may we more justly fear to be the event of such things in this nation,
where now, more than ever, every man stands from every other man,
so much divided in civil interest, but much more in matters of religion?
—There was a time indeed when monarchy and tyranny, Parliament
and liberty, were thought to be the same, but experience of our condition under that long, long Parliament, aye, and that little one since,
hath rectified our judgments. Let Parliament be made agreeable to
the name, *freedom to speak their minds, but not to do them.* For
while we do acknowledge that in the multitude of councillors there is
safety, we look for no such matter from a multitude of controllers."

And indeed, as every one saw, there was a more serious danger than
that from Parliament. What if the officers of the army, who now had
the upper hand, should claim the right to name the successor, as army
officers, similarly placed, had sometimes done in Rome? If they
could agree, that would mean army rule forever, otherwise civil war.
Colonel John Bridge, an Irish member, prepared an article for Major-
Generals Berry and Desborough, in which he argued that while every
man in the nation had the same right to succession on the Protector's
death there would infallibly be contest, great officers of the army
would compete with each other, and instead of dividing the realm
amongst them, as Alexander's generals had done, they would doubtless
come to blows. The one worsted would probably call in the help of
the Royalists, and come to an agreement with the King. And when
the nation found that each change of government brought on civil war,
it would conclude that "it's better to settle on the old bottom, and
better that some particular men suffer than that the whole be ruined."
So the old monarchy would be restored, without security for those
who had fought against it.

However, the question raised in October was allowed to rest for
three months, the House having been diverted from it by the case of
James Naylor, and the Major-Generals. But in January a new plot
against the Protector's life quickened the interest in the subject. The
Levelers were now working hand and glove with the Royalists. This
change of front need not in itself have surprised Oliver very much;
in that troubled time he himself had changed so often with changing
circumstances. Just as he had been willing to work with any one
who promised order and toleration, so they were willing to work with
any one through whom they might secure a commonwealth with manhood suffrage. But they were double in their dealings. They were

plotting with the Royalists for the Protector's assassination, not to secure the restoration of Charles II, but because they were convinced that "if he (Cromwell) were taken off, all things would come to a confusion, it being certain that the great men would never agree as to who should succeed but would fall together by the ears about it; then in that disorder the people would rise, so that things would be brought to a commonwealth."

So a certain Miles Sindercombe, a discharged soldier and a Leveler, attempted to fire Whitehall Chapel, hoping to kill the Protector in the confusion. The plot was discovered, and an account of it laid before Parliament. And on the twenty-third of January the house went in a body to Whitehall to congratulate Oliver on his escape. He answered them graciously, and on the twentieth of February, "which was a Thanksgiving Day," after hearing two sermons at St. Margaret's, they partook of "a most princely entertainment, at Whitehall, by invitation of His Highness." After dinner they withdrew to the Cockpit, and Oliver there entertained them with "rare music, both of voices and instruments, till the evening."

The discovery of this plot had tended to increase the Protector's popularity, but it had also strengthened the feeling that some certain provision must be made for carrying on the government, in case of his sudden death. "Revolutions are dangerous, so are elections," James Wainwright had written to Richard Bradshaw, English agent at Hamburg. So Ashe, an inconspicuous Parliament man, moved a startling addition to the note of congratulation, "It would tend very much to the preservation of himself and us, if His Highness would be pleased to take upon him the government, according to the ancient constitution." That is as a king.

Not much attention was paid to the suggestion at the time, but four weeks later, on Monday the 23rd of February, three days after Oliver had entertained the House, Sir Christopher Pack, one of the members for London, asked leave to introduce "somewhat tending to the settlement of the nation," that is to read a paper that had come into his hands, (he would appear not to have written it), in the form of a Remonstrance from Parliament to His Highness. After considerable debate the House decided that it might be read. It proved to be an entirely new Instrument of Government; a second House was suggested, and Cromwell was asked to assume the "name, style, title and dignity of King," and to appoint the person who should succeed him in the government of the nation.

It found considerable support. "All the long robes are for it," wrote

Thurloe to Henry Cromwell. So he says were some of the army officers, but Lambert, who had some hope of either displacing or succeeding Cromwell, led the opposition. "He had nothing but an unworthy pride," says Mrs. Hutchinson, "most insolent in prosperity, and as abject and base in adversity." Indeed to many the greatest objection to retaining the elective Protectorate was the fear that John Lambert would be the next Protector. He himself however maintained that the choice was not between Richard and John, but between progress and reaction. "He will, if it can be done, put the army in a ferment," wrote Thurloe.

And it looked as though it might be done. That very night some of the Major-Generals called upon the Protector, "tarried a quarter of an hour in the room before one word passed between them." Then they began to complain of the Parliament. Oliver answered hastily, "What would you have me do? Are they not of your own garbling? Did you not admit whom you pleased, and keep out whom you pleased? And now do you complain to me? Did I meddle with it?" And then he withdrew.

Four days later on Friday, the 27th of February, one hundred officers waited upon him, and petitioned him not to accept the title of King. "What entertainment these dissatisfied officers had at Whitehall," Vincent Gorkin wrote to Henry Cromwell, "though I heard it not, I may safely say that it was good, for the next day they were much quieter, and very willing and desirous to be satisfied."

We know something of what the entertainment was. Cromwell told them that he cared nothing about the title, that he liked it as little as they, to him it was but a feather to stick in his cap. But why should *they* object to it now? They had been sufficiently reconciled to it at one time. When he dissolved the Long Parliament, they had wished to make him King. And again when they prepared the Instrument of Government, (Lambert had been the principal author of it), they had proposed it. Why should they stick at it now?

Then he went over the whole history, showed how everything that had been tried so far had failed, yet in every instance he had acted upon their advice, had followed, not led. It was they who had made him dissolve the Long Parliament, 'twas against his judgment. (Was he quite fair in this? They had certainly urged him to do so for a long time, when it was against his judgment, but in the end he seems to have done it of himself, in anger and alarm. The question is whether he was more alarmed by what the Parliament might do, or by what, under the circumstances, the army might do.) Then when

they would have him choose ten persons to assist him in his government, (that again was Lambert's plan), he had proposed a hundred
and forty, and they, not he, had chosen them. "Not an officer of the
degree of a captain but named more than he himself had named."
And when these honest men could not govern, they had made an
Instrument of Government, but it had proved "an imperfect thing,
fitted neither to preserve their religious nor their civil rights." And
when the Parliament tried to mend it, they were sent home, again at
the advice of the army officers. "Then you would be mending it
yourselves, though you knew that I was sworn not to suffer it to be
altered but by Parliament, and then you might have given me a kick
in the breech, and set me going." Then against his judgment they
would have this Parliament called, and when they were chosen they
kept out and put in whom they pleased and now they were complaining of those they admitted!

Evidently it was time to take other advisers. He had always been
in favor of Parliamentary rather than army rule, if only he could
find a Parliament that would work in harmony with him in the things
that were dearest to him. It looked now as though he might. "It is
time to come to a settlement," he said, "and to lay aside arbitrary
proceedings so unacceptable to the nation. I have never courted you,"
he ended, the harsh, untuneable voice perhaps more harsh and untuneable than usual, "nor never will. They (the members of Parliament) are honest men, and have done good things. You are offended
at the House of Lords. I tell you that unless we have some such
thing as a balance, we cannot be safe. Either you will encroach upon
our civil liberties, by excluding such as are elected to serve in Parliament, or they will encroach upon our religious liberty. I abhor James
Naylor's principles, yet interceded. You see what my letter signified.
This Instrument of Government will not do your work."

It seemed as though it had come over him in a flash that not only
the nation, but even he himself with it, had been under the control
of the sword, and he wanted to free himself as well as the nation.
"You that are here (in Ireland) may think that my father has power,"
Henry Cromwell had said to Ludlow, "but they make a very kickshaw
of him at London." He had once said that it was better to serve under
a General than under a Parliament. But he had not been serving
under a General, he had been the General serving under the army.

And for a time Lambert and his followers subsided. Jephson writes,
"Lambert hath been silent, both Saturday, yesterday and to-day. I
suppose he hath now given up the buckler."

The House decided to postpone the discussion of the title, and consider the other proposals of the Remonstrance. And on these there was fair harmony, those opposed to kingship hoping that if they agreed to the rest, the question of the crown would drop, those in favor of it hoping that kingship would follow. But on March 25th, by a vote of 123 to 62, it was resolved that the Protector be asked to assume the title of King. And on March 31st, the new plan of government, now called Petition and Advice, was submitted to him for acceptance.

He was to assume the title of King, but his powers were to be restricted rather than enlarged. Parliament was to meet at least once in three years, oftener if necessary, and he was not to break or interrupt it, or suffer it to be broken or interrupted. No one elected to it was to be excluded, except by the consent of the House of which he was a member. A revenue of £1,300,000 was provided for ordinary expenses. Other temporary supplies were to be subject to Parliamentary grant, there were to be no gifts, loans, benevolences, tax or tallage, except by consent of Parliament. There was to be another House of not more than seventy, or less than forty members, to be nominated by the Protector and approved by Parliament. The standing forces were to be disposed of by the Chief Magistrate with the consent of Parliament; in the intervals of Parliament by the Chief Magistrate, with the advice of the Council.

These articles not only restricted the Protector, but implied a criticism on some of his former actions. But from these he was only too glad to refrain, if order and religious freedom could be secured without them. And the Petition and Advice seemed on the whole to provide for these.

There was to be an Established Church, in which "the true Protestant Christian religion, as contained in the Holy Scriptures, was to be held forth and asserted for the profession of these nations." For this there was to be a Confession of Faith, to be agreed upon between His Highness and Parliament, and "none was to be permitted, maliciously or contemptuously, to revile or reproach this Confession." But all who professed faith in God the Father, Jesus Christ, His Eternal Son, in the Holy Spirit, and acknowledged the Scriptures to be the Word of God, though differing in other things as to doctrine, worship and discipline, were to be protected in the full exercise of their religion, and to be considered fit and capable for any civil trust, employment or promotion open to members of the Established Church. Only the godly ministry, established by the Government, was not to be openly reviled in their assemblies, or disturbed in the worship of God.

Not quite so much religious liberty as Oliver could have wished, but more than he could have expected Parliament to grant. And it meant very, very much to him that it was Parliament that was proposing a plan that was acceptable at all. Now it would be possible "to divest the sword of all civil authority," to put his government on a legal parliamentary basis.

"I think," he said, "it is an Act of Government that in the aims of it, seeks the settling of the nation on a good foot in relation to civil rights and liberties, which are the liberties of the nation. It also exceedingly well provides for the safety and security of honest men in that great natural and religious liberty which is liberty of conscience."

He must needs bear testimony to the authors, "that they have been zealous of the two greatest concernments that God hath in this world. The one is that of Religion, of the just preservation of the professors of it; to give them all due and just liberty, and to assert that Truth of God as you have done in this paper, and do refer it to be done more fully by yourselves and me. And as to the Liberty of men professing godliness under a variety of forms amongst us, you have done that which was never done before," (by a Parliament at any rate)." And I pray God it may not fall upon the people of God as a fault in them, or any sort of them, if they do not put such a value upon this that is now done, as never was put upon anything since Christ's time, for such a Catholic interest of the people of God. The other thing cared for is the Civil Liberty and Interest of the Nation, and which, though it is, and I think ought to be subordinate to a more peculiar Interest of God, yet it is the next best thing given to man in this world; and if well cared for it is better than any rock to fence men in their own interests. Then if any one whatsoever think the interests of Christians and the interests of the Nation inconsistent and two different things, (for some time it had seemed as though they were), I wish my soul may never enter into their secrets,—He sings sweetly who sings a song of reconciliation between these interests." The song that Oliver had been waiting for a long time, and now he thought that he was beginning to hear it.

But about the Crown he hesitated, did not give Parliament and his friends a decided answer until May 8th. The thing was of weight, he said, the greatest weight that was ever laid upon any man. It ought to beget in him the greatest reverence and fear of God that ever possessed a man in the world. It was of high and great importance, "the welfare, the peace, the settlement of three Nations, and all that rich treasure of the best people in the world being involved in it." And he asked for time to deliberate and consider.

He took five weeks. During these weeks Parliament was constantly sending committees to him, and "time after time," says Clarendon, "they parted, all men standing at gaze and in terrible suspense, according to their several hopes and fears, till they knew what he would determine." Part of the time he was ill, could not see the committees when they came to him. After refusing to see them for two days, he "came out of his chamber, half-unready, with a black scarf about his neck."

And he had conferences with personal friends about it. He "often advised about this of the Kingship, and other great businesses, with the Lord Broghill, Pierpont, Whitelocke, Sir Charles Wolseley and Thurloe, and would be shut up three or four hours with them together in private discourse, none were admitted to come in to him. He would sometimes be very cheerful with them, and laying aside his greatness, he would be exceedingly familiar; and by way of diversion would make verses with them, and every one must try his fancy. He commonly called for tobacco pipes and a candle, and would now and then take tobacco himself, which was a very high attempt. Then he would fall again to his serious and great business of the kingship, and advise with them in these affairs. And this he did often with them."

And he could not decide the matter. Sir Francis Russell, Henry's father-in-law, wrote to him, "And now I would be a little merry with your father, and his temper and complexion, suppose I should tell you that he often knows not his own mind, 'twere but to affirm he is but a man, and like with many of his best friends and servants, who truly love him." "I need not tell you what His Highness' exercise is at this time," wrote Fleetwood. "There is no question," Clarendon says, "but that the man was in an agony." And he was. "You have urged me with reasons," he said to one of the committees that waited upon him, "I have thought rather to tell you my grief, and the sorrow that I am under. Any man can give me leave to die!"

The arguments presented for it were that the title of Protector was not known to the law, that of King was, the people knew their duty to a king, and his to them. Whatever else there was would be wholly new, would be "nothing else but a probationer," and upon the next occasion would be changed again. Moreover the name of Protector came in with the sword, and therefore would never be the ground of any settlement, "nor will there be a free Parliament so long as that continues, and as it savours of the sword now, so it will at last bring all things into confusion."

There was another argument, one that concerned their own safety. In case the Stuarts came back, there was an act of Henry VII, by which all persons who had obeyed a king *de facto* were to be held guiltless, not so if they served a Protector *de facto*. Also would not the assumption of the title be a protection against the return of the Stuarts? "The Imperial Crown of this country and the Pretended King are indeed divorced," said Lord Broghill, "nevertheless persons divorced may come together again, but if the person divorced be married to another, there is no chance left of that!"

As for Oliver's reasoning with himself and with others, he realized the force of all these arguments, he knew that the nation was "big with expectation of something that might add to their better Being," perhaps this would. If he had walked in darkness for a long time, so had the nation. "Surely none except the Israelites were ever led in such dark paths and ways as we hitherto have been," Fleetwood wrote to Henry Cromwell.

He had twice refused the title, largely because it had been offered by the army, but now Parliament offered it, and he "would rather have any name from Parliament, than any other name without it." And he believed that all men were of his mind in that, he believed that the nation was very much of that mind, "though that be an uncertain way of arguing of what mind they are of."

He had undertaken the Place that he was in, not in the hope of doing any good, but because he saw that the nation was running headlong into confusion and disorder, which would necessarily run into blood, and he might prevent imminent evil. And now, so far as he could, he was willing to serve under any name, as a constable, if they liked. "For truly I have, as before God, thought it often that I could not tell what my business was, in the place I stood in, save comparing myself to a good Constable to keep the peace of the Parish."

But then,—was he the right person to take the Crown? Might not his doing so prove a curse to the nation, as one who makes love to the wrong person, might bring a curse upon himself and his friends? He was adding himself all up.

He knew that he was no longer as popular in the nation as he had been after Worcester, and after the dissolution of the Long Parliament. At either of those times it was possible that he might have done it successfully. But not now, there were the Major Generals, and other things that might count against him. And was it not too late any-how? In choosing him, had they not chosen a man who was at the end of his work? And who would take it up after him? He knew that the infirmities of age were creeping upon him. These frequent illnesses were alarming.

And finally—he had to put his own doubt and questioning before them—was it not possible that they had chosen "a man in whom God took no pleasure"? For the blessedness that was his "when first he knew the Lord" seemed to have left him. As a practical statesman he had had to be so mundane, had had to compromise so much, sin so much against his own ideals! And his God no longer went before him as a pillar of cloud by day, and as a pillar of fire by night, he was in danger of losing his way. Had he fallen from grace? That was what was to trouble him even upon his deathbed.

And then, turning from his personal fitness, had not the providence of God laid aside this title of king, seeming to strike out not only the person and the family that had borne it, but the name itself, blasting the very title? Ought he to seek to build Jericho again?

While he was meditating about these things, there were two inter-ruptions. There was a rising of the Fifth Monarchy men, led by one Venner, a wine cooper. They planned to rise on Thursday, the ninth of April, and expel all carnal sovereigns. Cromwell knew about it, Thurloe kept him informed of everything. So as they were preparing a rendezvous on Mile End Green, a troop of horse seized Venner and twenty others. They were lodged in the Tower. Cromwell himself was with them until two or three o'clock in the morning, making ex-amination of them. No one was put to death for it, but two years later Venner died on the scaffold for a similar attempt against Charles II.

And on April 27th Sir Francis Russell wrote Henry that in spite of the fact that the weighty question of the Crown had not yet been decided, "the affair of Mr. Rich and Lady Frances seems to me to trouble the minds of both your father and your mother more than anything else."

For Lady Frances, Oliver's youngest child, only seventeen, had be-stowed her affections upon Mr. Robert Rich, grandson of the Earl of Warwick. Henry knew all about it, for in the preceding June his sister Mary, next older than Frances, had written him, "Truly, I can truly say it, for the last three months, I think our family, and myself in particular, have been in the greatest confusion and trouble that ever poor family was in." There had been some difficulty with Lord

Warwick about the settlement, but Lady Mary surmised that it was not so much the estate "as some private reasons that my father disclosed to none, but to my sister Frances and to his own family; which was a dislike to the young person, which he had from reports of his being a vicious man, given to play, and such like things"; reports spread "by some one who had a mind to break off the match." But Lady Frances, who was "so much engaged in affection before this that she could not think of breaking it off," had bestirred herself, and found that there was no truth in them, "so that she engaged me and all the friends she had, who truly were very few, to speak in her behalf with my father." And Oliver had promised that, if he were satisfied as to the report, he would make no difficulty about the estate. But now the young man's father was making trouble, "having no esteem at all of his son, because he is not so bad as himself." Yet "truly," Lady Mary ends, "I must tell you privately that they are so far engaged that the match cannot be broken off."

Poor little Frances! though her affair was much on her father's mind, she must wait until greater affairs were settled. It was not until May 8th that he made the great refusal. "But truly this is my answer. That although I think the Act of Government doth consist of very excellent parts, in all but that one thing of the Title, I should not be an honest man, if I should not tell you that I cannot accept of the Government nor undertake the trouble and charge of it, as to which I have a little more experimented than everybody what troubles and difficulties do befall men under such trusts and undertakings. I say I am persuaded to return this answer to you, That I cannot undertake this government with the title of King. And that is mine answer to this great and weighty question."

What had decided him? Up to the last moment Parliament had hoped that he would accept, and he himself had about made up his mind that he would do so, had even told Desborough that he would. But Desborough had replied, that in that case, though he would not work against him, he would never again work with him. And when the day for the final answer came Fleetwood, Desborough and Lambert threatened that, in case of his acceptance, they would lay down their commissions. That morning thirty officers presented a petition to Parliament protesting against the revival of the Kingship, and begging them to press the Protector no longer.

That was the immediate occasion for the refusal, the last straw that turned the balance, but it was not the real reason. Oliver was not afraid of the great officers, he had sent Harrison into disgrace, and

was soon to send Lambert.   But he knew that a large number of the
lesser officers and of the common soldiers that he loved were opposed
to it, would misunderstand it, would think that he was grasping at
greatness for himself.   "My Lord," Captain William Bradford had
written to him, "though the major part in Parliament hath voted this
upon you, yet those that loved you, hoped you would have disowned
it.—I am of that number, my Lord, that still loves you, and greatly
desires to do so, I having gone along with you from Edgehill to Dunbar.—My Lord, neither my life, estate nor relations were ever any
thing to me, in comparison of the public, nor yet is; yet I would not
be prodigal of them, or your Highness's favour.   My freedom proceeds
from a large proportion of love and no bye-ends."

That was the kind of thing that really moved Oliver.   On April 13th,
just after the discovery of Venner's plot, he had opened his heart on
the matter to the committee of Parliament, that waited upon him.
He went back over his history, told them how, beginning as a Captain
of Horse, he had been preferred and lifted up from lesser things to
greater, recounted his conversation with Hampden, told of the troops
that he had raised.   And then, his heart swelling with pride and affection, "I must say to you that they were never beaten, and whenever they were engaged against the enemy, they beat continually."

And now for the bearing of this upon the present question.   It
swayed with his conscience that there were godly men in the army who
opposed his taking the title that had been offered to him.   "And I deal
plainly and faithfully with you, when I say I cannot think that God
would bless me in the undertaking of anything, Kingship or whatever
else, that would justly and with cause grieve them."   It was true that
they might be troubled without cause.   And yet since he knew, as
indeed he did, that there were good men who would not swallow this
title, even though it was no part of their goodness to be unwilling to
submit to what a Parliament should settle over them, yet it was his
duty and his conscience to beg that no hard things be put upon them,
things so hard to them that they could not swallow them.   If the
Nation could be provided for without that, he thought that it would
be no sin to them, no grief of heart in time coming that they have a
tenderness, even possibly if it be to their weakness, for it was the
weakness of those who have integrity and honesty and uprightness.
And he would not have them lose any servant or friend who might
help them, not even one who might seem to be of an unmannerly or
forward or womanish spirit, he would not have even such an one to be
offended by that which meant no more to him than that which he had

told them it did. The thing was not necessary, it was a "circum-
stantial," not a "fundamental."

That was the real reason that he refused the Crown. He had refused
it before because it was offered to him by the officers of the army, he
refused it now because many of the army opposed it.

The rest of the Petition and Advice, slightly modified at his suggestion, he accepted. He was still to be Protector, but Protector by grace
of Parliament, rather than by grace of the army.

CHAPTER XX

The Parliamentary Protectorate

"Misrule is better than No Rule, and an Ill Government, a Bad Government, is better than none."—OLIVER CROMWELL.

ON the twenty-sixth of June 1657, Oliver was installed as Protector under the new constitution, with all the pomp and ceremony that might have attended his coronation as King. The chair containing the Stone of Destiny was brought from Westminster Abbey. There was the robe of purple velvet, the Bible "richly gilt and bossed," the sword of state, the scepter of massive gold, the foreign ambassadors on the right hand and the left, the people shouting and the trumpets sounding.

It seemed right to him that the Government, now once more on a Parliamentary basis, should be inaugurated in such a way as to make an impression. But for himself, he came to it, "not as to a triumph, but to undertake one of the greatest tasks that ever was laid upon the back of a human being." Nothing would have induced him to "undertake this insupportable burden to flesh and blood, had it not been that he had seen in this Parliament all along a care of doing those things, that might truly and really answer the ends that we have engaged for."

Parliament took a six months' vacation, but for the Protector there was no vacation. He was, of course, watching the movements of the army and navy abroad, and to a certain extent directing them. The prestige of England was very high, for in alliance with France she was making successful progress against Spain. At Santa Cruz Blake had dealt her the blow, from which she has never recovered, either as a continental or maritime power. And Oliver was taking a romantic interest in the career of Charles X, the new King of Sweden who, he fondly hoped, would prove another Gustavus Adolphus. Again, he was dreaming of a great Protestant league. But the various Protestant States, Holland, Denmark, Brandenburg and even Sweden, were more bent upon fighting each other for commercial gain, than upon uniting to fight Rome. "It may be said," wrote Jephson, English envoy to Sweden, "with as much truth as it ought to be with grief, that religion among States is much oftener pretended for their own interests than really embraced for the honour of God." Even Oliver, sincere as he was in his desire to advance Protestantism, generally managed to do it in such a way as would redound to the material advantage of England.

Thurloe was still ferreting out, and informing him of Royalist and Leveler plots. These strange allies continued to make common cause. But John Lilburn could no longer trouble him. On giving assurance that he would be peaceable, he had been removed from the Isle of Jersey to Dover Castle. Thence he announced that he had become "one of the preciousest and most contemptible people called Quakers," and had given up his militant career. The Protector did not release him, he would be too formidable a reviler of ministers and breaker-up of meetings. He was, however, given his liberty on parole, that he might be present at his wife's confinement at Eltham. There he died, on the twenty-ninth of August, just before the parole ended. The career of turbulence, entered upon before he was twenty, ended at forty-two. But there were other turbulent spirits.

There were family affairs also for Oliver to attend to, his "two little wenches," Frances and Mary, must be given in marriage. Frances was at last to be allowed to marry the man to whom "she was so much engaged in affection that she could not think of breaking it off." So on November 11th, 1657, "the most illustrious Lady, the Lady Frances Cromwell, youngest daughter of His Highness, the Lord Protector, was married to the most noble gentleman, Mr. Robert Rich, Son of the Lord Rich, Grandchild of the Earl of Warwick, and the Countess Dowager of Devonshire, in the presence of their Highnesses, and of his Grandfather and Father, and the said Countess, with many other persons of high honour and quality." On Wednesday Mr. Scobell, as Justice of the Peace, tied the knot "after a godly prayer made by one of His Highness's divines, and on Thursday was the wedding feast kept at Whitehall, where they had forty-eight violins and fifty trumpets, and much mirth and frolic besides mixt dancing." "The discourse of the Towne was much filled up with that great marriage."

And on Thursday of the following week, at Hampton Court, the Lady Mary was married, "to the most noble Lord, the Lord Fauconberg." For their wedding Andrew Marvell composed two pastorals, in one of which there is a musical dialogue in which the bride took the part of Cynthia, the bridegroom that of Endymion, and Oliver himself is said to have come on the stage in the final chorus, in the character of Jove.

Mary seems to have had a propensity for love affairs. We have
seen the interest that she took in the course of true love in her sister
Frances' case. At an earlier date she had tried to bring about a
marriage between her brother Henry and a daughter of Lord Wharton.
The Protector, sensing that this would not be agreeable to Lord Wharton, had written to him, "Let this affair slide easily off, and not a
word more to be spoken about it, as your Lordship's own thoughts are.
So hush all, and save the labour of little Mall's fooling."

But she had very little to say about her own marriage. That had
been arranged by her parents, and in such a hurry that it seems to
have taken her breath away. "The hurry that I have been," she writes
to Henry, "being so suddenly concluded as this business hath, has put
me into so great a confusion, as that truly I could not tell how or
what to write to my friends.—I cannot but hope," she adds, "God
has given me this as a blessing, although He has been pleased to
dispose of my heart, so that I have been obliged to my parents."

Yet she alone of all the Protector's children was destined to live a
long life in prosperity and comparative happiness. If she had not
made a love match, it turned out to be a love marriage. In less than
two weeks she announced that she had been married "to a person that
hath greater kindness than ever I could have expected. Lord Fauconberg was Oliver's favorite son-in-law, and later he acquitted himself
honorably as a statesman down into the reign of William and Mary.
A man of fine tastes too, fond of books, gardens, and works of art.
Mary lived on into the reign of Anne, the main stay of her family,
most of whom were in poverty, and needed assistance. Burnet thought
that she was more likely to have maintained the post of Protector
than either of her brothers, according to a saying that went of her,
"that those who wore breeches deserved petticoats better; but if those
in petticoats had been in breeches, they would have held faster."

These marriages were a happy relaxation, but Oliver's main work
during the recess of Parliament was to select the members of the
Upper House. He was, as we have seen, well pleased that there
should be such a House. There had been a time when he had been
called the greatest anti-lord in England. Had he not said that he
hoped to see never a lord there? But that was in a moment of irritation, he was conservative by nature, and perhaps had always believed
that some kind of second chamber was desirable. In the Heads of
Proposals, prepared in 1647 under his direction, the authority of the
lords was scarcely diminished. In the debates in the Army Council
in 1647 and 1648 he opposed the abolition of the Upper House, though

he said that if there had never been one, and it were free before him whether he should set it up, he probably would not do so. When the Lords finally were abolished in February 1649, "Lieutenant General Cromwell appeared for them, having already had a close correspondence with many of them."

And by this time his experience of the Long Parliament "assuming to itself the authority of the three estates that were before—the horridest contrariness that ever was exercised in this world," the difficulties that he had had with subsequent Parliaments, and finally James Naylor's case, had convinced him that another House was needed as a balance. So in a conference with members of Parliament concerning the Petition and Advice he had told them that he could not undertake the government, unless there might be some persons that might interpose between him and the House of Commons "to prevent tumultuous and popular spirits." So another House, not to be hereditary, was decided upon.

The choice of the members had been left altogether to him, the Commons not even insisting upon the right of approving. Men, it was said, might refuse to serve if they were in danger of being tossed up and down in the House, and their lives ripped up there. Then many in the Commons wished to be Lords themselves, and "if His Highness should send you a list of names, and they lie before you, and some think that they ought to be named that are left out, they will stir up obstruction to the approval of others."

And so he set to work to make his selection. It was a very difficult task, even though, as Thurloe said, "his Highness had the reputation of knowing men better than any other man." For there were "those who were fit and not willing to serve, and there were those who were willing and expected it, but were not fit." And "a mistake here will be like war or marriage, it admits of no repentance."

He at first drew up a long list of names of all possible candidates, then he reduced it to eighty. "These must go through the furnace again, and which will prove gold, and which dross, a little time will show." On the first of December Thurloe wrote that there was not one name fully decided upon yet.

But by the tenth the list was completed, and a form of summons, similar to that used in summoning Peers to Parliament, was sent to sixty-three persons. Among those selected were seven of the old nobility, and in the minds of many the dignity of the new House depended largely upon whether these peers obeyed the summons. Only two did so, Cromwell's own son-in-law Lord Fauconberg, and

George, Lord Eure, whom a Republican pamphleteer characterized as "a poor peer not very bulky, or inspiring for a lord."

Out of the sixty-three summoned, forty-two accepted. The selection was probably as good as, under the complicated circumstances, it could have been. As was almost inevitable, the military element had too large a place. There were seventeen officers actually in command of regiments, and in addition there were titular colonels.

On the twentieth of January 1658 Parliament reassembled after the six months' vacation. Not the same Parliament, however, there was the new House of Lords, and the House of Commons was as much altered as it might have been by a general election. In the first place many of Cromwell's best supporters had been transferred to the Upper House, and unfortunately they were the men who possessed the powers of management and leadership; in the second place the excluded members, almost a hundred of them, largely Republicans, came back to oppose the form of government that had been concocted during their absence. No doubt Oliver, to some extent at least, saw the danger, but there was no help for it. He could not fill the vacancies in the Lower House, caused by the removal of members to the Lords, except as the Speaker issued writs for that purpose, and that could not be done without the order of the House. And he had been obliged to accept the Petition and Advice as a whole, and that had forbidden the exclusion of any one elected to Parliament, except as it was done by the House to which he had been elected.

Yet there was a strong note of hopefulness in his opening speech. His was a sanguine temperament, hope crushed to earth always rose again within him, especially when there was a new experiment to be tried. And now he felt that there was abundant reason to rejoice and be glad, to thank God and take courage, for they were getting back on a legal and constitutional basis, there was at last a constitution really framed by Parliament, even though it was a packed Parliament, from which his opponents had been excluded. And this constitution was a long step toward the old order of things, probably the only order that England would accept.

That the return was slow was perhaps not altogether to be regretted, it might on that account be all the more sure. He probably agreed with his son Henry who wrote, "I confess I like gradual proceedings best, and this the better, because it seems such; for I take the late Instrument and way of government to have been a real relief against the wild courses of the Little Parliament; and am glad that no alteration in that Instrument was effected, till time and experience had taught us both its faults and its remedies. Wherefore I am contented that the finishing of our settlement be also deferred, till a competent trial hath been made of the present way. And although we should at last return to that very form which was of old, yet I do not think these several tossings and tumblings have been in vain, for by them men will be the better convinced of the danger of levity, and take heed how they are too wanton and bold hereafter with long settled constitutions. Besides these things come to pass that the works of God may be made manifest."

The Protector's speech was made in the Upper House, and he addressed his hearers in the old fashion, "My Lords and Gentlemen." It was brief, for he was not well. "It is very well known to you all," he said, "what difficulties we have passed through, and what we have now arrived at. We hope we may say we have arrived at what we aimed at, if not at that which is beyond our expectation. How hath God redeemed us, as we stand this day! Not from trouble and sorrow and anger only, but into a placid and happy state and condition, comprehensive of all the interest of every member, of every individual. Peace and Rest out of ten years of war, and given us what we would desire!" And now "if God should bless you in this work, and make this meeting happy with this account, you shall be called the Blessed of the Lord. The generations to come will bless you. You shall be the repairers of the breaches, and the restorers of paths to dwell in; And if there be any higher work that mortals can attain to in this world, I acknowledge my ignorance of it!"

"Being under some infirmity," he could not speak to them at length, and had asked Nathaniel Fiennes, the Commissioner of the Great Seal, to discourse more particularly. His address was a rhapsody in glorification of the new constitution. "Some years since we had not thought to see a Chief Magistrate again among us, and lo! God hath shown us a Chief Magistrate in His two Houses of Parliament! Now may the good God make them like Ephraim and Manasseh, that the three nations may be blessed in them, saying, "God make thee like these two Houses of Parliament which two, like Leah and Rachel, did build the House of Israel! This Constitution of a Chief Magistrate and two Houses of Parliament is not a pageantry, but a real and well-measured advantage to itself and the Commonwealth; and so consonant to reason, that it is the very emblem and idea of reason itself, which reasoneth and discourseth by a medium between two extremes. If there be two extremes, and one vary from the other, how shall they be reconciled, if there be no medium to bring them together?"

He dwelt upon the importance of the Protector and Upper House as safeguards against hasty legislation. "If anything inconvenient should chance to slip out at one door, must it not pass two, before it come abroad to the detriment of the people? How exact, and of how great respect and authority will be all your acts when, after they have passed the examination of that great body which sees with the eyes of the three nations, and is acquainted with the conditions, and sensible of the necessities of every individual part thereof, they shall then pass a second scrutiny, and be polished and refined by such as during life shall make it their business either to fit themselves for, or be exercised in things of that nature!"

But alas for these high hopes! The Opposition members were coming back to make trouble! "Here are very many strange spirits come amongst us," says a newsletter, "and there are daily more flocking in." They were perfectly willing to swear to be true and faithful to the Lord Protector, the only oath required of them. "I shall heartily take the oath," said Sir Arthur Haselrigg, who had been one of those summoned to the Upper House, but disapproving of such a House altogether, had preferred to retain his seat in the Commons, "I will be faithful to my Lord Protector's person, I will murder no man."

On the twenty-second of January, just two days after the opening, the New House sent the Old a message. Immediately the question came up as to whether, in the answer that was to be sent, it should be addressed as the Lords or the Other House. The Petition and Advice had styled it the Other House, but Oliver had addressed Parliament as "My Lords and Gentlemen."

The debate was not confined to the title, the very existence of another House was called in question. "We called the King of England to our bar and arraigned him," said Thomas Scott, member for Aylesbury. "He was for his obstinacy and guilt condemned to be executed, and so let all the enemies of God perish. Upon this the Lords' House adjourned and never met, and hereby came a farewell to all those peers, and it was hoped the people of England should never have a negative upon them.—They were by the providence of God set free from any negative. Will they thank you if you bring such a negative upon them, the people that have bled for you? What was fought for, but to arrive at that capacity, to make your own laws?"

And Haselrigg who, it will be remembered, was one of the Five Members whom Charles I had sought to impeach, chimed in with,

"Well is it for Pym, Strode and Hampden, my fellow-traitors, impeached by the King, that they are dead! Yet I am glad that I am alive to say this at this day. The Lords willingly laid down their lives, and the army desired that they might have a decent interment, which was done accordingly. And shall we now rake them up, after they have so long lain in the grave?" It was the matter of highest concernment ever debated in the Parliament of England. For himself he would rather be torn in pieces than betray the liberties of the people of England.

Some one complained that the new lords had not sufficient landed property to qualify them for their position. To which Major Boteler replied that they had better qualifications than land, religion, piety and faithfulness to the Commonwealth. "These are the best balances. These persons have them. It is not estates that will be the best balance." Major Burke thought they could qualify even in a material way, "The sword is there. Is not that also a balance? He that has a regiment of foot to command an army, he is as good a balance as any that I know, and can do more." He meant this as a defense, but it was really the gravest objection to which Oliver's choice of lords lay open. The military element was too well represented, even yet he had not succeeded in transforming the military state into the civilian state.

And the whole discussion was throwing him into a state of excited anxiety. He regarded himself as "set on a watch tower to see what might be for the good of these Nations, and what might be for the preventing of evil." This debate did not tend toward either, it was mere child's play, and dangerous child's play. And if this meeting did not succeed in lengthening tranquillity and peace, he did not consider that there was "as to men, so much as a possibility of discharging that trust that was incumbent upon them, for the safety and preservation of these Nations."

So on January 25th he sent for the Two Houses, and made them what one member calls "a very long plain and serious speech, relating to the state of our affairs at home and abroad, inviting us to unite, and not stand upon circumstances."

He had not taken time, he had not had time, to prepare this speech carefully, and when, a few days later, he was requested by the Commons to send them a copy of it, he replied that he could not remember four lines of it in a piece, but as it has been put together from the notes of some of his auditors, it is very forceful, without the frequent digressions that usually characterized his parliamentary addresses, and raises the question as to whether he did not, under strong excitement, speak better when he had not prepared than when he had.

He began, "My Lords and Gentlemen of the Two Houses of Parliament," as though that matter were settled, and yet not quite, for he added, "For so I must own you, in whom, together with myself, is vested the legislative power of these Nations."

He had had it in his thoughts to make it the method of his speech to have let them see the things that hazarded their Being, and the things that hazarded their Well-Being. But when he had come to consider it, he had decided that he could not make this distinction. As affairs now stood, all things resolved themselves into very Being for "You are not a Nation, you will not be a Nation, if God strengthen you not to meet with these evils that are upon us."

He had at first thought that the profession of the Protestant religion abroad was only a question of Well-Being, but, taken with all its concomitants, he had come to the conclusion that it was a question of Being. For the question to his mind now was whether the Christian world should be all Popery. The House of Austria, both in Spain and Austria, was planning to destroy the whole Protestant Interest. Leopold, King of Hungary, likely to become Emperor of Germany, was the son of a father who had exiled all Protestants out of his own country. The Protestants had been tossed out of Poland into the Empire, and thence where they could fly to get their bread, and in many cases had failed to get it. There was a Pope, Alexander VII, who was fitted to accomplish bloody work. He hoped that he had been born out of, rather than in good time. They knew what Spain was. So in all parts of Europe there was a consent, a coöperating at that time and season of all Popish powers to suppress everything that stood in their way.

Against this mighty torrent, the King of Sweden, "a poor Prince, indeed poor, but a man in his person as gallant and truly I think I may say as good as any these late ages have brought forth," had held up his hand. But he was now reduced to a corner, and men of their own religion (Dutch and Danes) were seeking his ruin. That was more grievous than anything that he had spoken of before.

And if they were not moved by religious considerations, then let them reflect upon the mundane aspects of the case. "If these warring powers can shut us out of the Baltic Sea, and make themselves masters of that, where is your trade? Where are your materials to preserve your shipping? Or where will you be able to challenge any right by sea, or justify yourselves against a foreign invasion on your own soil?" This certainly concerned Being!

And all the time they were threatened by a landing of Charles Stuart. How could they, so situated, "discourse of all things at pleasure," as though it were a time in which they might sleep, and take their ease and rest and draw one another off from considering these things, which were very palpable things? For if they should meet tomorrow, and accord in all things, it was to be feared that too much time had elapsed already to deliver themselves from the dangers that hung upon them."

For look at affairs at home. When he would speak of them, he hardly knew where to begin. "We are as full of calamities and divisions among us in respect to the spirits of men as we could well be.—Consider what is the variety of Interests in this nation, if they be worthy of the name of Interests!—What is the general spirit of this Nation? Is it not that each sect of the people, if I may call them sects, whether upon a religious or civil account, what is it which possesseth every sect? What is it? That every sect may be upper-most? That every sort of men may get the power into their hands, and they would use it well!"

And there were "men going about who could not tell what they would have, yet were willing to kindle coals to disturb others!" There were men who were "summoning men together to take up arms, and exhorting men, each sort of them, to fight for their own notions, every sort thinking they were to try it out by the sword.—Some of these, yea some of these, they care not who carry the goal, nay, some of these, have invited the Spaniard himself to assist him." "Peace-breakers, do they consider what it is they are driving towards? He that con-sidereth not the woman with child, the sucking children of the nation, that know not the right hand from the left, he who consid-ereth not these must have a Cain's heart, who was marked and made to be an enemy to all men, and all men enemies to him. The wrath and justice of God will prosecute such a man to his grave, if not to Hell!" [Oliver found it difficult to consign any man to Hell.] For "really, pretend what you will, if you run into another flood of blood and war, the sinews of this Nation being wasted by the last, it must sink and perish utterly.—It will be said of this poor nation, Actum est de Anglia."

Under these circumstances it would be a happy thing, if this Nation, so full of sects, would be content with rule. Content with rule, if it were but in civil things, and even with those who would rule worst, because MISRULE IS BETTER THAN NO RULE, AND AN ILL GOVERNMENT, A BAD GOVERNMENT, IS BETTER THAN NONE. And "have you any frame or model that would satisfy the minds of men, if this be not the frame that you are now called together upon, and have engaged in? I mean the two Houses of Parliament and myself. What hinders this Nation from being made an Aceldama, a field of blood, if this do not?"

He had said at the beginning, that when he had told them what occurred to his thoughts, he would leave it to such an operation upon their hearts, as it would please God Almighty to work upon them. That operation was disappointing. The futile debate on the Other House was continued as though he had not spoken to them. He had not frightened them out of it, they simply refused to look facts in the face, to see where they stood. So instead of trying to allay the forces of discontent, the men who were "kindling coals to disturb others," Fifth Monarchists, ultra-sectarian clergy and army malcontents, the Opposition members actually sought an alliance with them. A petition to the House of Commons was drawn up addressed to "the Parliament of the Commonwealth of England," the "Other House" being ignored. Who the author was is not known, but it was certainly supported by opposition members in the House, Hazelrigg, Scott and Weaver. It demanded a Parliament representing the people of England, limited neither by written constitution, Other House, or Protector. To win the support of Fifth Monarchy men, Quakers and Unitarians, it asked that provision be made for all sincere professors of religion, so that tender consciences should not be oppressed. This might be interpreted as a promise that there should be no Established Church. An alarming bid for the support of the discontented in the army was embodied in the demand that "the officers and soldiers, who have hazarded their lives for the nation's liberty, may not be turned out of their respective regiments, without a legal trial by a court martial, that so the military power may be preserved in the hands of those who are not merely neuters or disaffected." All very well for a modern army confining itself strictly to military affairs, but not for an army that was a great political power, in which there were Harrisons and Lamberts, trying to dictate not only the form, but every action of the government, and ready, perhaps able, to stir up a military insurrection when they were not listened to.

Fifty copies of this Petition were printed, and circulated in London for signature. How many signatures were obtained is not known, one estimate says twenty thousand, and adds that they were rolling up like a snowball. It was arranged that on February 4th twenty persons, (there was a rumor that Lord Fairfax would lead them), should present it to the House of Commons. And this was the plan of ultra-Republicans, at a time when Charles II with a small army was waiting in Flanders to cross the water, when the Marquis of Ormond, his emissary, was hidden in London, and the Royalists in England were preparing for a rising!

Oliver was fully informed. He knew that no time could be lost. So the mind that worked so slowly in council with others, so slowly in counsel with himself, again leaped to a decision as on the battlefield. This Parliament must be dissolved on February 4th, and before the Petition could be presented.

That was an exciting morning for him. What had been decided quickly must be executed quickly. So about ten o'clock he left Whitehall telling Thurloe that he was going to Parliament, but not telling him why. He intended to take a boat to Westminster, but finding that there was too much ice in the river to go that way, he came back, ordered a guard to call the first hackney coach that he could find. There was no time to prepare a state coach. On reaching the House, he went to his withdrawing room, where he sought to fortify and calm himself with a cup of ale and some toast. There his son-in-law Fleetwood and Fiennes came to him. He told them that he had come to dissolve the House. "I beseech your Highness," said Fleetwood, "consider well of it first; it is of great consequence." "You are a milksop," answered the excited and determined Protector, "as the Lord liveth, I will dissolve this House." It took a great deal to make Oliver swear, and when he did, he swore after the fashion of the Old Testament prophets.

The Commons were still engaged in that dreary, long-drawn-out debate "touching the appellation of the Other House," when the Speaker announced that Black Rod was at the door. Scott, supported by Hazelrigg, who said that he did not care for Black Rod, was trying to speak. Nevertheless, Black Rod was admitted, and delivered his message. "Mr. Speaker, His Highness is in the Lords' House, and desires to speak with you." So Speaker and Members trooped out to the Other House. There Oliver, standing under the cloth of state, addressed them.

He had had, he said, very comfortable expectations that God would make the meeting of this Parliament a blessing. He had thought that this new constitution would put them upon a foundation, upon a bottom. Because they had been so unsettled until they arrived at it, and the consequences would necessarily have been confusion, if it had not been settled, he had felt himself bound, when petitioned and advised by them, to undertake this government, a burden too heavy for any creature. He could say in the presence of God that he would have been glad to have lived under his woodside, and kept a flock of sheep, rather than undertake such a government. But having undertaken it, he had looked that they who had offered it to him should make it good. [It was not on the whole those who had offered it to him who were refusing to make it good, but those who had been excluded at the time that it was offered.]

They had permitted him to name another House that should stand between him and the Commons. He had named it of men that should meet them wherever they went, and shake hands with them, and tell them, that it was not Titles nor Lords nor Party that they valued, but a Christian and an English Interest. "Men of your own rank and quality, who will not only be a balance with you, but a new force added to you, while you love England and Religion."

But he would not have accepted the Government, if he had not hoped of a just accord between the Government and the Governed, if he had not felt that they would keep the oath that they had taken, as he meant to keep his. Instead "it is evident to all the world and to people living, that a new Business hath been seeking in the Army in this actual settlement. I do not speak to these Gentlemen (pointing to the Other House) or Lords, or whatever you will call them. I speak this not to them, but to you (the Commons). You advised me to come into this place. Yet instead of owning a thing taken for granted, some must have I know not what, and you have not only disjointed yourselves, but the whole nation. Through the intention of revising a Commonwealth again, That some of the people might be the men that would rule all! [With his memories of the Long Parliament, his experience of Hazelrigg and Scott, Lambert and Harrison, Cromwell did not believe that such a commonwealth would be a step toward democracy.] And most horrible and incredible of all, they are endeavouring to engage the Army to carry that thing! —And while it is doing, there are endeavours from some who are not far from this place, to stir up the people of the town into a tumultuous, what if I said into a Rebellion!" He had told them before, and it had been confirmed within a day, that the King of Scots had an army at the water side, ready to be shipped to England. "And some of you have been listing persons by commission of Charles Stuart to join with any Insurrection that may be made!"

Therefore "if this be the end of your sitting, and this be your carriage, I think it high time that an end be put to your sitting! And I do dissolve this Parliament! And God be Judge between you and me!" To which many of the Commons cried "Amen!"

That was the way that Oliver dissolved his last Parliament.

There can be some question as to whether he was wise in dissolving other Parliaments. There can be none about this one. As a contemporary put it, "His Highness broke up the Parliament, because they, instead of settling the nation, were endeavouring, a great part of them, to unhinge all things, and to bring us into blood and confusion."

Yet it was the first Parliament since Pride's Purge that had had anything resembling a legal or constitutional basis, or that in any sense represented the people. And the session had lasted only two weeks.

CHAPTER XXI

The End

"Indeed we are a crazy company, yet we live in His sight, and shall work the time appointed to us, and shall rest after that in peace."—OLIVER CROMWELL.

FROM the dissolution of Cromwell's last Parliament," says Clarendon, "all things at home and abroad seemed to succeed to his wish, and his power and greatness to be better established than ever it had been."

But that was not the way in which any one, least of all the Royalists, looked upon it at first. There was one of them who wrote that "his doing such desperate things of his own head, and being secret even to his own secretary, meant that he was at his wits' end, and all things pointed to the speedy deliverance of the nation." Had not he himself declared in his speech to both Houses of Parliament, that the army was affected with sedition, and that the people were possessed with an unwearied spirit of innovation, desiring they knew not what? And his treasury was empty, the King was in Flanders with a considerable force, ready to set sail, and they counted upon twenty thousand men in London, said to be listed for him.

Yet Oliver was Oliver, his resourcefulness and good fortune had so often surprised them, they might do so again. So it was well not to hope too much. "To speak freely to your Lordship," Broderick wrote to Hyde, "the man is seemingly desperate, any other in his condition would be deemed irrecoverable, but as the dice of the gods never throw out, so there is something in the fortune of this villain that renders ten to one no odds."

He himself seems to have been much discouraged. The failure of this last Parliament preyed upon his health, "drank up his spirits," his steward tells us, "of which his natural constitution yielded a vast stock." It was perhaps the greatest blow that had come to him. For it had come at a time when it had seemed as though he had most reason to hope, at a time when affairs seemed to be getting back into the old and tried ways, and that too upon a legal and constitutional basis. There was no one to whom he could look for advice, so he shut himself up for a week, trying to think it out apart from his Council. Only once during that time did he even appear in his family circle.

He was such an isolated man, every year becoming more and more so! Did the thought of that weigh upon him that week? There were so many old friends and fellow workers, men whom he had esteemed and even loved, Vane, Harrison, Haselrigg, Overton, Cooper, Lambert, all separated from him now, all distrusting him, he himself had driven them from public life. The trouble had generally been not that they were not good and honest men, but that they were all wedded and glued to a particular form of government, and he was not. They had all been doctrinaires, not willing to forsake their pet theories even temporarily, to meet a dangerous crisis. They had not even been able to see that the crisis existed.

And ever since the close of the First Civil War there had been nothing but crises, and he had had to meet each one as it came up in the best way that he could. He had at times done everything that he had objected to in Charles and Strafford, and more. The difference was that they, like the Republicans and Levelers, were doctrinaires, they had tried to carry out their pet theories, as Harrison and Ludlow would now like to carry out theirs, and it was their intention to make that line of action permanent. Cromwell had made mistakes sometimes, notably in the matter of the Major Generals, but he had done what he had done, not because he thought it ideal, but simply because he had felt that he had no other choice at the time, and he did not mean to make it permanent. Just now his job was to keep the peace and avoid anarchy. "Any government is better than no government," he had said. For "if you run into another flood of blood and war, it will be said of this poor nation, Actum est de Anglia." But it was natural for good men, fast wedded to their own theories, to regard his inconsistencies as proofs of insatiable ambition and moral turpitude.

It was not his nature to, and he had no time to consider what was the ideally best form of government. It was no time for any one to do that. But he had clung to the old forms longer than almost any one else of his party had, and now having tried other things, he wanted to get as near back to them as circumstances would permit.

He was not a Republican. The idea of a Parliament always sitting, and arrogating to itself all power, executive, legislative and judicial, was repugnant to him. Therefore Lord Morley thinks that he would have disliked parliamentary government, as it exists in England today. I am not so sure of that, the development of the Cabinet system, which he could not have foreseen, would perhaps have made it palatable to him.

And he was not a Democrat, at least not in the common acceptation of the term. He would have maintained the social gradations that he found in the England of his day. "A nobleman, a gentleman, a yeoman, and the distinction of these, that is a good interest of the nation, and a great one." But he put men of very humble birth into his House of Lords, and he believed that a nobleman should always be "one that shall meet you wheresoever you go, and shake hands with you and tell you it is not Titles, nor Lords, nor Party that he values, but a Christian and an English Interest."

And as matters then stood he did not believe in manhood suffrage. There were crises in which he did not even consider a Parliament, freely elected by those who had the suffrage at the time, safe. But he was a Puritan, he believed in the possibilities inherent in every human soul, it was a matter of time and education. "Who can tell how soon God may fit the people for such a thing? None can desire it more than I. Would that all the Lord's people were prophets!"

The first thing to be done now was to get rid of disloyal officers in the army. That could not wait, and for that he needed no advice. So only two days after he dissolved Parliament, he called together the two hundred officers in and about London, explained why he had dissolved Parliament, went over the story of the Civil Wars, in which he and they had gone along together, until he had come to his present place, a place not of his seeking. He could not understand, he said, why they should differ now. They answered with applause, declaring themselves ready "to stand and fall, live and die, with my Lord Protector." He drank to them and they to him. But he was not satisfied. "Deal plainly and frankly with me," he said, "if any of you cannot in conscience conform to the new government, let him speak."

And then, to this body-sick and heart-sick man, the answer came from his own regiment of horse, that regiment that he had raised when the war began, those godly men that "had the fear of God before them, and made some conscience of what they did," that "lovely company that was never beaten, no, not once." It was true that the personnel had changed considerably, but the officers were, for the most part, the same. Their commander, Major Packer, expressed dissatisfaction and said that all his captains felt as he did. So Oliver sent for them, six of them. They talked of the goodness of a commonwealth. He had several interviews with them, they said that they were still dissatisfied, but were willing to follow him upon the grounds of the good old cause. When he asked them what they meant by the good old cause, and in what particulars he had departed from it, they were silent. So he told them that, as their temper and spirits now were, he thought it neither for their good, nor for the safety of the nation, that they should continue in their commands.

That seemed to give him almost complete control of the army. Declarations of loyalty from various regiments and garrisons in Scotland came pouring in. From England there was one general declaration from the whole body of officers: "We remain, notwithstanding base calumnies and lies your and our enemies have dispersed throughout the whole nation, firmly united to one another, and all of us for your Highness, as our general and chief magistrate.—We make it our earnest request to your Highness that, as a mighty man strengthened by the Lord, you will run, and not be weary in that race God hath set you in, till you have settled the great ends of all our former engagements, our civil and spiritual liberty; which we hope is in a good measure well provided for in the Humble Petition and Advice. And in all your actings tending thereunto, we heartily engage to stand by your Highness with our lives."

There was a similar declaration from the general and field officers in Ireland. "We did not take up arms as a trade.—Wherefore to prevent the same for the future, and to deter such as would again embroil us therein, we do heartily and unanimously declare, in the presence of the Lord, that we will stand as well against the particular animosities of turbulent spirits, as against others, our professed enemies." So it seemed as though all danger of sedition in the army had been removed. Oliver had again become the master, no longer the servant of the soldiers.

The next step was to secure the loyalty of London and its citizen soldiers. Therefore on March 12th, the Protector summoned the Lord Mayor and Aldermen to Whitehall, spoke to them of the danger to city and nation, by the contrivance of Charles Stuart and his party at home and abroad. And on March 17th there was another address to the Protector, pledging the support of the City, expressing the hope of a "happy, lasting and well-grounded form of government, which the Petition and Advice had aroused in their hearts.—The old restless enemy was hoping to execute his wrath and malice against the good and peaceful people of these three nations, relying upon the discontents of a brain-sick party at home, and on the popish inveterate enemy abroad," but they would stand by His Highness with their lives and their fortunes.

There were still Fifth Monarchy men and Anabaptists trying to make trouble, and although they were rather ineffectual, it was considered expedient to arrest and imprison a few of them for a short time. For the Government was aware that the Royalists had not given up hope, that there was still a plot on foot that might be dangerous.

The plan had been that Charles II should come over from Flanders, and that there should be risings in various parts of England in his favor. The Rev. Dr. John Hewitt, who had been allowed to hold the living of St. Gregory's in St. Paul's Churchyard, was collecting money for this, and keeping up a correspondence with the King. Sir Henry Slingsby was attempting to persuade some officers of the garrison to betray Hull to him and the Spaniards. Ormond had been sent over from Flanders to make connections with the conspirators. But he found so many divisions among them, such lack of a concerted plan, that he decided that it was not wise for him even to see Hewitt; the conspirators needed to be restrained, rather than encouraged. To encourage a rising would be "to expose them to inevitable ruin, and the King's counsels to irreparable and shameful division." There was "no want of will, but there was want of skill." He returned to Flanders in March and reported that while there was considerable opposition to Cromwell, the idea of a successful Royalist uprising was at present moonshine.

And so the plan that Charles should come over was given up for a time, but risings in London, Surrey, Sussex, and other counties were still planned. The Government was, as usual, fully cognizant of the preparations, took various means to head them off, and the principal conspirators were arrested. About a dozen of them were tried by a High Court of Justice specially created for the purpose. Two, Dr. Hewitt and Sir Henry Slingsby, were found guilty and beheaded on Tower Hill. Six others were sentenced to be hanged, but of these three were reprieved at the foot of the gallows. Cromwell was not a man of blood, it seemed necessary to make an example of the principal offenders, but he was only too glad to pardon the others.

There was considerable sympathy for Slingsby, based partly upon the fact that evidence against him had been obtained in ways not accounted altogether justifiable. It did not make it easier for the Protector that this sympathy extended even to his own family. Slingsby's wife, now dead, had been Lord Fauconberg's aunt. Fauconberg was in France at the time, but Lady Fauconberg, Mary Cromwell, made an effort to save him, even appealing to the French Ambassador to ask Mazarin to intercede with her father on his behalf. The Cardinal however declined to intervene unless he had evidence that Oliver really wished to spare him, and would therefore welcome the pretext afforded by his intercession. As a man, Cromwell may have wished to spare him, but as Protector he could not. Slingsby had planned to betray the most accessible landing place in England to forces coming from Flanders to Charles II and the Spaniards. In pronouncing judgment upon him Lisle, the President of the Court, had said that natural considerations should have deterred him from such a treason. Charles Stuart was in confederacy with Spain against England. Was it natural that an Englishman, that a Protestant should affect such a conspiracy as that?

Abroad that summer England's arms were victorious everywhere, Oliver's fame was at its height. The victory of the Dunes came on June 4th, Dunkirk surrendered on the fourteenth. There were gains of the Allies in Flanders such as to remove all fear that Charles II and the Spaniards would land in England. When Fauconberg was sent to Calais with letters of congratulation to the French king, he was received by him and Mazarin with marks of respect such as had never been given to the ambassador of any crowned head. And Louis XIV dispatched a magnificent embassy to the Protector, and but for an attack of smallpox, would have come himself. In less than ten years the country that all foreign nations had despised had become the one that all honored and courted. "The Lord is pleased to do wonderful things for His Highness, and to bless his affairs beyond expression," Thurloe wrote.

That was the bright side of it, but the dark side of it was that the treasury was empty, and financial necessities were constantly becoming more pressing. The revenue was £1,900,000, the expenses of the government about £400,000 more, the debt £1,750,000. The Protector's foreign policy had been very expensive. The pay of the soldiers was in arrears, it was feared that they would have to take free quarters upon the people. And while it was evident that Spain would soon be forced to make peace, it was not certain that the consequent decrease in expenditure would not be more than balanced by the cost of holding Dunkirk.

No one had as yet thought of the expedient of funding the debt, and raising loans to cover deficiencies. In the Council Desborough and perhaps Fleetwood were for raising money by force. "I hope

God in His mercy will not lead us into that temptation," Henry Cromwell wrote from Ireland. Fortunately there were enough moderate men in the Council to vote it down, to decide that whatever was obtained, must be obtained by Parliamentary grant.

Almost as soon as the old Parliament was dissolved, there were rumors that there would soon be a new one. But what manner of Parliament would it be? There were those who thought that it might be a nominated assembly, this time not of saints, but of notables. And there was also a report that it would be like the Parliaments of old, that the change in the system of representation involved in the Instrument of Government would be abandoned, that the old peers of the nation who had not forfeited their right, would be summoned along with the new lords.

As for the opinion of the Council on the subject, Thurloe wrote: "They incline to a Parliament, if they can agree what to ask a Parliament.—If you ask what are the difficulties of coming to this resolution, I answer I know none but the fears in some honest men that they will settle us upon some foundation, and the doubt of some others that if these fears should prevail, and so disappoint a settlement, that then a Parliament will ruin us." Which is, being interpreted, a Parliament was certain to again press the crown upon Oliver, and if the opposition to it was so strong that he again felt bound to decline, it would probably grant no money.

Throughout the nation most men were sure that the Protector would soon take the title of king, perhaps even before Parliament met. "Our state here is for a king, and none fitter for it than His Highness," James Waynwright wrote to Richard Bradshaw. "It is certain," the French Ambassador informed his government, "that the re-establishment of royalty is agreed upon. A large part of the officers have already supported it, recognizing that it is the only way to secure the peace of the nation, and to extract money from it. All persons of quality wish this change, and only the inferior officers of the army seem opposed to it." Addresses were coming in from various counties, asking the Protector to assume the title of king.

What he himself thought about it, we cannot know. The call seemed stronger than it had previously been, much of the opposition had been removed.

In May the deliberations of the Council were interrupted by the Hewitt-Slingsby plot that had to be attended to. When this was out of the way the season was too far advanced to make it worth while to try to bring a Parliament together until after the harvest.

But in the summer Oliver determined that another Parliament must
be summoned in the autumn, and he put the deliberations on the
subject of how it should be constituted, and what should be asked of
it, into the hands of a junto of nine. Republican opposition was not
greatly feared, it was realized that the Republican strength in the
last House of Commons had been due largely to the removal of so
many of the Protector's supporters to the Lords, while their places
had not been filled by new elections. And now the victories of the
summer had made the government popular. The main difficulty was
that the question of the Crown would have to be faced.

Nothing much came of the deliberations of the junto. Oliver grew
impatient, decided that he must take his own resolution, he could
sit still no longer, and make himself guilty of the loss of all the
honest party, and of the nation itself. But what his resolution was
no one knew.

The only thing that his advisers could agree upon was that he should
be asked to name his successor. That was imperative. "Does not
your peace depend upon His Highness' life?" Henry Cromwell was
writing from Ireland. "If no settlement be made in his lifetime,
can we be secure from the lusts of ambitious men?"

It was a very difficult thing to do. "Where is that person of
wisdom, courage, conduct and reputation at home and abroad which
we see necessary to preserve our peace?" Yet he had already done
it. Shortly after his second inauguration he had written the name
on a sheet of paper, and put it in a sealed envelope addressed to
Thurloe. But he had not delivered the letter, no one knew what
was in it. Perhaps he feared that it might create further dissensions,
perhaps he thought it possible that he might change his mind. And
now his mind and heart were too occupied with other things to
give proper attention to it. On the twenty-seventh of July Thurloe
wrote that little or nothing had been done these last fourteen days.
"His Highness' constant residence at Hampton Court, and the sick-
ness of the Lady Elizabeth, which hath been and is a great affliction to
him, hindered the consideration of these matters;—which makes all
men stand at a gaze, and to doubt very much what will be the issue."

And the Lady Elizabeth's illness was not the only affliction that
had come to him during these months so full of glory and of perplexity. "We have been a family of much sorrow all this summer,
and therefore we deserve not the envy of the world," his son Henry
wrote. Only a few days after the dissolution of Parliament his son-

in-law Robert Rich died, little Frances had been able to keep the man upon whom her heart was set only three months. And "his Highness mourned three days in purple, as is used by persons of his quality." In May, the Earl of Warwick, the only one of the old peers still friendly to the Protector, followed his grandson to the grave. "Go on, my lord," he had written to him a short time before, "go on happily to love religion and to exemplify it. May your lordship long continue an instrument of use, a pattern of virtue, a precedent of glory."

It was not to be long. Constant vigilance, labor and anxiety had been sapping his strength for many years. "It has been heretofore a matter of, I think, but philosophical discourse that a great place, a great authority, is a great burthen. I know that it is," he had said. And although he had once dreamed that a time might come when he could lay aside that great place and great authority, he had soon come to realize that that would be impossible in this life. "Our rest we expect elsewhere. That will be durable."

In June Elizabeth Claypole, who had been hoping to spend the summer in Ireland, lost her youngest child, Oliver. And now Betty herself lay stricken with a cruel internal malady at Hampton Court. He himself moved out there to be near her, there the meetings of the Council were held, there he received foreign ambassadors. He was all father now. What mattered public affairs when the dearest of his children was dying? Most of his time was spent by her bedside, his "sense of her outward misery in the pains she suffered took deep impression upon him." All the family were gathered about her, except Henry and Bridget, who could not get from Ireland. Frances the child widow, Mary and the husband who had been so greatly honored, Richard, so soon to succeed, were with her. At three o'clock on the morning of August 6th she died. On the tenth the body was taken by water to Westminster, and buried in the chapel of Henry VII. There it was allowed to rest even when the bodies of her kindred were disinterred.

Her father, for some time troubled with insomnia, such as makes men regret the past and fear the future, had scarcely slept during her illness. On August 3rd there was a hope of her recovery. That night "he had a very good refreshment by sleep, and was much recovered." But "her long illness had made a great impression upon him," and when she was gone, the reaction was too great for him, he was sick in body and mind, and lay abed five days. He bethought himself of the Scripture which had comforted him almost twenty years ago in the little house at Ely, when his eldest son died, "I can do all things through Christ, that strengtheneth me." "He that was Paul's Christ is my Christ too," he said.

He got better, and although not able to be present in Council on August 12th, the next day he "gave evident tokens of that health, which is of so grand concernment to the peace and prosperity of these nations." On the seventeenth, he "seemed reasonably well recovered, took the air for an hour, and was much refreshed by it." Three days later George Fox, who had come to London to speak with him about the sufferings of the Friends, met him riding into Hampton Court Park. "Before I came to him," he says, "as he rode at the head of his life-guards I saw and felt a waft of death go forth against him; and when I came to him he looked like a dead man." He told Cromwell what he wanted to talk to him about, and was invited to come and see him the next day.

But when he came next day, the Protector was unable to see him, he was sick of an ague. Others were alarmed, but he himself was hopeful. "Banish all sadness from your looks, and deal with me as you would with a serving man," he said to his physician. "You can give great help by your skill, yet nature can do more than all physicians put together, and God is far above nature." There were so many praying for him, their prayers must be answered! "I shall not die, but live this bout," he told his wife, "I am sure of it."

On Tuesday the 24th he was taken to Whitehall, he could have better care there, and the change might benefit him. But he grew worse instead of better, and the body affected the spirit. "It is a fearful thing," he was heard to murmur at times, "to fall into the hands of the living God." "Tell me," he said to one of his chaplains, "is it possible to fall from grace?" "It is not possible," was the answer. "Then I am safe," he cried, "for I know that I was once in grace." His mind went back to the days when he had written to Mrs. St. John, "My soul is with the congregation of the first-born, my body rests in hope, and if here I may honour my God, either by doing, or by suffering, I shall be most glad," to the days when God had seemed to say to him, "Up and be doing, and I will stand by you," to the days when he had not been called upon to sacrifice one ideal to another, to the days when it was easy for him to keep himself unspotted from the world, for he had not had to overcome the world. "Pray for me," he had written to his cousin, "that He Who hath begun a good work in me may perfect it to the day of Jesus Christ." And now his chaplain had assured him that, in spite of some fallings by the way, He would.

There were prayers throughout the nation for his recovery. The officers met for prayer, and to discuss what should be done in case of his death. For all felt that "though his loss must needs carry weight in itself, yet the consideration of the miserable posture he leaves these nations in is stupendous."

Shortly after he fell ill, while still at Hampton Court, he had sent one of the gentlemen of the Bedchamber to Whitehall for the letter addressed to Thurloe in which he had nominated his successor. He told him that it lay on his study table, but it could not be found. On the night of Monday, August 30th, Thurloe, alone with him, discussed the matter. He probably at that time named his eldest son, but his illness "disenabled him to continue the conversation fully." On Thursday, September 2nd, it was evident that he was dying. Thurloe asked him if he continued of the same mind as when he had last spoken to him about it. He replied that he did. Some members of the Council were sent for to attest it, and in their presence Cromwell nominated Richard as his successor. Not a very good nomination, but perhaps the best that could be made. Henry was abler, but he had many enemies in the military party. There was no one outside of the family who could be thought of as a candidate. And there was a great desire to assimilate the Protectorate to a monarchy by means of the hereditary succession.

The Protector's mind was clear, and for himself he was happy. But he thought much about the country that he was leaving, about God's cause and God's people. On the night of August 31st he was heard to pray: "Lord, though I am a miserable and wretched creature, I am in covenant with Thee through grace, and I may, I will come to Thee for Thy people. Thou hast made me, though very unworthy, a mean instrument to do them some good, and Thee service; and many of them have set too high a value upon me, though others wish and would be glad of my death. Lord, however Thou dost dispose of me, continue to go on and do good for them. Give them consistency of judgment, one heart, and mutual love, and go on to deliver them, and with the work of reformation, and make the name of Christ glorious in the world. Teach those who look too much upon Thy instruments to look more upon Thyself. Pardon such as desire to trample upon the dust of a poor worm, for they are Thy people too. (Fifth Monarchists, Levelers, Anabaptists, they might be dangerous to England just now, but they were still His people.) And pardon the folly of this short prayer, even for Jesus Christ's sake, and give me a good night, if it be Thy pleasure." Less than four years ago his mother's last words to him had been, "My dear Son, I leave my heart with thee. A good night!"

On Thursday night, after nominating his successor, he was restless but happy. "God is good, indeed He is," he was heard to say often. And once, "I would be willing to live to be further serviceable to God and His people.—But my work is done.—God will be with His people." To one who would give him a sleeping draught, he said, "It is not my design to drink or to sleep, but my design is to make what haste I can to be gone." Later he spoke "some exceeding self-debasing words, annihilating and judging himself," mingled with broken texts "implying much consolation and peace."

Toward morning he fell into a coma, and between three and four in the afternoon, the crowd that waited for news at the palace gates were told that the Lord Protector was dead. Those sad eyes that once "shed a piercing sweetness" were closed forever. It was the third of September, the day of Dunbar and Worcester, his fortunate day. He had no more fortunate day than the third of September, 1658, when he "reached the bound of life where he laid his burden down."

He had been a good constable, he had kept the peace, he had saved England from anarchy. He had not hoped, he had said, to do much good, but only to prevent some evil. And he had done that.

The old order of things, in its general outline at least, came back, it was right that it should. And the short period of his power soon came to seem but "a strange interlude" in his country's story. But by his sword he had saved Parliamentary government, he had made absolute monarchy impossible in England. He had done it by force, but back of the force lay the will of the people of England. And yet he himself had not been able to make parliamentary government workable. Partly because there had not as yet been sufficient political experience, partly because the cabinet system and the civil service that make it workable had not at that time been evolved. But largely because, Parliament willing or unwilling, he had insisted upon religious toleration, at least for "the people of God in England."

Religious toleration for all the people of England came in time, but it is difficult to say whether he hastened or retarded it. What he gained in that direction during his lifetime, he gained by force, and back of that force was not the will of the people of England.

One cannot force a people ahead of their time. "First the blade, then the ear, afterward the full corn in the ear." That is Nature's way, that is man's way.

As for his foreign policy that made his country glorious, and kept her poor, it is sufficient to say that he was England's first great practical Imperialist. Opinions will differ as to whether that imperialism has been good for England and for the world. But even the most ardent Imperialist must admit that this first Imperialist made mistakes. His alliance with France against Spain served to strengthen the country with which England was destined to have a long series of bloody wars. And had he lived, his determination to hold Dunkirk, combined with his desire for a Protestant alliance, might have led to another bloody and expensive foreign war. He looked forward to getting Gibraltar, and the later acquisition of that has probably been an advantage.

But the great thing to which he looked forward was a spiritualized England, an England in which all the people would be the Lord's people, and in which all the Lord's people would be prophets. Will England or any other country ever attain to that?

Dr. Gardiner tells us that his chief interest in Cromwell arises from the fact that he sees in him England writ small. My own interest in him arises chiefly from the fact that I see in him every one of us writ large, every one of us who, in dealing with complicated circumstances, strong passions, limited knowledge and imperfect men (we are all of us imperfect men, and our knowledge is always limited) has to sacrifice one ideal to another, every one of us who finds "It should be, baulked by Here it cannot be." Perhaps too a study of Cromwell may make us a little more charitable toward those who are trying to bring order out of the present chaos.

For, although, as Carlyle puts it, there are centuries that separate us, and it is hard to speak together, although his language is not our language, and his faith, in part at least, is not our faith, his struggles are our struggles, his victories our victories, his defeats our defeats.

INDEX

INDEX

313